BUTCH WILKINS

AND THE

SUNDANCE KID

A TEENAGE OBSESSION WITH TV SPORT

NIGE TASSELL

D1385962

First published in 2018 by

ARENA SPORT
An imprint of Birlinn Limited
West Newington House
10 Newington Road
Edinburgh
EH9 1QS

www.arenasportbooks.co.uk

ISBN: 9781909715615
eBook ISBN: 9781788850926

British Library Cataloguing-in-Publication Data
A catalogue record for this book is available on request from the British
Library.

Designed and typeset by Polaris Publishing, Edinburgh

Printed in Great Britain by Clays, Elcograf S.p.A

To Ma, for that first door key.

And to Jane, for all the door keys since.

Nige Tassell writes about sport and popular culture. His work has appeared in the pages of *The Guardian*, *FourFourTwo*, *Esquire*, *The Sunday Times*, *The Independent*, *Q*, *New Statesman*, the *Times Literary Supplement* and *The Word* among many others. His most recent books are *Three Weeks, Eight Seconds: The Epic Tour de France of 1989* (Polaris Publishing, 2017) and *The Bottom Corner: A Season With The Dreamers Of Non-League Football* (Yellow Jersey Press, 2016).

CONTENTS

THE CONVERSATION always went the same way. It was a predictable screenplay.

[A knock at the door]
HIM: You coming out?
ME: Bit busy.
HIM: We've got no homework though. What are you doing?
ME *[gazing back over my shoulder into the living room]*: Stuff.
HIM: What stuff? Chores?
ME: No.
HIM: Why are the curtains closed? It's one in the afternoon. Come on, let's go out on our bikes.
ME: But the Lombard RAC Rally highlights have just come on.
HIM: The highlights of *last weekend's* Lombard RAC Rally?
ME: Er, yeah. Still good though.
HIM: After that then? I'll come back in half an hour.
ME: The snooker will be on. UK Championships. Alex Higgins is playing this afternoon.
HIM: But we could actually *play* snooker if you came round ours.
ME: Not the same really, is it? Plus I'd miss the half-times.
HIM: It'll be four o'clock by then. Getting dark. I haven't got any lights on my bike.

ME: Best leave it then. The World Masters darts is on before the vidiprinter anyway.

HIM *[sighing]*: OK, I get the message, you boring sod. Tomorrow?

ME: Yeah, probably. *[Pause, then a barely audible whisper]* But it'll be the same answer . . .

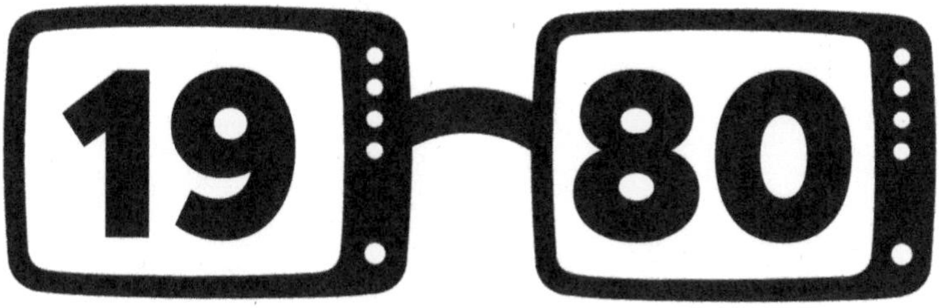
19
80

HOME ALONE

THE GOLDEN ticket was actually a brass door key.

It spanned most of my 11-year-old hand, a chunky front door key made by Chubb of Willenhall and handed to me, without ceremony, by my mum. It was the afternoon of 12 June 1980 and I was in her clothes shop, having just walked the five minutes from primary school, a walk I only had to do for little more than another month.

I had the key for a specific purpose. That afternoon, England were playing Belgium in their opening match of the European Championship, their first game in a major tournament since West Germany had cancelled out, and then eclipsed, their 2-0 lead in the World Cup quarter-final of 1970. That was a full ten years before. Half a generation ago. It felt like ancient history, especially to those of us too young to remember it. All bar three of England's starting line-up that day in León – Martin Peters, Alan Ball and Terry Cooper – had retired. This was a measure of how starved England football fans had been. In short: the Belgium match was a very significant one. To 11-year-old eyes, it would be nothing short of historic.

Maybe my mum understood its significance. More likely, she probably just didn't want the moans of a grumpy pre-teen, starved of watching the game, scaring off her customers as they browsed the kaftans and cheesecloth blouses that remained strong sellers in our village, despite it being several years since their mid-70s fashionability.

The key turned out to have significance way beyond that particular day. It was never made clear whether my mum meant me to have possession of it permanently or just for the afternoon. Either way, I wasn't going to give it up. That key would open the door to mild independence, to allow me to come and go as I pleased during the forthcoming summer holidays and for ever more. No more being held hostage in the clothes shop for six long weeks, twiddling my thumbs, kicking my heels. The release papers had been signed. My sentence had been commuted. Cry freedom.

(One handwritten sign in the shop, fixed to the fitting-room mirror with yellowing Sellotape, scarred me deeply and I was delighted to be getting away from it. The fact that I can recall its precise wording almost 40 years later suggests it to be a scar that never completely healed: 'Customers are requested to keep panties on while trying on bikini bottoms'. Twelve words that would unfailingly turn any primary-school-age boy's cheeks to a deep crimson, especially when these words were in your mum's handwriting and were an instruction to the mothers of your friends.)

Key held in a tight fist, I bolted home, past the bakers, the garage, the fire station, through the shortcut across the waste ground and all the way down to the far end of the street. Our end of the street.

There was no fanfare when the key went into the lock. The clouds didn't part. There was no glow of heavenly light. But the door opened, I was over the threshold and the TV was on in seconds.

It would take 26 minutes before the pictures coming in from Turin confirmed my grounds for optimism. England were ahead and it was an extraordinary goal that had put them there, unlike any I'd seen up until then and unlike any I've seen ever since.

As the Belgians partially cleared a Trevor Brooking cross, the ball fell to Ray Wilkins about 25 yards out. He deftly chipped the ball over the advancing line of defenders, patiently waited for it to land before lobbing the Belgian keeper Pfaff. There were a couple of seconds of silent incomprehension on my face and, presumably, the faces of those who were also home alone, whether these were schoolkids returning home or office workers who'd excused themselves from work early while mumbling something about a life-threatening condition coming on.

Wilkins himself seemed genuinely surprised that his boot could create such an artistic, beautiful goal. For a moment or two, he casually walked away as if displaying such unbounded flamboyance was an everyday occurrence for him. Then it hit him – just at precisely the same millisecond that it was hitting us back home in front of the telly. Once the enormity of what he'd just done had dawned on him (this was England's first tournament goal since Martin Peters had put them two up in León ten years previously, of course), he bolted off towards the corner flag, pursued by a posse of equally dumbstruck teammates.

It seemed that in one swipe of Wilkins' right boot, England's place at the top table of international football was confirmed. It had clearly been reserved for us throughout that ten-year blip; no one had been allowed to sit in our seat. We were back.

This new era very quickly revealed itself to actually be the first of those many false dawns I'd become familiar with over the following decades. That mild sense of invincibility lasted precisely three minutes. It was the Belgian striker Jan Ceulemans, a player for whom the word 'burly' was surely invented, who burst the balloon, barging his way through the

England defence to equalise. And then, to show their contempt for anyone who dared to doubt their God-given right to breezily stroll through life, the more impatient quarters of England fans began to attack neutral Italian spectators who had shown the brazen cheek to applaud Ceulemans' goal.

The England fans, though, more than met their match in the local *carabinieri* who, with ammunition to hand, swiftly deployed tear gas. Yellow smoke flooded the terraces and the match was held up while several players – most notably Ray Clemence, the player closest to the unrest – were treated for the effects.

Wilkins and the tear gas aside, the match was nothing to write home about. It didn't feel historic. And it certainly didn't prove to be the foundation from which England would launch their assault towards the tournament's final stages. While Belgium unexpectedly went all the way to the final, England's subsequent 1-0 defeat to hosts Italy meant their fate was sealed after just two group matches. The nation slipped back into the default position of dejection and disappointment, the mode its football fans had occupied throughout the previous decade.

England's early exit didn't end the fun for me, though. I still had that door key, the passport to all those afternoon kick-offs throughout the tournament. And I had sole control of the family TV. No one else around. Wonderland.

The die was cast that June afternoon, setting in motion an adolescence spent sidestepping the familiar and expected teenage pursuits of girls, house parties, illicit substances and general arsing about. Free to come and go as I pleased, I never used this licence to roam, not even to embark on a series of more innocent adventures. I was no freewheeling Huckleberry Finn.

Instead, my new-found freedom was invested in staying put, in sitting on my backside in front of the goggle-box for an incalculable amount of hours a day. Weekends, evenings and school holidays had but one master: TV sport. And the rest of that year – and the rest of that decade – generously gave me top-class sporting occasion after top-class sporting occasion fed directly into my home, largely thanks to the good burghers of the BBC choosing to invest a goodly portion of the licence fee into sport broadcasting. The department's output was relentless. Good relentless, that is. Amazing relentless.

During these peak years of sporting coverage on terrestrial television (with the notion of directly paying for what you watched a distant dollar-shaped Murdochian pipe dream), it was all on tap. And I more than had my fill. From my front-row seat on the sofa, I drank it all in. Whether a middle-distance record attempt in an exotic European capital or a low-ranking table tennis tournament in some municipal leisure centre in the Home Counties, I didn't care. I just wanted the sweet smell of success – and the awful stench of failure – in my nostrils. And I wanted the thrill of witnessing these amazing global events at the precise moment that they happened, albeit via a television screen in a bedroom in a house in a village in deepest, darkest Sussex.

As I approached teenagehood, I was making the conscious decision not to push outwards and upwards in life. I was heading indoors instead. The boy was creating his own bubble, dancing out of the sunlight and closing the curtains behind him. The Sundance Kid was born.

NO PARTICULAR PLACE TO GO

IT WASN'T as if I would only be able to get my fill of TV sport when no one was else in the house. That wasn't the limit of my allocation. There was no rationing. Far from it, in fact. If there was sport on the box of an evening or weekend, that would be the default choice of programme round ours. There was a clear hierarchy. Non-sport programmes almost always took second billing. International athletics had priority over *Hi-de-Hi!*. The darts outscored *Knots Landing*. This suited me just fine. No complaints whatsoever. The obsession was open all hours.

As families went, we were pretty sporty. Until the papers arrived calling him up for national service, my dad had been playing for Charlton Athletic in some capacity. Exactly what capacity was never properly revealed to me (and, strangely, I never bothered asking), but it seemed to go beyond the 'I had a trial for them' default. Everyone's dad had claimed to have had a trial with some club or other, after all. When he was discharged from active service, my dad had been away from the game at a high standard for two years so, until his mid-thirties, he contented himself playing down at county level. He was also the coach of the village boys' team. My team.

My brother, two and a half years older than me, wouldn't have described himself as a sportsman, though. Not team sports, at least. If you regard it as a sport (and it is in the Olympics so I guess we have to concede it does qualify as such), target shooting was his thing. He was something of a dead-eyed marksman with a rifle in his hands. This had been discovered during his time in the Combined Cadet Force at school, but he never really pursued it. The odd competition, perhaps, but that was it. Instead, he was keener to be the outdoorsman, preferring field and forest over pitch and track. I could still persuade him to play the odd game of darts in the garage. It was a bit like target shooting, I suppose. Just a little quieter. And marginally less deadly.

My mum wasn't mad-keen on sport, but tolerated it. Wimbledon fortnight was her thing, though. If she felt she couldn't get away with closing the shop for a couple of weeks to soak up the action, she'd lug the portable black-and-white set down the road on the first Monday and would be engrossed for the tournament's duration. Who knows how low the takings – and how high the incidents of shoplifting – were while she was transfixed to the screen. There may even have been some panties/bikini bottoms-based misdemeanours occurring in the fitting room while she was otherwise occupied watching Connors or Evert or Goolagong.

The sporting genes on her side of the family must have jumped a generation, for her mum, my gran, was as enthusiastic about sport as she was about whisky and cigarettes (and she was very enthusiastic about whisky and cigarettes). Her passion for sport was quite possibly born out of the fact that she was very good at it. As a young woman, she'd represented England at badminton. As a woman well into her seventies, she was ladies' champion at her golf club year after year, scoring her first hole-in-one at the age of 72. Her husband – Mum's stepfather, my step-grandad – was also a sport fanatic. One sport, that is. Cricket. A player, a spectator, a club chairman. It was in the blood. His cousin was the much-garlanded England wicketkeeper-batsman Les Ames.

But while the balance of power in the family did definitely swing towards sport, we never swore our allegiance to one club and one club only. I wasn't born into a generations-old tradition of being blindly recruited into supporting the team of my father, which had been the team of his father, and his father before him. That was a tradition that didn't exist in the branches of our family tree. And there was no obvious local team to follow. Living out in the sticks, we didn't have the luxury of an easy-to-catch-every-home-game club at the other end of a 15-minute bus ride.

My dad had a tenuous interest in Spurs which didn't manifest itself sufficiently into actually ever going to see them. My brother had arbitrarily plumped for Arsenal, a connection that, again, barely went deeper than supporting them if they happened to be in the Cup Final (which, of course, at the tail end of the '70s, they were on a regular basis).

As a six-year-old, I had a Chelsea shirt, but I don't remotely remember actually picking them as my team – and, as we've ascertained, no one would have imposed them on me either. I do, though, vaguely remember something about a clearance sale of fire-damaged stock at the local sports shop. That might explain why I had the shirt. It was the cheapest.

There was a flirtation with Terry Venables' Crystal Palace in their short-lived and much-scoffed-at 'Team of the Eighties' phase; I did actually go to a couple of games at Selhurst Park, at least. But this swapping of sides did naturally leave me open to accusations from other kids of being a glory-hunter. These taunts would have been perfectly reasonable in any other circumstances, but as they were usually made by an Arsenal fan on the school bus who couldn't remotely tell me which part of London you'd find Highbury, I chose to ignore them.

In my first couple of years at university, I did go to a fair few Colchester United midweek games. And in my final year, I didn't miss a home match as the U's charged towards the GM Vauxhall Conference/FA Trophy double. This was the closest I got to being a proper fan diligently following a team – a season of getting to know the players from close quarters, becoming familiar with their strengths and their weaknesses, and being able to recognise them when they were sitting on the 62 bus from Wivenhoe to town.

I can still name the squad – and whom they were signed from and whom they went on to sign for – nearly three decades on. And if being told, 'Why don't you just fuck off?' by the player-manager halfway through a match – after I loudly jeered his decision to substitute his doing-OK strike partner and not his doing-rather-shit self – isn't a badge of honour that proved I truly belonged to this club for nine or ten months, then I simply don't know what is. (Any ongoing affection has been paper-thin. I've only been back to the old place once in 25 years.)

That one season aside, such a lack of undying commitment to one team, such ambivalence to a cause, is of course heresy to most sport fans. In my defence, thinking back I suppose I was upholding a family tradition as much as those of my friends who had inherited a particular club. It was just that our family tradition was one of non-affiliation. I have plenty of friends for whom the weekend is ruined, and the early part of the week too, if their club's result isn't a favourable one come 4.45pm on Saturday. Me, I'm missing that gene. It's not in my DNA.

Accordingly, my adolescent sporting life isn't a tale of endlessly queueing for the autographs of my idols. Or religiously collecting programmes from every match, both home and away. Or undertaking long journeys on board one of British Rail's football specials, round trips of 500-odd miles to watch a goalless match that was abandoned in the 83rd minute when the floodlights failed – or when the referee lost the will to live. Part of me wishes I had these tales to tell. But then I think about how these loyalists missed out on a particular Philippe Sella try in the Five Nations. Or those innumerable victories by June Croft at the national swimming championships. Or pipe-sucking David Bryant's domination of the bowls world. Who really lost out, eh?

Commitment on my part stretched to nothing more than being the objective observer in front of the box, chewing over the action as a neutral and reaching a verdict without the blinkers of partisanship to colour my judgement. Perhaps, if I quizzed a psychoanalyst who also had a sideline in careers advice, I'd discover that it was actually all subconscious preparation for a future life as the impartial journalist I'd later become.

So maybe I hadn't just lazily stumbled into the mindset of someone who didn't care enough to swear eternal allegiance.

Maybe there was purpose behind my non-affiliation. Perhaps, after all, I knew exactly what I was doing.

VERUCA SALT

THE BLACK-AND-WHITE TV set was providing sterling service in the clothes shop in the last week of June and the first week of July. Meanwhile, during the after-school hours of that Wimbledon fortnight, I was in the prime spot: at home in front of the big colour set. In the men's singles, there seemed to be a sense of inevitability about how the draw would unfold. It was hard to see beyond a final contested between defending champion Björn Borg and second seed/US Open champion John McEnroe. And this was how it panned out, a final that represented – as billed in both the press and the saloon bar – nothing other than a gladiatorial clash between good and evil. Ice versus fire.

If I'd been two or three years older, I'd probably have identified a little more with McEnroe. My hormonal imbalance would have kicked in by then and I might have understood his angst and anger. I could have felt empathy with the way he challenged authority and I would surely have howled my encouragement whenever he stuck it to the man. As it was, at the non-hormonal age of 11, I thought he was a bit of a dick.

He was petulant and pedantic, bawling and whining when something – some little thing, *any* little thing – didn't go his way. The Veruca Salt of international tennis. To me, his behaviour appeared disproportionate to whatever comparatively minor occurrence had wronged him. He'd been issued with an official warning during his semi-final against Jimmy Connors, another player who didn't always go quietly into the night. Maybe that indicated some method in his madness. Perhaps

McEnroe carefully picked the matches in which he could act up, knowing bad behaviour would get right under the skin of a player who could be drawn, or at least distracted, by what was happening on the other side of the net. After all, the petulance seemed to stay zipped up whenever he played Borg. Even if he had set it free, no amount of psychology could penetrate the Swede's mental suit of armour. And McEnroe knew this.

I wanted Borg to swiftly put him to the sword, a quick dispatch to silence the gobby boy from New York City. There was another reason why I needed him to take him in this manner, ideally in straight sets. We had to go out as a family at 5pm to watch a carnival parade in which we had some kind of (now forgotten) vested interest. With the match starting at 2.20pm, this shouldn't have been too much of an issue. There was plenty of time for a vanquishing to be administered. I'd need not miss a shot. We all settled down to let the grandfatherly tones of Dan Maskell describe the vanquishing.

McEnroe had other ideas. He took the first set 6-1, giving our presumptive tendencies more than a little wobble. Borg, chasing his fifth consecutive title, was his usual unflappable self, though. He knew he could retrieve the situation, a mindset that caused the American to slightly unravel. Every time McEnroe put an easy volley into the net or beyond the baseline, our house erupted, especially when one such error gave Borg the second set. He had put him back in his box.

Borg seemed to understand about our family's prior engagement. At 4.53pm, seven minutes before we needed to leave, he was two sets to one up and, at 40-15 and 5-4 up in the fourth, was serving with two championship points in hand. He had one hand and four other fingers on the trophy again. *His* trophy. But McEnroe rallied, winning four successive points to break back. On the stroke of 5pm, at 6-6 the pair headed into a tiebreak. We couldn't leave now. Anyway, a tiebreak would only last five or so minutes. Little harm would be done. We wouldn't miss much.

The tiebreak actually lasted 22 minutes. Thirty-four points were won and lost, including a few more championship points for Borg. The back and forth was relentless. 'They've both looked down the gun barrel,' said John Barrett in the BBC commentary box, 'and they're both still alive.'

McEnroe eventually edged it 18-16, arguably one of the greatest tiebreaks in tennis history; I was relieved we had delayed our exit to see it, even if I was concerned that Borg's fifth title was very much in doubt. We had to go now though, despite my protestations. Why couldn't I stay home? I'd been home alone throughout the European Championship, so what was the difference? Was I more likely to be bludgeoned to death by a merciless burglar on a Saturday teatime than I was on an after-school Thursday afternoon?

It was a three-line whip. I quite possibly had a minor McEnroe-esque strop, but I had to go. We had the commentary on in the car, but naturally it wasn't the same. It was very different, in fact. The radio commentators didn't stop talking, having to describe every phase of play in tight detail: what kind of shot it was; what part of the court the ball had been dispatched to; which flavour of Robinsons Barley Water each favoured in the turnaround. Tennis commentators on television knew to keep their mouths shut during each point, only bursting into appreciation or analysis once the ball had gone dead. Dan Maskell might be primarily remembered for the exclamation 'Oh, I say!', but the irony is he didn't actually say that much. He knew we could see for ourselves.

It was even-stevens throughout that final set, poised at five games apiece as we took our roadside vantage point. Mum had brought a transistor radio along, but it wasn't powerful enough to be of communal use. She had it glued to her ear, relaying each line of the commentary with a half-second delay. Other people edged closer, keen to listen in on this second-hand reportage.

Then she let out a whoop.

'Borg?' asked a man just along from us.

Mum nodded.

'Yessssss!'

He had finally clinched it, after nearly four hours of the most intense play. The word quickly spread. It seemed as though everyone currently perched on the kerb of this roundabout, waiting for some dismal carnival procession, was in Borg's camp. The smiles broke out all over. We weren't the only ones. Watching the TV highlights later, the relief on the officials' faces around Centre Court was far from disguised. It was writ large for all to see. The final – in danger of going off script in a couple of places – had delivered the result that had been largely hoped for. The loudmouth had been silenced; Veruca Salt was sulking. Until 12 months' time, that is.

RISING DAMP

IF A cricketing novice was looking for a Test series to draw them into the sport, to have its talons sunk well and truly into their skin, the five-match England-West Indies encounter of 1980 was most certainly not it. While the tourists took the first Test, the remaining four all petered out into draws, each badly affected by a soggy British summer. There was, of course, more than enough dazzling talent on show to hook even the most reluctant onlooker – not least the fast and furious West Indian pace attack, a bowling tag team so strong that even a player with Colin Croft's immense skill and speed couldn't make the cut for the first Test. It was just that the frequent interruptions by the weather rendered play disjointed and ultimately fruitless.

To someone already committed to the cause of cricket, someone familiar with its folds and creases, rain-affected sessions weren't necessarily bad news. The last two Tests of this particular series fell within the summer holidays and so, once the precocious child presenters of *Why Don't You...?* had disappeared off our screens for the day, it was over to Peter West at The Oval or Headingley. With West invariably introducing the coverage from the pavilion balcony, straight away you knew how the morning was going to pan out from looking over his shoulder to the pitch beyond. If the ground staff were making last-minute adjustments to the wicket, it was game on. If the overnight covers were still in position, there was likely to be a sizeable, possibly even day-long, delay to proceedings.

As curious as it might sound, rain stopping play wasn't necessarily a bad thing to my eyes. Yes, it might mean a protracted on-screen debate about the cricketing matters of the day between ageing former players in blazers and ties, which was likely to be less than scintillating to a young kid. But it would almost certainly also mean, once conversation was exhausted, that a production assistant would have been dispatched to the archives to retrieve the tape of a classic encounter from yesteryear and which would soak up some of the scheduled broadcast time. This was hog heaven, especially if the revived match was of a vintage that predated my TV sport addiction – possibly David Steele battening down the hatches against the Australians in 1975, or a classic Benson & Hedges Cup tie from earlier in the decade. For the historically inquisitive lad who spent plenty of time nose-deep in stats and records, a 40-minute highlights package featuring a particular event in the middle-distant past was exactly the primer he needed. Whisper it, but sometimes watching archive action was actually preferable to soaking up the live coverage, especially if the snail-slow pair of Geoff Boycott and Chris Tavaré were at the crease at the same time, digging out their respective innings with paint-drying flair.

With the rain limiting the amount of time the great West Indian bowlers had to impose themselves on England's top order (and thus the time I had to study them), the next best thing was to pretend to be them in real life. And even if it were drizzling at Headingley or Old Trafford, there was a reasonable chance that the conditions were much drier down in Sussex. There was an alleyway that ran down the side of our house and, as luck would have it, it measured almost exactly 22 yards from its entrance to the gate at the far end. This became my own personal wicket. One day I'd be Michael Holding, the next Malcolm Marshall. I didn't need someone to bat against me; until play had resumed in the Test, I'd hurl a tennis ball towards the makeshift stumps that had been fashioned from three wooden shelving slats liberated from the airing cupboard. If I hit the stumps three times in an over, I viewed that as a success.

And every time I did hit them, I raised a single arm to the invisible crowd as another imaginary England batsman headed back towards the pavilion.

GOODY TWO SPIKES

YOUR AFFILIATION with either Borg or McEnroe wasn't just based on character type or playing style. Nationality also played a part in determining which side of the net you fell. So, when it came to choosing your favourite world-beating middle-distance runner – the leading two of whom were both British-born and British-bred, and about to finally go head-to-head over two distances at the Moscow Olympics – nationality was one less criterion to consider. It was, though, replaced by another: social class.

According to the *Daily Mail* – the bugle for the aspirant lower-middle class and thus a staple of our breakfast table – Sebastian Newbold Coe was the one to follow. A young man of poise and pace and *properness*. Strait-laced. Decent. Middle England in a vest and spikes.

Steve Ovett, by contrast, was the scruffy loose cannon, the cocky showman who would invariably salute the crowd if he hit the front with 50 yards still to run. I'm sure, if my dad at the other end of the sofa was a reliable sample of the nation, there were plenty willing Ovett to come a cropper in the home straight of a major race. (It turned out that they were in luck, too. A week after the 1500m Olympic final in Moscow, at an evening meeting at Crystal Palace, Ovett performed his usual trick. Despite having moved up to the unfamiliar 5,000m, he gave that victory wave more than 80 metres from home. John Treacy wasn't having it. The Irishman pursued him all the way to the line, his dipping torso pipping the decelerating and soon-to-be-embarrassed Ovett. 'Steve has only got himself to blame,' tutted the BBC's Ron Pickering. Laughter was the utterance of choice from the western end of our sofa.)

At the age of 11, you're no class warrior. You tend to tune into whatever the prevailing mood around the house and the family is, one itself that was tuned into the prevailing mood of the morning paper. So it was that three weeks before Crystal Palace, as the athletes defied the government by refusing to boycott the Games and boarded their flights to Moscow, I just fell into line. Thanks to my conditioning, I was a Coe man. For now, at least.

So when Ovett beat Coe in Moscow over the latter's preferred distance of 800 metres, I feared that the man from Brighton would claim double gold by winning the 1500m too. After crossing the line in the 800m final, he raised his arms in celebration (he'd wisely shown enough caution to do so only as he crossed the line), lifted a forefinger to the sky and began an action as if he were writing a message on a condensation-heavy window. When it emerged what he was doing – spelling out the letters ILY, aka I Love You, to his girlfriend back home – I was even less impressed with him. Any athletics meeting, let alone the precious Olympic Games, was no place for public displays of affection. Love and all that stuff. No thanks, said the 11-year-old. Not today. And probably not ever.

Coe got his revenge over Ovett's favoured distance, the 1500m. Ovett trailed in in third place, meaning Coe's gold and silver represented the better medal haul. He had won the personal battle, just shading it on the athletics equivalent of goal difference.

THE FLYING SCOTSMAN

I WAS a short-sighted kid. I wore glasses from the age of eight, an affliction blamed on watching hours of TV perched on the edge of a coffee table no more than three feet from the screen. I knew this not to be wholly true. The myopia was hereditary. Almost all of us in the family wore glasses – or, rather, almost all of us *should* have worn glasses; my mum refused to comply. My brother escaped the genes, though. The 20/20 vision of a marksman, he had. Still does. Me? I was Magoo. Four Eyes. Joe 90.

Despite wearing glasses in every waking moment that I wasn't on a football pitch, my eyesight was amazingly sharp when soaking up TV sport at full speed. Useless in the observation round of *The Krypton Factor*, I boasted the vision of a hawk when it came to spotting a hairline offside decision or when correctly – and instantly – calling the winner of a photo finish Olympic 100m final. And this was how, at teatime on my final day at primary school, for a few moments I felt superior to those experts in the BBC commentary box.

Admittedly, the result of the 1980 Olympic men's 100m final was a difficult one to call. Not only did the two fastest men – Silvio Leonard of Cienfuegos, Cuba and Allan Wells of Edinburgh, Scotland – record identical times to the hundredth of a second, but the lane draw had kept them well apart. Leonard was in lane one, Wells in lane eight. Leonard was at the top of the screen, Wells at the bottom. Were they next to each other in the middle lanes, it would have been easier to call, to spot which vest broke the tape first. As it was, the lane draw meant the human eye couldn't focus on one without the other becoming even slightly blurred.

Despite this, I just knew Wells had pipped the Cuban. The Scot had thundered through the last 40 metres and, timing his dip over the line perfectly, had taken gold. I was sure of it. Even if the commentary team weren't committing either way, I was. The fact that Wells didn't break his stride and continued straight into a lap of honour was, to me, vindication. It was only later that he admitted he wasn't completely sure of the result himself and, while soaking up the applause and accolades along the back straight, was concerned he might very quickly become the most embarrassed Olympian of all time.

It was the easiest thing to denigrate Wells's win, that it had only been achieved thanks to the absence of the Americans. That those 10.25 seconds represented the slowest winning time for the men's Olympic 100m since 1956 only added fuel to the flames of disquiet. Wells, to his credit, accepted a post-Olympic invitation to silence his critics, travelling to Germany to race against a collection of the world's very best sprinters, both those who had and those who hadn't boycotted the Games. He put his reputation and his Olympic gold medal on the line and he beat them all. (That impressed me greatly, as did learning he had a fabulous middle name: Wipper. And, in more recent times, he went even higher in my estimation by making a cameo appearance in a Belle and Sebastian video.)

Perhaps I felt a close affinity with Allan Wells and his achievement simply because I'd called his victory before David Coleman and his colleagues had. To be fair, they were positioned high up in the stands at the Olympic Stadium. Sitting on that coffee table, with my nose practically touching the screen, Joe 90 had more than a slight advantage.

O GUBBA, WHERE ART THOU?

THE MOVE into secondary education is both seismic and normal at the same time. Everyone does it, after all. It's just that from the outside, especially during the closing weeks of the summer holidays, it appears like a giant step, one that your mind makes greater every day you get closer to the start of term. It's a world potentially crammed with bullies and thugs and antisocial behaviour – and that's just the teachers. The pond in which you were happily swimming at your own pace, the one whose dimensions and parameters had been so familiar for more than half your life, was being replaced by a comparative ocean whose depths were dark. You would be swept up in a gulf stream that rendered you disorientated and dizzy. It was all down to the scale of the beast. In September 1980, my new school had 80 classrooms, plus metalwork and carpentry workshops, a working farm, and acre after acre of sports pitches. A world apart from the cosiness and closeness of primary school.

There were about 80 teachers in my secondary school too, 80 personalities you had to decode to understand their respective characters and boundaries. Like everyone else at this point, I came from an environment where a single teacher taught you the entire curriculum in just one classroom. Moving on up was such a change in culture. But, in understanding this new, strange, multi-layered hierarchy, there was already a similar structure that I could refer to and use as a comparison. It was the only hierarchy from the adult world I'd come across thus far in my life: that of the BBC's football commentating team.

David Coleman was undoubtedly the all-powerful headmaster – stern, authoritative, intimidating. As a result of both seniority and force of personality, he was the one to get first dibs on everything, as well as being the man, I always presumed, who had a strong say in how the remainder of the work was divvied up. Then came Barry Davies, younger than Coleman but someone with sufficient experience and authority to make a comfortable appointment as head of year. As boyishly enthusiastic as Coleman was deadly serious, John Motson was the newly qualified teacher yet to be worn down by the system, the bright-eyed, chirpy graduate whose lesson preparation was undertaken in the kind of depth that would never be needed in the classroom. You suspected he'd spent the entire week before a match compiling a bespoke dossier on every player taking to the field. In short, he was a keener.

And then there was Tony Gubba. His role was undoubtedly that of supply teacher, brought in to plug a gap when the others higher up the food chain were indisposed. He was required to fill in as and when, no matter the subject, no matter the sport. As a result, Gubba was deserving of our sympathy – the man without tenure, without a permanent parking space, without his own coffee mug in the staff room cupboard.

DEPARTURE LOUNGE

WHEN YOU'RE 11, you don't really understand much about death. The notion of finality is a concept that's hard for your brain to analyse and compute. Life at that age is all about possibility and endlessness. Nothing can stop us.

Something stopped Grandad. He didn't see much of the 1980s, just ten and a bit months. On Bonfire Night, he collapsed at the dinner table and died, an abrupt end to his innings. The news came through in a solemn phone call, one that silenced our house. I remember spending the next hour staring into the fire. No tears, strangely. Just numbness.

As shallow and selfish as it might appear, the following day my overriding thought was that this meant the end of the cricket matches I would force him to play whenever he and Gran came visiting. He was frail, with numerous physical complaints, but I'd always insist he played. To be fair to the old fellow, he didn't take much persuasion. He was up from his chair and out into the front garden in a shot.

And he was still an elegant batsman. Despite his rickety bones, and despite being armed with a child's cricket bat, he swatted each of my deliveries high and handsome over the house. In a proper match, he wouldn't have played such a shot; the ball would have gone right down mid-on's throat. But for the purposes of our game, his target was clear. He'd get four runs if he successfully landed the ball on the postage stamp of our back garden, or six if he was able to pinpoint his shot even more precisely to land on top of the chicken run. Two noises alerted us to whether he'd achieved the latter: the metallic ping of tennis ball on chicken wire, instantly followed by the squawk of hens believing themselves to be under attack.

Those hens were safe now.

I don't remember being stricken with grief, but my teacher offered sympathy by making me captain of the house table tennis team. The timing was good. Our first match was scheduled for the following Tuesday and, in between, *Grandstand* was showing a tournament from some European city – it may even have been an exhibition match, actually, one where the players earned their passage by playing the kind of extravagant, indulgent shots they'd steer clear of in proper competition. Studying the greatest British player, the mighty Desmond Douglas, would be the ideal preparation.

As he cruised to victory, Douglas made it look so easy, as if the ball contained tiny ball bearings that were attracted by an invisible magnetised panel on his bat. His accuracy was astonishing, a tall man able to deftly control a bat and ball that looked tiny in his hands. His head was still, his footwork mesmerising and his devastating smash hit the target almost every time.

As much as I told myself I had risen to the lofty position of captain on the basis of my own mesmerising footwork and devastating smash (which my teacher, who taught history and not PE, had never seen), my appointment was undeniably an act of charity. This was abundantly clear from my first showing with the figurative skipper's armband on. I appeared to have no knowledge – or ability – of how to cope against a player who not only had unzipped his own super-smart, super-smooth bat before the match, but who introduced me to a new type of spin with every shot. Twice the ball hit my glasses before flying off across the gym. I was trounced, savaged, humiliated. Captains are supposed to be the leader of the pack, and almost certainly their best player. I was relieved of the job later that day.

Another reminder of how belief in your own abilities can pull up well short of the mark came the following week at the inaugural meeting of the lunchtime Subbuteo club. I'd diligently brought my favourite brown-shirted team into school, which I believed made them Dumbarton, despite a complete lack of evidence that this was actually their shirt colour. (My players could, of course, have been Coventry City in their shit-brown away kit of the time. But, you know, who wanted to be Coventry?)

I'd even brought my Subbuteo 'electronic' scoreboard in for the occasion, a technological wonder that was actually as analogue and non-electronic as they come. I soon wished I'd left it at home. In the first game, I got thrashed in the same manner as I had seven days earlier at table tennis. Worse, in fact. The scoreboard – *my disloyal scoreboard* – showed I hadn't moved off nil. In an echo of the lyrics to The Undertones' 'My Perfect Cousin', it turned out my grasp of Subbuteo's rules wasn't as deep as the instruction booklet dictated. I didn't know.

Twelve-nil in a five-minute game. Relegation certainties from the off. Poor Dumbarton.

DRAWING A BLANK

I DON'T remember inheriting anything from Grandad. Perhaps a little bit of money went into a savings account, but none of his belongings came my way. I wasn't now the guardian of his sacred cricket bat, nor had I taken possession of a collection of fastidiously compiled scorecards from Test series past.

I had been up for some kind of sporting inheritance. I was an avid reader of 'Billy's Boots', a cartoon strip in one of my favourite publications of the day, *Tiger & Scorcher*. The premise was simple: a young lad called Billy Dane turned into a footballing sensation every time he played in the old boots of 'Dead Shot' Keen, a deceased goalscoring legend whose footwear Billy's grandfather had once bought as a souvenir and which the young lad found in his grandmother's attic. Grandad's death was too recent for me to go rummaging through his possessions, so I made a commitment to scour the village's regular Saturday afternoon jumble sales (only while some duff sport was showing on *Grandstand*, of course – ice dancing, perhaps, or dressage) in search of a pair of rotten old boots that would turn me into a free-scoring local superstar.

I was in need of some assistance. The previous season, I'd scored ten goals from left wing for our village under-11s team. The move to under-12s had proved troublesome; deep into November, I was still to get off the mark and in danger of being demoted to left back. No one wanted to play left back.

I never did find what I was looking for. The ultimate prize would have been the boots of someone like Dixie Dean, the man about whom every football reference book on my shelves gushed over, thanks to his legendary 60 goals for Everton in the 1927-28 league season. I admit I was naïve when drawing up my wish list. Why on earth would such an historical artefact not be in a museum cabinet somewhere? Plus, Dixie Dean had plied his trade 300-odd miles away at Goodison Park. What were the chances of his boots turning up among piles of unwanted clothing and footwear at the far bottom of the country?

Reassurance about my lean spell in front of goal came before the year's end when I saw an interview with Garry Birtles, either on *Football Focus* or the ITV equivalent, *On the Ball*. The young striker – scoring for fun at Nottingham Forest, with whom he had already won two European Cups – had recently earned himself a seven-figure transfer to Old Trafford, but things weren't progressing as planned. He too was experiencing a goal drought, yet to find the net for his new club. He said he wasn't unduly worried. Goals would come. It was just a case of relaxing. I heeded his advice and yes, nabbed my first of the season the following morning. A toe-poke from three yards out, but the duck was broken.

Birtles' advice didn't work for himself, though. He failed to score for United that entire season, drawing a blank in 25 matches and only finally getting off the mark 11 months after signing.

It was never revealed whether he'd had to scour the jumble sales of Stretford and Salford to help him make the breakthrough.

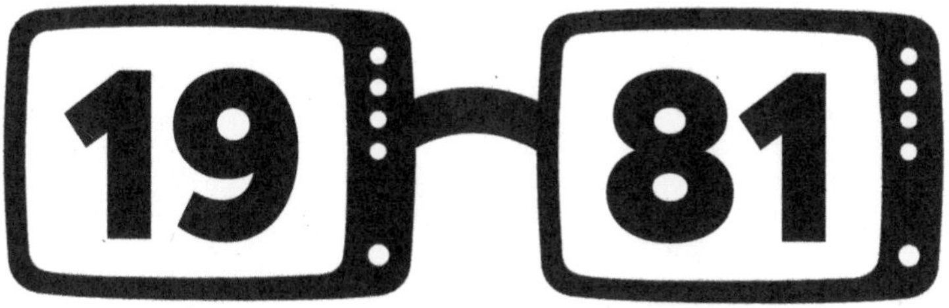
19
81

THE LONELINESS OF THE CROSS-COUNTRY RUNNER

ONE OF the plus points of ascending into secondary education was the chance to participate – albeit compulsorily – in a new sport: cross-country. This to me was proper athletics. The only concession my primary school had made to the art of running was a 200m grass track marked out every June, in wobbly lines of white emulsion, for sports day and for sports day alone. Not only did my secondary school boast a 400m track, but its provision for cross-country was much more than running endless laps of plain, dull, flat playing fields. We were sent off out of the school gates, along the canal, under the dual carriageway, up through the woods, past a row of shops, across the looping footbridge, over the canal, through a gap in the fence, and back via the sports pitches.

The shape of the course lent itself to a little skulduggery. In one episode of *Grange Hill*, Tucker, Benny and Alan hopped on a bus to foreshorten their efforts on their cross-country run. That wasn't an option for us; bus companies tended not to run services along canal towpaths. But no matter. Our route was a broadly drawn figure-of-eight, so miscreants could shelter under the dual-carriageway bridge – the crossover point of the two loops – to catch their breath before climbing up the bank and rejoining the pack as they went over the top ten minutes later. If the teacher – perhaps angry Mr Turner or chirpy Mr Gill – got wise to them, the inevitable 'You're only cheating yourself' lecture would get yet another outing. Let the record show I only cheated myself on one occasion.

The romantic life of the long-distance runner – and its fabled loneliness – greatly appealed to me. It was a pursuit that came with distinct benefits for the socially less confident. If you weren't up to the grade performance-wise, it was only yourself you had to answer to, unlike a team sport where any inadequacies would be loudly dissected by teammates and coaches throughout those long minibus journeys home. (After one particular cricket match a few years later, that same Mr Turner made sure I overheard the comment 'I can't believe Tassell took two wickets bowling that shit'. One straight out of the motivational textbook.)

I had the right physique for running distances: lithe, skinny and, as puberty approached, sufficiently leggy. I could even wear my specs while taking part. Seeing where you were going was a definite advantage, after all. But despite making the school team – based on my ever-present attendance at after-school cross-country practice more than anything, setting in motion the making-up-the-numbers theme of most of my subsequent sport participation – I was far from a natural. When I did run for the school at a couple of Saturday morning races, it was a personal triumph that I didn't come last in either. I was second to last both times.

I simply didn't have the stamina; it turned out that sharing a house with a couple of smoking enthusiasts wasn't great for developing strong lung capacity. And there was a psychological barrier, too. Whenever I started to run out of puff, I found it hard to overcome my inner demons. These inner demons continually asked a simple question: 'Why don't you just walk instead?'

So, again, my appreciation of a sport – and my admiration for sportspeople with the necessary ability, physique and psyche to excel – was shown through the dedication to park my backside down and watch long-distance runners on the small screen. And there were plenty of opportunities to do just that. On the last weekend of March 1981 alone, there were two televised events that allowed me to doff a metaphorical cap towards athletes with a far superior lung capacity to me.

First up were the World Cross-Country Championships, that year being held in Madrid. A racecourse in springtime Spain wasn't quite my experience of the sport. Where were the narrow towpath and the vertigo-inducing footbridge, for starters? Nor, I suspect, was it the experience of too many of the British runners competing in the worlds. Madrid didn't offer the muddy slopes and wind chill factor of Gateshead, where most of the BBC's cross-country coverage seemed to be broadcast from. (While my head is certain that Gateshead hosted the national championships year after year, I've just checked the record books – aka the internet – and have found that *exactly the opposite* is the case. It turns out they were held pretty much everywhere else but.)

Not only were the Madrid temperatures not as bracing as north-east England, but I also suspect that, when the starting gun sounded, the gathered Europeans, North Americans and East Africans had it somewhat easier than us gallant souls in our school cross-country championships. After all, they didn't have to contend with Dean Harwood, the star centre-forward of our year's football team, zigzagging back and forth across the back of the bunch kicking everyone's legs out from under them.

From my position on the sofa, I enjoyed watching cross-country more than long-distance track events for obvious reasons: the varied terrain, the different tactics, the possibility of someone going arse over tit on a particularly muddy section. It was also revealing to watch athletes taking themselves out of their comfort zones, competing in a different environment with its own variables. The second major long-distance event of the weekend did exactly that too.

Even today, it does still seem like woefully misguided planning to schedule a brand-new long-distance running event (to which the cream of the world's runners had been invited) the day after a very established long-distance running event (at which the cream of the world's runners were competing). But, on that damp Sunday morning in late March, the London Marathon took its bow.

No matter the scheduling. No matter if some of the world's elite runners had plumped for Spain instead. The athletes were of secondary concern. In that debut year, the location was undoubtedly the star. And the organisers pretty much got it right from the start. Yes, subsequent years saw the finishing line shift its position, but the general Greenwich–Tower Bridge–Isle of Dogs–Tower Bridge–West End route has survived for the best part of four decades. And it gave a country boy like me his first proper inkling of how that massive metropolis fitted together. Within a couple of years, I was fairly certain that should I ever need to find my way from Greenwich Park to the Cutty Sark, I could do so successfully (even if that meant following the race's six-mile detour rather than taking the much shorter, as-the-crow-flies route).

While the sporting purist in me could do without the chicken costumes and the trad jazz bands playing on street corners, the whole thing was undeniably an absorbing spectacle right from the start. The scale was vast, both in the number of London landmarks it took in and the number of eager participants willing to publicly put themselves through torture on the capital's streets. Even better, it brought sport on to Sunday morning TV, albeit for a single weekend each year. Even better still, the BBC coverage had its own enduring theme tune to which it would be wedded in perpetuity – Ron

Goodwin's regal-sounding 'The Trap', originally composed for the 1966 film of the same name.

Despite all of these ingredients, I had a particular issue with that first race. Approaching the finish line on Constitution Hill, along the northern flank of Buckingham Palace, the leading pair in the men's race – Dick Beardsley of the US and the Norwegian Inge Simonsen – gave each other a conspiratorial nod and crossed the line holding hands. David Coleman's straight-bat commentary showed he was clearly in favour of the gesture, declaring how the pair had extended 'the hand of friendship' and personified 'the true spirit of a people's marathon'. I didn't agree. This wasn't sport. This wasn't competition. I wanted to see a death-or-glory battle for the line. Agony and ecstasy. Triumph and despair. This was why we'd got up early on a Sunday morning. To see winners. To see losers. After more than two hours of committed racing – and two hours of committed viewing – all we got was a lousy draw.

TAKE ME TO THE RIVER

WATCHING SPORT in the flesh can often fall short of what you expect the experience to be. For instance, position yourself on a French roadside come July, wait a few long, sun-baked hours and then the peloton of the Tour de France is likely to zip past you in a blur before you can say 'EPO'.

A week after the London Marathon made its first appearance on the British sporting calendar, as a family we found ourselves in the capital, standing among the throng on the banks of the Thames, a few hundred yards east of Chiswick Bridge. The throng spoke with the kind of cut-glass accents I'd never heard before, the voices of those I would later identify as Sloanes and yuppies. These weren't my natural companions, but we were thrust together cheek by jowl, all gathered to watch the closing stages of that year's Oxford-Cambridge Boat Race. The fact that most were drinking as if they had a Saharan thirst on should have been a warning.

The Boat Race was never the most gripping event on TV. My personal highlight was always the point at which the two crews would row past Craven Cottage, when the director in the BBC gantry would treat us to an aerial shot of the best example of a Victorian stadium in all the Football League. Or, perhaps, there was the outside prospect of one of the boats sinking. The Cambridge crew had disappeared beneath the waterline just three years previously; that was the best edition of the race I'd ever seen.

In 1981, though, there was no dramatic sinking. There was no drama at all. Oxford's winning margin was the widest since the nineteenth century. Positioned close to the finish, we saw one boat pass us as they slowed to victory and then another boat pass us as they slowed to defeat. They might as well have been on a training session. The alcohol that the rest of the crowd were sucking down had a purpose; it was a deathly dull occasion otherwise. For the second weekend on the trot, I felt somewhat short-changed by the capital's sporting offerings.

MICKEY THOMAS'S CHEWING GUM

TWELVE-YEAR-OLD boys aren't the usual students of causation theory. I certainly wasn't. In fact, I wouldn't know of its existence for many years to come. But had it been explained to me on the morning of the second Saturday of May 1981, events that afternoon would have made perfect sense.

Here was the scenario: Manchester City were leading Spurs in the Cup Final, thanks to a crashing thunderbolt of a header from

Tommy Hutchison, their Scottish midfielder who looked every bit his 33 years – plus at least another decade on top. I'd been rooting for Spurs, not just because of my dad's loose affection for them, but also because of their flair players: the likes of Glenn Hoddle, Ossie Ardiles and one of my favourite strikers, Steve Archibald. Plus, I had a distrust of City's bejewelled manager John Bond. I wasn't one for flash Harrys. Or flash Johns.

There was quarter of an hour left and something needed to change. I knew there was still time; the last five minutes of the '79 final, with its three late goals, had taught me that. Perhaps, all those miles away, I could be an agent of change. I tried doing a few things differently to help the Spurs cause. Like turning my back on the screen. Like leaving the room entirely. Like even feigning an admiration for City and John Bond. Nothing doing, though. Nada. Zip.

Or, as my gran would say, 'sweet Fanny Adams'.

I'd read plenty of Q&As in *Shoot!* magazine, in which players downplayed their own talents and revealed the superstitions they subscribed to. It was as if the scaling of their personal peaks and summits had simply been down to the repeated observing of irrational rituals. I remember Man Utd winger Mickey Thomas's superstition involved spitting out his chewing gum as he ran out onto the pitch and then trying to volley it. If he made contact, it meant he was going to have a good game. If he missed, he wouldn't. Most players' rituals were less gross, and usually involved the sequence in which they put on their kit. The left sock on first. Their shorts on last. That kind of thing. There was even one who went public with the fact he wore his underpants back to front.

I thought such things to be largely mumbo jumbo, to be excuses made for poor performances that were actually quite clearly within a player's control. But, with Spurs requiring an injection of good fortune, who was I to cast aspersions on the collective wisdom of football's finest? That afternoon, I decided to join them in their curious, attire-based superstitions. I had no intention of switching my underpants around, so instead elected to swap my sweatshirt. Off came the grey-blue one that had been put out for me that morning, with its discreet Levi's logo on the left side of the chest. On went a black one emblazoned with the legend 'Hawks' in white, blocky letters.

Had Tottenham's nickname been the Hawks rather than Spurs, it might have made sense, but as it began with an H, like Hotspur, it would have to do. And do it did. Almost immediately, Spurs were awarded a free kick when Ardiles was chopped down on the edge of the area. Up stepped Hoddle (another H) whose shot hit the shoulder of Hutchison (a third H – are you seeing the signs too?). The ball's path altered dramatically and now arced towards the net in precisely the opposite direction to that chosen by Joe Corrigan in the City goal. 1-1. I had saved Spurs. I had secured them a draw. They lived to fight another day.

That day came five days later, when my tactical genius again worked its magic. It was a Thursday, a school night, and I only got to stay up to see the whole replay after some intense, high-level negotiation of which the likes of ASLEF and the NUM would have been proud. After much deliberation – over milk and digestives, rather than beer and sandwiches – an agreement had been thrashed out with my parents that, as long as I was in my pyjamas and had brushed my teeth by 9pm, I'd be able to watch the rest of the game. (I had deliberately not mooted what would happen in the event of extra time. Should the scores have still been level after 90 minutes, that would have needed further high-level negotiations that may have required the intervention of the arbitration service ACAS.)

The obvious thing to have done was to have fulfilled my contractual requirements during half-time. The trouble was, I spent half-time watching every-angle replays of Steve MacKenzie's stupendous 11th-minute volley that had cancelled out Spurs' early lead. At about 8.45pm – and with Spurs 2-1 behind to a Kevin Reeves penalty – I shot upstairs to keep my side of the bargain. I was back within less than a minute, now resplendent in burgundy paisley pyjamas and with teeth that had had barely cursory attention. A future believer in matters supernatural, Glenn Hoddle again seemed to acknowledge my change of clothes and immediately went on the offensive, exactly as he had done in the first match. Within seconds of my reappearance in the living room, he played a delicate chip over the statuesque City defence and a combination of Steve Archibald and Garth Crooks conjured up the equaliser. I'd turned the tide again.

Six minutes later – and possibly because I had put on *two* items of clothing – Spurs struck again, Ricky Villa's lazy, mazy dribble culminating in what would later be named the greatest-ever Wembley goal, fittingly coming in the 100th Cup Final. This six-minute passage of play was incontrovertible evidence that what had just occurred in a house in deepest Sussex had a direct line to a football pitch 80-odd miles away. Had I put my dressing gown on too, I dare say Spurs would have added another goal before full time.

Mickey Thomas was right. There was something in this superstition nonsense after all.

DIZZY HEIGHTS

THE ABILITY to alter the course of a distant football match simply by changing my clothes was an impressive superpower that, if proved reliable over a larger sample than two matches, would surely make me the envy of my friends, family and bookmakers alike. But this didn't seem to be a legitimate route into the sport. I knew what would, though. I wanted to be a commentator.

In later years, once we had a video (we were late adopters), I would record matches and, when no one else was in the house, play them back with the sound turned right down so that I could commentate over the top of them. It was the sporting equivalent of singing into a hairbrush in front of the bedroom mirror. In his book *Outliers*, Malcolm Gladwell explains how success tends to arrive only after the individual has put 10,000 hours of practice into their chosen vocation. Had I known that at the time, that would have been an awful lot of video tapes I'd have had to fork out for. It would have probably been cheaper for me to put myself through five years of medical school.

These imagined commentaries also provided the soundtrack to solo kickabouts on the driveway. I was always much happier on my own – re-enacting, with this audio enhancement, the goals from the previous weekend's matches – than I was playing three-and-in with a friend. When I was with someone else, out of embarrassment and shyness, I'd keep my mouth shut.

That shyness to commentate in front of others wasn't the only obstacle to joining Motson and Moore and Davies and Gubba in the ranks of the sheepskin-wearing mic men. In the same way that the footbridge on the cross-country run was capable of inducing the medical condition known as the collywobbles, the idea of taking a precarious perch on a rooftop gantry atop a club's main stand wasn't a fear I was rushing to overcome.

At the end of the 1980-81 First Division campaign, Tony Morley's brilliant solo goal for Villa at Everton – where he charged down the left wing before planting the ball out of reach of the Toffees' keeper Martin Hodge – won *Match of the Day*'s Goal of the Season competition. The footage, though, set the vertigo going again, with the BBC's cameras set up on a gantry in the gods at such a steep angle to the pitch that, when Morley gathered the ball on the touchline beneath, the cameras seemed to be directly above him. Even on the telly, and a few months after the goal was actually scored, the footage continued to provoke mild nausea in me.

I tried to make peace with this, figuring out how I could avoid this occupational hazard, how I could keep my feet closer to terra firma in this imaginary future career of mine. Perhaps, I thought, so rapid and irresistible my ascendancy through the commentator ranks would be that I could pick and choose exactly which grounds I would grace with my presence. I'd worked out that David Coleman was likely to have retired by the time I reached the unfathomably ancient age of 25. At that point, I reckoned Barry Davies would be handed Coleman's gig as athletics commentator, leaving a vacancy in the football ranks. I'd fill the gap and rise up the *Match of the Day* hierarchy with such speed that I'd be in a position to call the shots. Goodison Park, and its death-drop commentary position, could be left well alone.

Elsewhere, the cameras and the commentary perch were positioned at a more civilised level. Portman Road in Ipswich was one such stadium, a ground of intimacy and atmosphere, and where the football was first-rate. Ipswich were almost everybody's second team. Most fans had a soft spot for them – at least those who didn't call Norfolk home. With a style of play authored by the twin Dutch pivots in midfield – Arnold Mühren and Frans Thijssen – they played exciting, open football and, in May 1981, secured their one and only European title: the UEFA Cup. Compared to the recent successes of Liverpool, Nottingham Forest and Aston Villa in the premier competition, the European Cup, Ipswich's triumph over AZ '67 Alkmaar went curiously under-celebrated. Perhaps, by being held over a two-legged final, the

UEFA Cup couldn't match the one-night-only drama of its more prestigious sibling. But there was drama by the gallon in the '81 final, especially during the second leg in Amsterdam.

Bobby Robson's team flew to the Netherlands with a comfortable three-goal advantage after the first match at Portman Road and, when Thijssen fired them into an early lead on his return to home soil, victory seemed assured. The Dutch had other ideas, coming from behind to win on the night 4-2. It was Ipswich's 66th game of the season. There were no winter breaks, no squad rotations for the Tractor Boys. A game too many, perhaps, but there was the insurance policy of that 3-0 home victory to give them both a 5-4 aggregate winning margin and the trophy.

John Motson had been on commentary duties in Amsterdam for the second leg, as well as being first choice for the FA Cup Final and its replay. So good sense and fair play prevailed in the corridors of power at the BBC when Barry Davies was handed a division of the spoils – that is, he was given the nod for the European Cup Final at the Parc des Princes in Paris where, exactly a week after Ipswich's trip to the Netherlands, two-time winners Liverpool would be taking on six-time champions Real Madrid.

The Motson/Davies rivalry wasn't a rivalry as such. There were no bitchy words exchanged publicly, no pistols at dawn. But it was another of those perceived face-offs that studded the sporting landscape of the early '80s. Athletics had Coe/Ovett, while tennis had both Borg/McEnroe and Evert/Navratilova. Beyond the BBC commentary box, football had its own one too: the battle between Ray Clemence and Peter Shilton to claim the number one shirt for England on a permanent basis. Just like this particular duel where both goalkeepers were given plenty of time between the posts, Motson and Davies were both rostered for the big games, even if the younger Motson would receive the larger share.

Although most people didn't side with one commentator or the other in the way they aligned themselves with a particular middle-distance runner or tennis player, as a kid I preferred Motson, mainly for his ready supply of facts and stats, the possession of which earned respect in the school playground come Monday morning. As I got older, I grew more into Davies and his style, both for his more figurative use of words and for the odd acerbic observation. But, having a decent moral compass back then, I was perfectly accepting that the prime jobs were shared around, and so I welcomed Davies climbing into the commentary box in Paris. How good of me.

As it was, I only got to judge Davies's first half; a mediocre school report issued earlier that day gave me no leverage at all on the staying-up-late front. With only one television in the house at this point, I was hamstrung. I couldn't simply lie in bed oblivious to the ebb and flow of the match while my classmates, whose school reports were presumably less mediocre than mine, soaked up each and every tackle, shot and save. So I plumped for the next best thing: the tried-and-tested transistor radio under the bed covers.

It wasn't the same. Yes, I had a decent imagination and could visualise each phase of action in my mind's eye, but something was lacking – and it wasn't simply the moving pictures. I'd grown used to the pitch, delivery and vocabulary of Motson and Davies. If I closed my eyes, regardless of the actual words they were saying I would pretty much know where on the pitch the action was, simply from the level of excitement in their respective voices. The closer to either penalty area the ball came, the higher the needle climbed towards the red. But the radio commentary on that particular May evening didn't offer up those easy clues.

So when, in the dying minutes in Paris, Liverpool left back Alan Kennedy collected the ball from a throw and made a sudden charge into the Madrid penalty area that ended with him firing home the only goal of the game, I was almost non-plussed about the whole affair. I heard Davies's reaction a few days later and he'd been suitably excited as Kennedy's shot nestled in the Madrid net. 'Alan Kennedy . . . and he goes on . . . and he scores!'

But in his Radio 2 commentary, Peter Jones sounded utterly matter of fact about the goal. His words weren't exclamatory. They were sing-song at best. He sounded as though the goal was inevitable and never in doubt. Perhaps he was trying to keep a lid on his annoyance at not drawing Kennedy in the office sweepstake based around who'd score the first goal. Or perhaps he was an Evertonian.

I acknowledge now that Jones had a more difficult proposition: transporting a young lad who was covertly listening in the dark under the covers (and, I'm guessing, transporting hundreds of thousands of young lads doing likewise) to the noise and heat and drama of that stadium in Paris. It's just that, without the pictures, he needed to up the excitement levels somewhat.

From that moment on, I vowed to keep things a strictly audiovisual affair. There was a downside, of course. Half-decent school reports would be needed to make that happen.

SECOND BILLING

IF FATE didn't play fair when it came to career options, if I never made the grade as a football commentator, there was a Plan B, an alternative path to take.

Sport on television rarely got any more exciting than if you were watching through the in-car camera on board a rally car – possibly a Saab 99 or a Lancia Stratos – that was hurtling impossibly fast through mud and over gravel, the prospect of a spectacular crash just an ill-judged slide away. I fancied a piece of that.

To me, it was the co-drivers who were the true heroes of the rally world. The likes of Christian Geistdörfer, Walter Röhrl's wingman for two World Championship triumphs, and Arne Hertz, right-hand man of choice for both Stig Blomqvist and Hannu Mikkola, were surely the stars of the show.

After all, anyone could throw a car sideways around the dusty tracks of a forest at high speed. They had the advantage of a windscreen to look through. The co-driver had no such luxury. He or she had to show their magic with their eyes in their lap, matching a clipboard's scribbled, near-indecipherable instructions with the bends and hairpins that arrived and disappeared in the blink of an eye. A single miscalculation and the rally – and potentially more – was over.

They were a double act, the driver taking top billing while the co-driver played the straight man. Second-in-command role suited me fine. Less pressure but still indispensable. And you were still allowed to sit on your car's bonnet and spray champagne over anyone within range should you actually win.

There was just one problem. At this time, I could travel barely 200 yards down a less-than-arrow-straight road without experiencing rising waves of nausea and demanding that the car pulled over. You couldn't ask Björn Waldegård or Ari Vatanen to slip into the nearest lay-by so that you could regurgitate your breakfast. This created an obstacle to my second-choice sporting ambition. If the vertigo didn't get the future football commentator, travel sickness would surely extinguish the dream of the wannabe co-driver.

THE HOLY DAY

SUNDAY 17 May 1981 was a day that would shape my decade like few others. There it was, in black and white. The

Radio Times was saying it. It was going to happen.

BBC2
14.30 Sunday Grandstand
Introduced by Desmond Lynam
The first in a new series of Sunday programmes which will reflect the changing face of British and international sport with the emphasis moving to a Sunday conclusion of many major events.

Previously, BBC2 had broadcast sporting action on most Sundays, but on an as-and-when basis, and always as stand-alone programmes. Now, with Formula One increasingly favouring Sundays as their day of racing, the channel decided to package them up into one overall programme – and to commit to a run of this afternoon-long show throughout the summer months.

It effectively stretched Saturday – the undisputed best day of the week – across the weekend. Double impact. A guaranteed second full afternoon bouncing from golf course to tennis court, grand prix circuit to running track. A further bonus, too; there was no horse racing on a Sunday.

It meant, of course, more chances for me to learn the commentator's craft, to study the ways and words of those mic men who weren't necessarily heard week in, week out on the BBC. The likes of Alan Weeks for gymnastics, or Hamilton Bland for swimming, for whom the new programme presumably plumped up their pay packets with time and a half for unsocial hours. We all benefited.

For the first show, Jim Laker and Christopher Martin-Jenkins headed off to the shires for some decidedly relaxed John Player League cricket action, a five-man commentating deputation (Carpenter, Alliss, Clark, Critchley and Hay) had been dispatched to the West Course at Wentworth for the final day of the Martini International tournament, and that now-dependable pairing of Murray Walker and James Hunt held court at Zolder for a Belgian Grand Prix not short on either controversy or tragedy.

The quality of the events and the output remained high over the subsequent weeks. The pre-satellite 1980s were when the BBC was in its pomp when it came to securing broadcasting rights for sport, ensuring that nothing ever felt stretched thinly over a four- or five-hour programme. The second week of *Sunday Grandstand* gave us more golf and more John Player League cricket, but also athletics from Antrim and gymnastics from Rome. The week after was the Monaco Grand Prix and international showjumping from Hickstead. Later that summer would come the French Open and the Ashes and Wimbledon and plenty more besides.

Guiding and gliding us through Sunday afternoons, presumably also earning a little overtime, was the old smoothie himself – Des Lynam. He was undoubtedly the sporting anchorman of the era. No one was his equal. Not Coleman, not Davies, not Moore, not Carpenter, not Rider, not Bough. No one seemed as quite at ease with all and any sports as Lynam, a broad-brush – but never vacuous – amalgam of charmer and everyman. He was a fan of sport above being a presenter. It was just that he could combine and intertwine the two with ridiculous ease.

And he was inclusive, welcoming. Never snippy, never snide. Des could be your favourite uncle, the one who would slip a nip of something into your fizzy pop at a family gathering, serving it with a knowing wink that told you that you were in his club. That you were accepted. That you were all right.

Uncle Des and I were in that club together every single Sunday that summer. And for many years to come.

TRUE HORSEPOWER

OF ALL the sporting occasions that could have fallen during a week I was sofa-bound with tonsillitis, there were plenty I'd have put ahead of the Derby. As almost all the Saturday afternoons in the decade would prove, I never developed a strong bond with horse racing. Give me races on two legs or two wheels or four wheels, and I'd be first in line. But for some reason, the self-branded sport of kings left me colder than cold.

Even so, when ITV's afternoon programming on the first Wednesday in June went live to Epsom Downs, I reluctantly stayed tuned in. There were probably only schools programmes on the BBC. I was sure I could get something out of the race. It only lasted three minutes anyway. Being a far keener fan of motorsport, I was always distracted during the horse racing by the ambulance that would invariably be belting round the inside of the track, trying to keep pace with the pack, ready to attend to any imminent catastrophe.

I was in luck at the '81 Derby. Once the runners and riders were under starter's orders and off, not only did an ambulance lurch into view behind them, but also a Volvo estate, the two vehicles barrelling and bumping down the course after the horses. This was definitely a more riveting contest, with the Volvo in particular being driven in the same manner that Hannu Mikkola would throw his Audi Quattro around Kielder Forest. Whoever was behind the wheel – presumably the chief steward or head vet – seemed intent on beating the ambulance to the winning post. Peter Bromley's commentary fitted just fine with the four-wheel duel. 'That's the leader in the early stages . . . the favourite is beautifully placed as they go under the mile-and-a-quarter gate . . . He's opening up a lead now!'

As the horses turned Tattenham Corner into the home straight, the vehicles disappeared out of the camera's view, prematurely curtailing my fun. Rather than concentrate on the remaining 50 seconds or so of the Derby itself, I was then distracted by the line of double-decker buses parked in their usual formation on the inner rail of the track, musing at how many of them Eddie Kidd – the just-emerging motorcycle stunt rider, Islington's own Evel Knievel – could clear on his motorbike.

Only when Bromley's increasingly excited tones punched through this distraction – 'There's only one horse in it. You need a telescope to see the rest!' – did I realise something rather special was happening. And so it was that I missed all but the last few seconds of one of the most impressive Derby victories ever, the dominance of a horse named Shergar.

CHAINED TO THE SOFA

IF I cared to look over my shoulder, I could have seen the length of the needle the doctor was preparing. But I didn't need to see it. Within a few seconds I would be feeling it, boring deep into one of my buttocks, ripping its way into the muscle and bringing several tears to the eye.

I was no stranger to the doctor's needle that year. I was a pretty sickly child throughout spring and into early summer. If there was an ailment, I seemed to contract it. Had Big Chief I-Spy published an *I-Spy Book of Moderate Illnesses*, I'd have been earning points all over the shop. Before that dose of tonsillitis around the time of the Derby, I'd had a few days suffering from a particularly violent episode of gastroenteritis which, through the unceasing stomach cramps and frequent dashes to the downstairs loo, had initially raised a chuckle. When he first diagnosed it, I thought the doctor said I was suffering from Vitas Gerulaitis.

The subsequent tonsillitis then segued into a protracted bout of glandular fever that, despite the frequency of the injections in my backside, left me even more listless and feeble than usual. It meant a good few weeks off school and a good few weeks on the sofa, under a blanket and quaffing Lucozade by the quart.

But I was at ease with all the injections and the medicine and the listlessness and everything else. I saw it as the graft that gained the reward, the Faustian pact I'd signed. For while my peers were learning about the properties of potassium permanganate and studying *To Kill a Mockingbird*, I was watching pretty much every ball of the Ashes, the glorious Ashes of 1981. What a time to be seriously ill.

The first two Tests were disappointing: an Australian win at Trent Bridge and a draw at Lord's, after which Ian Botham and the captaincy went separate ways. In the third Test at Headingley – with England in such a perilous situation that the bookies quantified them as a 500/1 chance of winning the Test – the shackles were off and Botham began to spray the ball to all four corners of the ground. The BBC's commentators, in particular Christopher Martin-Jenkins and Richie Benaud, were purring at Botham's shot selection, both the immaculately timed and the improvised. Ably supported by Graham Dilley, whose stoicism bought his senior partner time, Botham ended up a free-hitting 149 not out. It was an innings that brought great tonic to me: not only was his display a welcome distraction from my illness, but it ensured that play would continue into a fifth and final day. That was good enough for me. At that point, even the medication I was on didn't present the kind of mind-altering scenario where England would actually win. That would require skittling out Australia for under 130, the same Australia who'd made a declaration beyond the 400-run mark in the first innings.

But win England did the next day, when they found another hero. Yes, Botham had saved the Test, but it was Bob Willis who won it, steaming in from the Kirkstall Lane End and destroying the Australian batsmen, in the process recording extraordinary figures of eight for 43. The last nine wickets fell for just 55 runs. I felt the best that I had in weeks.

Willis was the man of the hour for me, someone a little shyer and more self-effacing than his more public-facing fellow strike bowler. He was a man of depth, too. I was delighted to learn that the 'D' in his name as presented on the scorecard – R.G.D Willis – stood for 'Dylan', having changed his name to include the surname of his favourite guitar-toting balladeer. Indeed, it was a few years later, when I was fully music-savvy, before I realised that his magnificently thick thatch of hair was modelled on Dylan's own barnet circa *Blonde On Blonde*. This was refreshing. Going by the Q&As in *Shoot!*, the musical appreciation of most footballers extended little further than Luther Vandross, Barry White or Teddy Pendergrass.

Botham grasped the bull by the horns at Edgbaston where a not dissimilar situation – Australia had been set 151 to win – played out again. This time an extraordinary spell with the ball, where he took five wickets in 28 balls while only conceding a single run, gave England a 29-run win. A third victory at Old Trafford gave England the series, rendering the sixth and final Test at The Oval a dead rubber.

This was a shame as The Oval was, and probably still is, my favourite of England's Test grounds. Lord's to me felt too much the domain of the Panama-and-blazer brigade, while Kennington gave a magnificently prosaic backdrop to cricket south of the river. Not only was there the famous gasometer, but the ground was partially surrounded by those distinctive tenement blocks. I made a vow to live there when I became a responsible, tax-paying adult. The flats' open windows afforded their residents corking views of the ground which, combined with having the radio commentary turned up to 11, made for cricket heaven. (I later rescinded this ambition when I heard the flats' most famous resident, Ian Dury, refer to his top-floor abode as 'Catshit Mansions'.)

The series would be forever remembered as Botham's Ashes, a rather unfair branding bearing in mind Willis's massive performance in that pivotal third Test. That said, despite this injustice, when us neighbourhood kids inevitably picked up bat and ball in the aftermath of that glorious series win (and when I'd finally shaken off my own less than glorious series of illnesses), it wasn't Bob's brilliance we were trying to replicate.

The previous summer, in those occasional hours when I did emerge into sunlight, Alex Cooper and I had multiple games of 'Allan Wells' over the 100-metre stretch of pavement between his house and mine. The game consisted of nothing more than trying to run as fast as possible against the clock – aka Alex's new digital watch. We didn't need a photo finish to determine the winner. Alex made a decent Allan Wells, but I was no Silvio Leonard. There was plenty of daylight between the two of us.

In the summer of '81, 'Ian Botham' became the game of choice. The rules were as simple as 'Allan Wells'. You had to slog the ball in a Beefy-like manner across Alex's back garden and, whenever it landed in the sticky sludge at the bottom of a small, disused ornamental pond, you scored six runs. Each time Alex planted the ball in the sludge (which was plenty), my inner commentator would pop up and adapt one of Richie Benaud's most famous lines for anyone within earshot.

'That's gone straight in the confectionery stall. And stayed there.'

RETURN OF THE MAC

SEVERAL MOVIE sequels came out in 1981 – *Friday the 13th Part II, Halloween II, Mad Max 2* – but none of them reached the heights of their respective originals. It was a truth transferable to sport. In July, on American Independence Day, the second instalment of Borg versus McEnroe at Wimbledon couldn't possibly replicate the dramatic plot twists of the first chapter.

The signs were all there: not just that it wouldn't be another near-four-hour thriller, but also that the title could well change hands. Borg had already been put through a five-set match in his semi-final, when he rescued himself from two sets down to Jimmy Connors (who'd taken the first set to love) to reach his fifth consecutive final. McEnroe's passage to the final was much easier: he'd dropped just two sets, albeit while not having had to face a single seeded player. The New Yorker did his best to make it difficult for himself, though. His outbursts – more vocal and vitriolic than in 1980 – earned him reprimands and fines, and could have endangered his continued participation in the tournament.

Although McEnroe wasn't overwhelmingly dominant in the final, it felt like his name was on the trophy. He eased to a 3-1 triumph without much drama. Even so – when the final volley buried itself deep in Borg's court – there was a sense of shock that the champion's impeccable run at Wimbledon had been neutered. Dan Maskell's commentary felt loaded with this sudden realisation, seemingly needing to repeat himself to confirm McEnroe had indeed brought an era to an end. 'That's it. He's done it! He's done it!'

The following year, Borg competed in just one tournament before, 18 months after his loss to McEnroe in his last Centre Court appearance, he retired from the sport. He was 26.

OPEN ALL HOURS

IF OLD Father Time had cruelly ensured that my grandad would lose his final wicket less than a year before arguably the greatest Ashes series ever, his widow, my gran, had no such issues when it came to her favourite sport and her favourite competition. In mid-July, the energetic old bird saw the Open Golf Championship unfold not just from close quarters, but from the closest quarters imaginable. She was a scorer for all four days at the tournament in Sandwich.

Such proximity to the hard-hitting stars of the day obviously sounded deeply glamorous to her pre-teen grandson, as well as providing him with an indisputable, inarguable reason to watch as much live coverage of the event as possible. To catch even the most fleeting of glimpses of her on screen would be a family duty, no less. And despite her diminutive stature, it should have been easy to spot her: just look out for a grey fug of cigarette smoke at every tee, on every fairway, beside every green.

There was a problem, though. Gran was scoring the shots of Bob Charles, the left-handed New Zealander who, whether by coincidence or design, just happened to be her favourite player. He'd won the Open before, but that had been 18 years earlier. Now at what to me at the time was the ridiculously elderly age of 45, Charles never threatened the leaderboard. His first round alone would have tested Gran's powers of addition, carding a 77 that removed him from contention – and from the attention of the TV cameras.

While he did make the cut and thus provide four rounds of employment for Gran, I never caught the slightest glimpse of her. Nor of that attendant cloud of cigarette smoke. In truth, without the hunt for a sighting of her, the whole tournament would have been a somewhat dull experience, what with Bill

Rogers maintaining a long-term lead of several shots over the field after a second-day 66.

Not all high-level sporting events offer edge-of-your-seat tension and intrigue to keep you glued to the screen for a full four days. So perhaps the deployment of close relatives into the proceedings is the key to gripping the casual viewer, the insurance policy to guarantee their attention.

POWER TO THE PEOPLE

MOST OF the time I was content to be watching sport from home. It was a trade-off. If I wasn't there in the flesh, soaking in all the atmosphere, then at least I'd have a way better view of proceedings on the box than if I'd paid my entrance fee and been observing from a duff position. Plus, I'd be able to chew over slow-motion replays from multiple angles, as well as having the benefit of a commentator's insight. Obviously at that point I wasn't in a position financially or logistically to be able to choose between the two scenarios, but I definitely felt I had the sweeter end of the deal.

But there was one particular aspect of a sporting event that I, sitting on my own at home, was jealous of: the crowd invasion. Here I'm not talking about the type of incursion onto the pitch or track that's attention-seeking or motivated by a sense of injustice or outrage. I mean the kind of invasion that, once the action is over, expresses the unbounded joy that sport can bring, the ecstasy that has to be shared with others. A most vivid example of this had been the mass invasion by tens of thousands of Crystal Palace fans onto the Selhurst Park turf in 1979 after the club had secured their return to the old First Division. It was a wonderful sight – a peaceful, aggro-free articulation of relief, delight and celebration.

There was a similarly communal release of joy during the summer of 1981. And it came in an unlikely location. On the third day of the Open, the Saturday, I had allowed myself a couple of hours away from grandmother-spotting at Sandwich to take in live coverage of the British Grand Prix at Silverstone. It was quickly obvious how pumped up the crowd in Northamptonshire were. Throughout the race, as the Ulsterman John Watson thrillingly threaded his Marlboro McLaren through the field, the cheers of the crowd were very much audible over the buzz and roar of the cars' engines.

Their excitement was nothing compared to the post-race scenes. After Watson took the victory, the first UK driver to win his home race since James Hunt in 1976, he was ushered onto the back of a flatbed truck to be paraded before the British fans. But they had other ideas. In their scores, they climbed the high safety fences and took to the Silverstone tarmac. The truck wasn't going anywhere, swamped and stopped by this human traffic jam. While a motor-racing circuit, with the fastest cars in the world still being driven around it, didn't seem to be the most sensible crucible in which to express this kind of people power, their rapture at Watson's win overrode any concerns they might have had for their personal safety.

I'd have loved to have taken to the circuit too, taking my chances. Sometimes, maybe you did have to be there.

THE NINE-DAY DUEL

THERE'S LITTLE to beat a sustained, intense sporting event to lose yourself in. Ideally a competition that unfolds itself over the course of at least a couple of weeks. A World Cup, a Test series, a Tour de France.

Over the course of nine days in August 1981, a non-Olympic year, middle-distance running nonetheless felt this kind of white-heat intensity. The crucible was the world mile record. And, of course, the protagonists were the two usual suspects, between whom a cigarette paper could still barely be slipped.

Sebastian Coe struck first, on a Wednesday night in Zürich. It was the first time he'd run the mile for a couple of years. The last time he did, he broke John Walker's world record, one of three he grabbed over the course of 41 days during the summer of '79. The following year, before he flew to Moscow to claim Olympic glory, Steve Ovett took the mile record for himself. Now Coe was out to reclaim it.

Urged on by his father Peter, a conspicuous presence on the track's infield in a bright red anorak and gripping a stopwatch, Coe was forced to go it alone on the final lap once the pacemakers took their leave. The split time around the final bend wasn't good news; he was well off the pace. 'Ovett's world record survives,' declared David Coleman as Coe hit the home straight. But he dug deep and kicked like he'd never kicked before. Eighty yards later, the record was his.

A week later, Ovett was in Koblenz with one thing in mind. And he went for it. Led by his pacemaking chum Bob Benn, Ovett clocked 1:53:59 at the halfway mark. This was exactly – right down to a hundredth of a second – the same split as Coe's in Zürich. There was still nothing, absolutely nothing between them.

With the German crowd getting louder with every Ovett stride, Coleman helped to ratchet up the tension and excitement even further. 'He loves to race, but there's no one left to race against. He so enjoys the personal battle against fellow competitors, but now it's Ovett against the unforgiving finger of the watch.' And he beat that watch, reducing the record by 0.13 of a second. Coleman realised, as we all did, that this battle royal was shaping up to be a classic episode in athletics history: 'Steve Ovett, within seven days, gives Sebastian Coe his answer.'

Coleman's summer tour of European athletics stadia wasn't over yet. Just 48 hours later, he was in the commentary box at the Heysel Stadium in Brussels, an arena that would have tragic connotations for British sport four years later. Back in 1981, he was completely in his element, his true habitat. There might have been better football commentators, and possibly better *Grandstand* presenters, but give Coleman a mic and a top-class athletics field and no one could touch him for articulating the high drama of it all. No one.

Coe's performance that night in Brussels was the most majestic of the three record attempts. Without recourse to examining the split times, you could tell the pace was high. At the halfway mark, the field was nearly a full second inside the time that both men had previously clocked – although Coleman, getting over-excited in the stands, misread the split time and declared that they were *three seconds* inside world-record pace.

This time, Coe wasn't alone on that last lap. The Kenyan Mike Boit was just a couple of metres behind and his presence seemed to put extra fire in Coe's legs. He broke the tape more than a second inside the record; Ovett had held it for just two days. And Coe hadn't just shaved it. He'd taken a serious chunk out of it. 'A miracle run' was Coleman's verdict. Neither Coe nor Ovett ever ran the mile faster again.

While Coe's run in Brussels – and, of course, the one in Zürich too – was an extraordinary feat, this nine-day period marked the time that I switched allegiances. It was something that Coleman had said during Ovett's race that sold it to me, when he described him as 'the man who dislikes the clinical approach to record breaking'. I realised that Ovett simply had more soul. He loved to compete, to *race*. He saw it as an art form, while Coe and his father saw it as a branch of science. To me, science meant cold, calculated, dispassionate. The arts were warm, spontaneous, heartfelt. (Also, another plus point in Ovett's favour was that he seemed to have removed that cocky premature celebration from his locker.)

I didn't, and still don't, doubt that all of Coe's multiple achievements were deserved, the product of every daylight hour – plus several before sunrise and several after sundown – being devoted to the cause. He put the shift in. Went more than the extra mile. Several extra record-breaking miles, even. It was just the coldness, the emotion-free efficiency that came with it.

Ovett was my man now.

GOODNIGHT OSLO

THE POSITIVES first. They won't take long.

The last time England had successfully navigated the qualifying stages for a World Cup was when they reached the finals in 1962. In 1966, they'd been the hosts. In 1970, the holders. In 1974 and 1978, they'd been conspicuous by their absence. In September 1981, as they attempted to head to Spain for the following summer's tournament, they appeared to be doing their utmost to secure the hat-trick of non-participation. It shouldn't have been so; after all, they had the seemingly benign task of flying to Oslo to collect maximum points against the part-timers of Norway.

Everything was going according to plan, with an early Bryan Robson goal, his first for England, settling any nerves. Despite being fouled a couple of times during the build-up, he doggedly scooped the ball home while near horizontal. It was the first inkling of the never-say-die behaviour that would see him anointed as Captain Marvel in future years.

Then it all came undone. The first Norwegian goal gave us all a jolt. The second put us in a cold sweat, gasping for air.

'We've gone absolutely chaotic,' sighed the ever-neutral Ron Atkinson, Brian Moore's co-commentator in Oslo. But Big Ron's partisanship wasn't a patch on that expressed by Norwegian broadcaster Bjørge Lillelien. His riffing on the final whistle has been quoted extensively over the decades since, but it's such a delightful example of the art that it stands up to revisiting.

'It is completely unbelievable!' Lillelien screamed in his native tongue, before demonstrating he had paid attention in history lessons at school. 'We have beaten England! England, birthplace of giants. Lord Nelson, Lord Beaverbrook, Sir Winston Churchill, Sir Anthony Eden, Clement Attlee, Henry Cooper, Lady Diana. We have beaten them all!'

He then slipped into English to taunt our island nation and the troubled government of the day. 'Maggie Thatcher! Can you hear me? Maggie Thatcher! Your boys took a hell of a beating! Your boys took a hell of a beating . . .'

It was a beating that I sincerely hoped wouldn't affect my enjoyment of the next summer's tournament by denying England's qualification. We weren't a religious family, but I may well have whispered a secret prayer to an unspecified deity that night.

ONCE IN A LIFETIME

ONE OF the staples of the *Roy of the Rovers* comic was a strip called 'Mi££ionaire Villa'. It was the story of a successful businessman called David Bradley, who saves his local club Selby Villa from bankruptcy by writing them a cheque for

£1million. An honourable man, for sure. There was one caveat, though: he had to be picked for the side every week. This was a problem. David Bradley wasn't very good at football. He was complete shit, in fact.

There was one particular 'Mi££ionaire Villa' storyline that caught my eye. Named once again in the starting XI as per the club-saving deal, Moneybags Bradley played a blinder one particular Saturday, by far the best player on the park. He put it down to a bracelet he'd been given before the match by a gypsy, a lucky charm that had worked its magic over the subsequent 90 minutes. At the end of the match, with the cheers of fans and teammates still ringing in his ears, Bradley noticed the bracelet had broken. Obviously wanting to repeat his performance the following Saturday, he took it to a jeweller for mending, whereupon he was informed that it was a cheap piece of tat that would cost more to mend than to buy new. The take-home moral of the piece was that everyone – even lousy David Bradley – has one good game in their lifetime.

It remains unrecorded whether, one December Sunday in 1981, Konrad Bartelski was wearing a cheap lucky charm. Until that day, he was largely unknown to us. Tender his name to the average British sport fan at the time and they'd be forgiven for thinking he was either a Czech pole-vaulter or the second-choice goalkeeper for Legia Warsaw. But no, he was one of ours. He was Britain's number one downhill skier.

That afternoon, he tamed the vicious slopes of Val Gardena in a manner in which he'd never tamed any slopes before – and would never do again. His gung-ho style shot him into second place, with only a slight mistake in the last couple of hundred yards costing him top spot. This was history being made in arguably one of the most un-British of sports. Thankfully, David Vine's commentary did the occasion justice: 'Suddenly the Union Jack came down the hill like a rocket.'

At home, we could tell this run was an anomaly, a quirk. It wasn't about to launch Bartelski into the sport's upper echelons for anything longer than a Warholian 15 minutes. He himself almost certainly knew this too. In the post-competition interview with Vine, he was at a loss to explain what had gone on up on those steep slopes. 'If I knew the magic ingredient, I'd go and put it in a bottle and market it, wouldn't I?'

Magic ingredient or lucky charm, this was Konrad Bartelski's David Bradley moment.

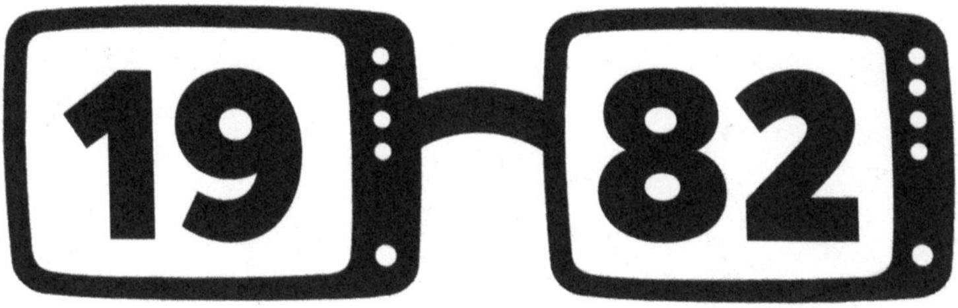
19
82

WILLIE CARSON'S LAUGH

THE EARLY weeks of a new year aren't the greatest for the TV sport addict. In terms of action, whether live or recorded, these slim pickings are usually divided between football and darts and little else. You have to get a fuller sporting fix elsewhere in the schedules. Not that this was too much of a problem in 1982. Throughout the year, there was plenty of a sporting hue beyond *Grandstand* and *Sportsnight*.

Superstars, Kick Start, We Are The Champions, the newcomer *Bullseye* – even with all its backslapping chumminess and the fact that it was closer to light entertainment than sporting drama. *Pro-Celebrity Golf* could provide the odd memorable moment too, not least the previous year when Terry Wogan sank a 100-foot putt at Gleneagles, earning him a place in the *Guinness Book of Records* for many years for the longest-ever televised holed putt.

In the first week of the year, though, all eyes were on the new series of *A Question of Sport*, which was due to unveil two new team captains. When the wraps came off, two men of contrast were revealed. There was soon-to-retire England rugby captain Bill Beaumont – a hulking mass of a man who seemed not to have much use for words of multiple syllables – and there was former champion jockey Willie Carson, a tiny chatterbox who would, when particularly excited, leap out of his seat as if rising from the saddle in the final furlong at Sandown Park.

In the regal pantheon of *A Question of Sport* captaincies, Carson's tenure remains one of the shortest. Not Brian-Clough-at-Leeds-United short but, in televisual terms, pretty fleeting. Just two series. I was more than content with that and I had my reason. It was simply down to that bloody laugh of his, a giggle the cadence of which would rise as it lengthened, as if the joke was getting funnier the further you were from it. No joke – and certainly no joke on *A Question of Sport* – was that funny.

Elsewhere on the schedules, there was always the chance of a sporting figure, either a player or a commentator, being surprised by Eamonn Andrews and his big red book on *This Is Your Life*, especially if they'd enjoyed significant success of late. Both Ian Botham and the Grand National-winning jockey Bob Champion, for whom 1981 was arguably their respective totem year, had been guests in the previous few months. The programme's producers didn't feel the need to hold back and honour the subject towards the end of their career. Get them while they were hot.

It was a policy that continued right into the show's later years. In 1990, when the just-crowned snooker world champion Stephen Hendry, a spotty sapling of just 21, was anointed by the programme, he pointedly reminded them that he'd 'hardly had a life . . .'

CAREER OPPORTUNITIES

IF I never graduated to being Motson's or Davies's successor perched on a cold plastic throne atop a wobbly camera gantry, or I never eradicated the motion sickness that jeopardised a future life as a rally co-driver, I had a fallback careers option. Sure, it was seasonal employment, as well as offering very limited part-time hours. But it accorded the employee a sainted disposition and enviable powers.

Plan C was to become a member of the Pools Panel.

After all, who was better qualified to pass judgement on the likelihood of a result of a not-to-be-played football match than a 13-year-old who'd witnessed a full two top-flight games in the flesh? I may have been occupying a solitary bedroom perch, one at quite some distance to the professional game itself, but my teetering piles of *Shoot!* and *Match Weekly* back issues had served me well, as had meticulously studying every highlight clip on *Football Focus*, every interview on *On the Ball*, every piece of transfer news in the back pages. This was my education. From this vantage point, I would be able to ascertain, with no fear of failure, exactly how each and every match would have panned out had a less reluctant referee not considered the presence of mountainous snowdrifts on the pitch to be something of a hazard.

Notts County to get a draw at reigning champions Aston Villa? Pah! Middlesbrough to sneak an away win at top-of-the-table Southampton? Not. A. Chance. Who were these monkeys suggesting such fanciful ideas? I suppose, though, if you gave an infinite number of monkeys an infinite number of Saturday afternoons and an infinite number of pools coupons, they'd get all the results correct eventually. And do so an infinite number of times, of course. But why take that gamble? Simply sign me up for the cause and prepare yourself for the gushing torrents of wisdom and knowledge.

The mysterious folk who made up the equally mysterious Pools Panel were in high demand between December 1981 and January 1982. That winter saw the lowest temperature ever recorded in the UK. The mercury had never plunged that low before – and, contrary to what Oldham fans might contend, it wasn't a measurement taken on the terraces of sub-Arctic Boundary Park. Every week, matches were postponed by the dozen. This meant that not only were the Pools Panel on to a nice little earner, but the operator of the vidiprinter wasn't exactly overburdened come Saturday at 4.40pm. There were so few results to come in. Conversely, both James Alexander Gordon, the voice of the football results on BBC Radio's *Sports Report*, and his television counterpart Len Martin had to do a little more, adding 'home win' or 'score draw' after 'match postponed'. Hopefully they were being paid by the word.

There was more than a masonic whiff about those Pools Panel members. I'm guessing they had to retain anonymity because they had the power to indirectly create millionaires, but just who were they? Where did they meet? And how did they manage to battle the elements to convene if the weather was sufficiently inclement for their services to be required? Indeed, if a particular sitting of the Pools Panel didn't have enough members to form a quorum, was a substitute panel required to sit in their stead to predict what the original panel would have predicted?

Such were the quandaries troubling a 13-year-old mind with little else to fill it.

THE MONOCHROME SET

AS 1982 began to defrost, the sporting calendar gradually righted itself and got back on track. Even the hard men of the Five Nations had surrendered to the weather, with Ireland's charge towards the Triple Crown kicking off a week late after heavy snowfall at Lansdowne Road for the scheduled match against Wales.

My enjoyment of the Five Nations, or of its key players, wasn't based on a sophisticated grasp of the game's finer points. By this stage, I'd now been forced to play rugby for a couple of winters at secondary school, although 'play' was a dubious description. I played rugby in exactly the way that Billy Casper played football in *Kes* – disinterested and distanced, keener to chat with the other lightweights than offer myself up as a sacrifice to those muscular, already-deep-into-puberty boys who would bear down on me like stampeding wildebeest. Hand into face, shoulder into chest.

This lack of engagement meant very few of the game's rules had filtered through. Accordingly, sitting in front of the box on a Five Nations weekend, I rarely knew what the infringement was whenever the referee's whistle was blown – and blown so frequently – at Murrayfield or Twickenham or Parc des Princes. It was complex and bewildering, too complicated, like chess or electrical engineering. But, contrarily, this ignorance actually enhanced my enjoyment. With everything appearing to happen haphazardly, I revelled in the organised chaos. In a mirroring of my deep analysis of every aspect of football, where I retained the ability to correctly call a marginal offside decision from an adjacent room, I was in the dark when it came to rugby union. And that was fine by me.

There was an issue with the 1982 Five Nations, though. It had nothing to do with the quality on the pitch; even my ignorant eyes could spot how special the likes of Ollie Campbell and Serge Blanco were, how brightly they illuminated any match they graced. It was a problem that was closer to home. One benefit of having a birthday just nine days before Christmas – the only benefit, actually – was that, more often than not, you were given a joint present that covered both days. You might have to wait those nine days before you got your mitts on it, but it would be a big present, a substantial one. One presumably worth double the value of a normal birthday gift, in fact, like the Scalextric Rallycross set ('with high-speed banking') that came my way in the end days of 1980.

On 25 December 1981, nine days into my teens, I received another double present. The box was sufficiently large for me to know it contained something special. And indeed it did: a white plastic cuboid, with metal fittings and a glass screen. My own TV – one that would beam sporting action from around the globe straight into my bedroom. I didn't need to share it with anyone. Mine, all mine.

The set had a suitably Japanese-sounding manufacturer's name. Not one of the big ones like Hitachi or Sanyo or Fujitsu. But it had enough F's and J's and I's in its name to sound credible and authentic, to give it that 'futuristic Tokyo' feel. I suspect, though, that the name might actually have been concocted during a marketing brainstorm inside an industrial unit on the outskirts of Bracknell.

As thrilling as my own personal direct line to the action was, there was one inevitable problem. Well, two actually. Firstly, the loop of flimsy wire that passed for an aerial meant that the picture rarely came close to the sharpness of the downstairs TV set (although for the first couple of weeks in late December and early January, I took its snowy reception to simply be those extreme weather conditions). The second problem was bigger. Its pictures were in black and white.

This new arrival took the beautifully vivid colours of TV sport and washed them out, flattening them, dulling them. Everything was now presented in 50 shades of grey. This soon became an issue when the Five Nations – which, aside from the World Darts Championship, was the first *proper* live sport on the BBC of 1982 – came around three weeks after Christmas. Matches involving either lily-white England or dark navy Scotland were fine. But when Ireland and Wales and France played each other, their mid-tone shirts were indistinguishable in my monochrome world. Those strong colours – Welsh scarlet, Irish emerald, French royal blue – had vanished.

I couldn't tell the sides apart. At times, it looked as though players were tackling their teammates. Admittedly, this was a state of affairs that further enhanced that sense of chaos I so welcomed, but still. . .

I soon learned to live with it. It was a deal I was prepared to strike. I might have been relegated back to a miniaturised, monochrome televisual world, but I was now in sole command of what was shown on the screen. Up in my room, I was master of all I surveyed. No more could *The Pink Panther Show* interrupt an evening of international athletics, nor could *The Dukes of Hazzard* call 'shotgun' over the final session of that day's Test match.

There was one sport, though, that still required me to watch with the rest of the family on the colour set downstairs. It was one that increasingly fascinated me and one, unlike rugby union, that I could understand perfectly well. I had sussed out its subtleties, nailed its nuances. I just couldn't watch it in black and white.

LIKE A HURRICANE

HE DRANK with enthusiasm, he smoked with enthusiasm, he swore with enthusiasm and he headbutted officials with enthusiasm. And he played snooker like no one else.

It didn't matter that Alex Higgins was a dishevelled mess of a man, an incorrigible amalgam of George Best and Keith Floyd. He was his own person, one with a medical note in his top pocket that excused him from wearing a bow tie when playing. Perhaps it had been issued by the same doctor who signed off Bill Werbeniuk's claim that he needed to consume multiple pints of lager during a match to maintain his natural equilibrium.

Higgins's scruffiness meant I was the only one fighting his corner in our house. Straight and respectable was usually the order of the day round ours but, to my eyes, being less than immaculately turned out wasn't a crime. If anything, it was a virtue, a signifier of someone who readily flicked the V's at convention. My teenage brain saw these things clearly. It wasn't what someone *wore* that made them special. It was what they *did*. The beautiful things they did.

After all, would Bryan Robson's second goal against France in the World Cup a couple of months later – where he floated in the air, like some angelic presence, to glance Trevor Francis's cross past the feet-in-clay French keeper Jean-Luc Ettori – have looked quite so magnificent if his socks hadn't slipped down his shins and coiled around his ankles? Of course not.

It was the same with Alex Higgins. The comparative casualness of his attire freed him up – to use the football commentator's vernacular – to express himself. Buttoned-down players produced buttoned-down performances. The Hurricane never did all his buttons up.

If it was good enough for a world title-winning snooker player, it was good enough for me. I put Higgins's Law into action the following Sunday morning, the last game of the U13s football season. We were playing Petworth Panthers who, confusingly, chose to play in luminous orange rather than feline black. As I moved to the edge of the box for a corner halfway through the second half, I surreptitiously untucked my claret-and-blue shirt out of my shorts. This act of sartorial rebellion wasn't surreptitious enough, though. The coach (aka my dad, of course) bawled at me to tuck myself in. I ignored him; the corner had already been taken. A half-clearance fell at my feet and I drilled the ball into the bottom corner with all the ruthlessness of Higgins dispatching that final black at the Crucible.

Vindication.

YIN, YANG AND THE GREEN
EYE OF JEALOUSY

UNTUCKED SHIRTS were the order of the day a week later as those majestic, and often majestically scruffy, practitioners of the midfield arts – Glenn Hoddle and Micky Hazard – took to the Wembley turf for Spurs' second successive Cup Final, this time against QPR. No matter the usual levels of excitement on this red-letter day, even at the age of 13 my sense of the world order was well defined. I knew that the heights of the previous May, when Ricky Villa and my paisley pyjamas had won the Cup so thrillingly for Spurs, couldn't be repeated. Anyone who thought lightning could strike on the exact same rectangle of turf was clearly delusional. I fully understood that yin had to be balanced with yang, that profit needed squaring with loss. For every moment of blood-pumping glory, there had to be a moment of unrefined mediocrity. We had to take our punishment.

And no one who had kept their Saturday free for all the hours of build-up, of pre-match speculation, of the game itself, could describe the 1982 final as remotely close to a classic. It turned out that we had been royally spoilt the year before, shown how a final could explode into bone-shaking brilliance rather than dissolve into misfiring anti-climax. Nonetheless, 12 months on, we still felt short-changed. The 90 minutes of normal time weren't overburdened by goals; QPR barely launched an attack, while Tottenham's finishing was far from clinical. As a marker of how flat the match was, I was almost – *almost* – compelled to see what classic Ealing comedy was showing on BBC2 instead. Sacrilegious behaviour on any given Saturday; the stuff of excommunication on Cup Final day, the holiest Saturday of them all.

(For the first half of the 1980s, the main temptation to lure me away from *Grandstand* was indeed the prospect of one of

Ealing's finest being given another airing on the sister channel. Only if certain sports were on, of course, and only if *World of Sport* failed to offer a credible alternative. I wasn't a monster, after all. But how wrong-thinking must someone be to *not* rank *The Lavender Hill Mob* above rhythmic gymnastics?)

Like his compatriot Ardiles, Villa – the hero in '81 – had made his excuses and hadn't returned to HA9. Or, rather, he'd had his excuses made for him – the small matter of the Falklands War. And he wasn't the only one for whom the war intervened that May day. Unbeknownst to me, my best pal Ab almost made an appearance on Cup Final TV that would have tested our relationship to near breaking point. Once the Peter Powell/Mark Curry vehicle *Get Set For Summer* had handed the reins to *Cup Final Grandstand* at 11.30am (via a three-minute weather forecast), David Coleman had issued a request for viewers to phone in to ask for a clip of Cup Finals past to be shown. The more personal that particular match was to you, Headmaster Coleman explained, the more likely you were to be successful and to get on air.

Ab's connection to this most famous of cup competitions fitted the bill perfectly. His dad, the ever-affable Fred, had been a ballboy at the 1956 final – the one where Bert Trautmann played on despite breaking his neck mid-match – and had never seen the goals from the game. It was a great story that made Ab's televisual debut an absolute shoo-in. He was next in line to go on, until he was bumped in favour of a Moira Stuart-fronted newsflash. She was delivering the latest on the conflict in the South Atlantic. The war was in full battle cry that particular week.

Ab never got on air and our friendship remained intact. Had I suddenly heard his voice chatting away to Coleman, it would have been impossible to keep the lid on my jealousy. It would have felt like a betrayal on the part of *someone*; I just wasn't quite sure whether it was best pal Ab or Headmaster

Coleman. *Grandstand*, after all, was mine and mine alone, clearly meticulously put together at great cost simply for my appreciation and no one else's. I couldn't cope with the notion that *other people* might also be tuning in, that *other people* had a similar connection to mine. The new telly in the bedroom, the screen built for one, conspired in this fantasy.

More so, I was annoyed that I too had a near-direct link to the FA Cup Final but had shown neither the gumption nor the inclination to phone the *Grandstand* switchboard that particular lunchtime. My grandad had been present at the first Wembley final in 1923, the famously over-populated White Horse Final (he'd gone, as he had always been at pains to point out, as a legitimate ticket-holder). Such a connection would surely have been attractive to the BBC researcher on the other end of the phone – especially if I bent the truth a touch, strumming the heartstrings by suggesting that the old fella had passed away only in the last few weeks.

A few days later, a carrier bag of various BBC goodies came Ab's way, which he cheerily showed anyone wandering past his school locker. This was to compensate him for not getting on air. For me, this was no replacement. How could a *Grandstand* mug and a handful of bumper stickers be an adequate substitute for a few seconds of awkward, nervous interaction with David Coleman, the sport department's leading man? Secretly, though, and rather selfishly, I was glad that that was all he got out of the deal.

EARLY DOORS

THE SIGHT of your dad in the reception area of your school isn't normally good news. It's an abnormal picture, the strange convergence of your two demarcated worlds. A familiar place and a familiar face that just didn't go together.

That you've been pulled out of Mr Preece's geography class ten minutes early, and that one of your parents is here to take you home before the final bell, can mean one of two things. One: that you've behaved so atrociously during a previous lesson that the school have requested your temporary suspension. I knew I'd not done that. The stories of corporal punishment that did the rounds in the school corridors were an effective deterrent. Legend had it that one particular head of year, cane in hand, apparently did several laps of his office in order to get a sufficient run-up for the beating he was about to administer on a poor unfortunate.

Two: that a close relative has died. As fit and healthy and formidable as Gran was, this was always a possibility. She was the oldest person I knew.

We walked out of school silently. I thought it must be the latter but that he just couldn't find or form the words. It was a good minute before either of us spoke, but I quickly learned the reason for the prolonged silence. The school walls might have ears. Being halfway to the car park meant we were out of earshot.

'The traffic will still be light. Not rush hour yet. We should just about make it.'

'Make what? Have I got the dentist?'

'No, we're going home. But tell everyone tomorrow that you went to the opticians.'

'Home? But the bus goes in 20 minutes.'

'You'll be late if you catch that. It goes the long way home. It'll be close to half-time by the time you're back.'

The penny slowly dropped. He had sagged off work early and fraudulently taken me out of school before the allotted time, for a third reason. There had been no bad behaviour and no one had died. And this third reason was the very best reason imaginable: England were playing their first match in their first World Cup for 12 long, barren, sunless years. An encounter against France – Platini, Rocheteau, Six and the rest – awaited. Of course, I hadn't remotely forgotten about the match. It was just I hadn't foreseen my dad's hitherto unrevealed capacity for mild rebellion. I wasn't complaining, though. Appreciating his sense of history, I sank into the passenger seat of his rust-coloured, rust-covered Hillman Avenger. He lit up a Piccadilly Filter De Luxe in satisfaction of a scheme well executed.

The traffic out of town was heavier than expected; it seemed that plenty of others had viewed England's return to World Cup Finals action to be worthy of nipping off early from work too. Nonetheless, we arrived home less than two minutes after the scheduled kick-off time of 4.15pm. However, it was two minutes too late.

'Do you want to know the score?' asked my mum. She was also home early, although her presence had less to do with catching the adventures of Ron Greenwood's boys and more with her shop observing the quaint tradition of closing early on Wednesdays.

'There won't be any score yet,' I said. 'It's only just started.'

'1-0 to England. Don't know who scored. Just heard the cheers.'

I dashed into the living room. The ongoing excitement of the England supporters in the far right corner of the stadium, plus the accelerated tone of John Motson, suggested it was true. 1-0? Already? How quick was that? Twenty-seven seconds?! We were going to walk this competition. A stroll in the park.

At this point, I would normally have made a beeline for my own room where I was free to form my own conclusions about what I was watching. But solitude didn't seem right in the circumstances. Father and son had just committed this act of subterfuge and, having sidestepped the sentries of both work and school, it didn't feel right that we then went our separate ways to watch the remaining 88 minutes apart. And certainly, in our joint appreciation of Bryan Robson's second goal halfway through the second half – that beautiful, gravity-defying header – we shared a moment. We'd beaten the powers-that-be and now England were beating the French. And all without Kevin Keegan and Trevor Brooking. Imagine how much better we'd be once they were back from injury. The world spun smoothly that evening.

The next day I plain forgot about the opticians alibi and excitedly suggested to my pals – I may have even directly stated – that I'd seen Robson's record-breaking opening goal live on the TV, while they were still kicking their heels in the bus queue. Such one-upmanship is the currency of the schoolyard, after all.

No one needed to know that we were still two streets away from home when it went in.

THE TWO BRIANS

LIKE *A Question of Sport* and the occasional sport-themed episode of *This Is Your Life*, *Superstars* also gave the viewer the rare chance of seeing their heroes off duty and out of context. The premise was simple but intriguing. Who'd be better at canoeing – a bantamweight boxer or a Grand Prix driver? Who could complete more squat thrusts in a minute – a 400m hurdler or a rugby league winger? And, most profoundly, was there a worse cyclist on the planet than Kevin Keegan?

While the show attracted A-listers from across the sporting spectrum, there were two lesser-known competitors who pretty much trounced all comers. Brian Jacks was an Olympic medallist in judo, but didn't become a household name until he reigned supreme in the British and European versions of *Superstars* in both 1979 and 1980.

While Jacks never managed to win the world crown, in 1982 pole-vaulter Brian Hooper did just that, one of six titles he bagged. Although the pair's respective *Superstars* careers didn't overlap, you still had your favourite one. I went for Hooper.

Proof that I'd picked wisely came a year or so later during a school trip to Crystal Palace for a floodlit night of international athletics. Our bus was making slow progress through the streets of Upper Norwood when we spied Hooper jogging along the pavement, warming up before that evening's pole vault event. Several of us banged on the window. The cheery wave we received in return showed he was one of the good guys.

Had it not been for *Superstars*, of course, that bus of schoolkids wouldn't have known him from Adam.

MARTINA AND CHRISSIE

THE 1981 defeat to John McEnroe was the last time Björn Borg graced a Wimbledon court. His subsequent – and surely premature – retirement cut down the rivalry in its prime. The story stopped there, ending abruptly after just a couple of chapters.

McEnroe lost his equilibrium when Borg hung up his racket. As the author Tim Adams has noted, 'great tennis players, like great chess players or great boxers, cannot exist in isolation: they require a rivalry, an equal, to allow them to discover what they might be capable of'. McEnroe was well aware of this and pleaded with the Swede to return to the game, to turn the permanent retirement into a temporary sojourn. At this, he failed. 'There was this void,' he confessed to Adams, 'and I always felt it was up to me in a sense to manufacture my own intensity thereafter.'

No self-manufactured intensity was required in the women's game. The rivalry between the top two players wasn't brought to a sudden and premature halt through the early retirement of one of them. The opposite, in fact. It ran and ran and ran.

While Borg/McEnroe gained intensity from the extremes of their respective behaviour, the extended Evert/Navratilova duel was viewed on purely sporting terms. There might have been an extra edge to the rivalry had Navratilova not defected from her native Czechoslovakia and become a naturalised US citizen. Sport has, after all, always loved a face-off between the Iron Curtain and the West.

Instead, they were two Floridians – one natural, one naturalised – fighting tooth and nail for overall supremacy of the women's game. But there appeared to be a genuine friendship at the heart of their rivalry. The respect they had for one another was far from grudging. Indeed, they had won the 1976 Wimbledon women's doubles as a pairing.

They certainly spent plenty of time in each other's company over the years, meeting 80 times in singles competitions. Navratilova had the edge overall, albeit by the narrow margin of 43 wins to 37; she had the advantage on grass, with Evert having more joy on clay. By their respective retirements, both had won 18 Grand Slam singles titles; furthermore, Evert had been world number one for six years, Navratilova for seven.

In short, there was very little daylight between them. And they rarely allowed anyone else a look-in. In 1982, it was the year that the pair properly made the women's game a two-horse race. The Wimbledon singles final was the third of 15 consecutive Grand Slam singles finals that either one of them won.

Navratilova triumphed in three sets that day, leaving me a little deflated. If I favoured one of them, it would have been Evert, an assessment I'm ashamed to say was solely based on fancying her (in my defence, I was a hormonal boy by this point). I only had eyes for her – although the emergence of Keren from Bananarama meant she had a love rival.

In 1982, though, there was an inconvenient truth that I was in denial about, one that would scupper any plans I might have secretly held of eloping with her. The Wimbledon scoreboard told it how it was, albeit in its formal and outdated way, informing us that Chris Evert wasn't on court that day. Martina's opponent was Mrs JM Lloyd.

THE BOYS OF SUMMER

IT IS far, far from an original thought but, back at the World Cup, the Italy-Brazil match was simply the greatest game I had seen at that point in my life. There was fairly universal agreement about this among my brethren, even if – despite being far closer to the glorious team of '70 than to the misfiring World Cup sides of '74 and '78 – Brazil lost that afternoon. Zico and Falcao and Eder were scintillating, and in Junior they had a full back with all the flair and vision of a number ten. The most regal of all was, of course, their captain – the chain-smoking, doctorate-owning Socrates, a player who glided across the pitch as sublimely as he caressed a football.

But no matter how glorious that '82 Brazil team was, how golden and sun-kissed and extravagant and irresistible their collective genius, that sunny Monday in Barcelona taught me there was no such thing as inevitability. No matter how you expected events to go, no matter how much you tried to bend them to your will (and I did change out of my school uniform when Italy went 3-2 up, even digging out the now-too-small Hawks sweatshirt to try to tempt history to repeat itself), there were no guarantees. The stars didn't always align. Obstacles could get in the way. And Brazil's main obstacle that afternoon went by the name of Paolo Rossi, the ex-jailbird whose hat-trick dumped Brazil and its pretty footballers out of the competition.

As the sun went down that day, the action turned to Madrid where England, after a goalless draw against West Germany in their first match in the second group stage, needed to snatch a win against the hosts to progress to the semi-finals. But they found the Spanish goal as impenetrable as the German one a few days before; a second 0-0 draw wasn't enough to stay in the tournament. It could all have been different. Kevin Keegan came on as a second-half substitute for Tony Woodcock, but those 26 minutes – the full extent of his World Cup Finals experience – will be forever remembered for the most famous miss of his long, trophy-laden career. Six yards out and with the huge target of an empty net before him, Keegan put his header wide. 'Well, if we were going to win this World Cup,' sighed ITV summariser Jack Charlton, 'this was the one.' In the playground the next morning, we tried to re-enact the moment with the aid of a tennis ball. We were unsuccessful. It proved ridiculously hard to actually miss such a gaping target.

The sense of disappointment I'd experienced after the twin exits of both Brazil and England would be eclipsed by the moral outrage I felt at the semi-final stage after West German goalkeeper Harald Schumacher's sickening challenge on Patrick Battiston put the Frenchman into a coma. The game itself was as gripping, possibly even more so, than the Italy-Brazil match had been, ending 3-3 and going to penalties. After Schumacher's assault (oxygen was administered to Battiston on the pitch, before the match unbelievably restarted with a West German goal kick), most of the football-literate world was willing France to win. And when they took a 3-1 lead in extra time, it looked as if justice had been served. But two late goals, one from party-pooper-in-chief Karl-Heinz Rummenigge, took it to a penalty shoot-out. You can guess the rest.

The Schumacher incident wasn't the only moment in the tournament's closing stages to burn an indelible impression on the collective hippocampus, a moment to eternally replay over and over in slow motion on the TV screens in our heads. There was also Marco Tardelli's very public display of untrammelled joy at scoring in the final – one of the truly great football celebrations of all time. Indeed, Tardelli's scream was one that, three decades later, I found myself unconsciously replicating as a 40-something on a dog-rough five-a-side pitch in south Bristol.

It all stays with you for ever.

THE SAD TALE OF BOBBY C

'THERE'S NO success like failure,' Bob Dylan once sang, before adding that 'failure's no success at all'.

Bobby Clampett knows both sides. He's most remembered by golf fans in this country for one of the saddest surrenders in the history of the Open. And he's surely spent a lifetime knowing that had he held his nerve at Royal Troon in 1982, the dice may have rolled differently, that he'd have been a fixture of the upper echelons of tournament leaderboards for the following decade or two.

I came home from school on the Thursday, the first day of that year's Open, expecting – and hoping – to see the likes of Ballesteros or Langer or Lyle leading the pack, but a new name greeted me. Clampett? Bobby Clampett? Who was he? Wasn't he the son from TV's *The Beverly Hillbillies*?

It turned out, Peter Alliss reassured us, that he wasn't some wildcard rookie who'd just landed from the back of beyond. Clampett had taken third place in the US Open the previous month, so this wasn't a random lightning strike. He had previous, making his lead more understandable, if still unlikely. I preferred the back story I'd created for him – that he was a chancer, a grifter, who'd hitchhiked his way to Ayrshire carrying nothing more than an old set of clubs, but also in possession of an inordinate amount of raw talent and a desire to upset the sport's apple cart.

His age was appealing to me. He was 22, seemingly a generation younger than the main guys who, to 13-year-old eyes, looked as though they were deep into middle age. Positively ancient. (In fact, they weren't. Tom Watson, with six Major titles to his name at that point, was still only 32. I'd have put him in his mid-forties at the very least.) Clampett didn't seem part of the neatly groomed pro golf set. His thick thatch of blond curls, bleached by the Californian sun, were a little unkempt, and he played with the freedom of a young man without too many responsibilities in life, with few concerns to distract him. At the end of the first day's play, his round of 67 gave him a two-shot lead. It was the first time he'd played golf in Scotland. I was sold.

I dashed home from school on the Friday, nervous that my new hero had sunk without trace while I had been sinking academically in a double bill of chemistry and physics. Clampett had done no such thing. In fact, he'd done even better than the previous day, an 18th-hole birdie giving him a 66. At the tournament's halfway point, he was five shots better off than anyone else.

On Saturday, I could give Clampett's entire round my full attention. He was continuing his form. After five more holes, he was now seven shots ahead and in danger of running away with the tournament. Then he made close and extended acquaintance with Troon's bunkers, his lead slipping through his fingers like the sand blowing in little clouds around his feet.

He took 12 more shots than he had done on Friday. The lead was still his come sunset, but it was a fragile one. A single shot, the pack gathering.

I kept my faith throughout that Sunday, but Clampett's collapse was as unrelenting as was Tom Watson's greedy surge for yet another title. The young man's 77 consigned him to a share of tenth place. It was heartbreaking to watch Clampett slumped to the ground on the edge of the final green, his eyes darkening into a thousand-yard stare. This was a young man learning a harsh reality from which his career never really recovered. It defined him as a player. While he would be a fixture on the circuit for many more years, he only won a single tournament. All that promise, all that expectation, had flowed away.

In middle age, Bobby Clampett would reflect on those four days at Royal Troon, on how one weekend derailed his career, how his presumed path to greatness was rerouted. 'That road got . . . [a pause] . . . interrupted.'

MUD ON THE TRACKS

GIVEN PAPER and pencil, as a sports-obsessed teen I could faithfully draw the outline of most Formula One circuits. Silverstone was a comparative doddle, while Monaco's twists and turns were a complicated pleasure to replicate. The old Nürburgring, however, 13 decommissioned miles of switchbacks and hairpins, was the most testing, plus its size definitely required a blank sheet of A3. While these drawings wouldn't necessarily conform to the kind of precise scale we were being taught to adhere to in our school technical drawing classes, any Formula One fan worth his or her salt would be able to discern one from another, to be able to put a name to each.

There was one racetrack, though, whose simple shape and comparative shortness I could actually replicate through the medium of Scalextric. It wasn't a Formula One circuit; it was the rallycross circuit at Lydden Hill, a fixture on the *Grandstand* schedules during the early part of the 1980s. Better still, rallycross was a sport even more gripping than Formula One, usually an egalitarian three-and-a-half-lap blast where a Hillman Imp was in with as much chance of victory as the occasional Porsche.

While the likes of Arnoux, Prost, Piquet and Rosberg stuck to their smooth Grand Prix circuits, the drivers of Lydden Hill bumped and rumbled their way through mud and chalk and dust onto tarmac and back again. Every lap was a doozy, the only element of predictability being that it would be unpredictable. Thrills and plenty of spills. There was one particularly memorable crash when two drivers – Paul Springett and John 'father of Jenson' Button – got too close for comfort, with the former's Mini going, in the poetic words of Murray Walker, 'end over end over end'. The back axle was ripped from its fixing on the car's underside and left hanging, just as it would be on either of my two Scalextric Minis if ever they took that high-speed banking at too enthusiastic a speed. (My version of Lydden Hill, of course, was an unfaithfully reproduced all-tarmac affair. I was rightfully advised not to sprinkle earth and sand over my Scalextric track in order to heighten the realism.)

When it came to rallycross, I suspended my usual backing of the underdog. My favourite driver was the excellently named Keith Ripp, a man whose devil-may-care mastery of the sport meant that he rarely disappointed. And when he tore off his helmet for a post-race interview, his droopy Jason King moustache didn't disappoint either. It gave him – an amateur sportsman with an Enfield accent – proper star quality. Just as much star quality, in fact, as the globetrotting matinee idols of Formula One.

TERRY-THOMAS'S KID BROTHER

DURING THE 1980s, *Grandstand* had several anchormen. Bough and Coleman and Lynam and Rider and Carpenter and even – very occasionally, when everyone else was indisposed – supply teacher Gubba. For the first half of the decade, when ITV still had a multi-hour, pan-sport Saturday afternoon show in the form of *World of Sport*, the network largely had just the one presenter. A man born Richard Davies but known to every household in the land as Dickie.

Dickie Davies rivalled Lynam when it came to smoothness. Having previously worked on ocean-going liners, he looked as if he knew how to tie a cravat, the method required to mix the perfect vodka Martini, and where to find the Monte Carlo casinos that offered the most generous roulette wheels. He was Terry-Thomas's kid brother, in all but name and blood.

He didn't exactly look like a man of the muddy pitch or the tightly packed terrace. His sporting pedigree wasn't obvious. It was Clive James, in his role as the market-leading acerbic TV critic, who suggested that dear Dickie didn't have the ability to grade the relative importance of whatever sporting event he was reading out loud about from the autocue. Whether football's World Cup or the World Target Diving Championships, his delivery on one link was indistinguishable from the next: 'He folds his hands,' wrote James, 'he leans forward and smiles at you from under his moustache.' Repeat and repeat.

Inherent in that delivery, though, was his silent acknowledgement that, if you changed channel, there would be proper sport on the other side. But by giving *World of Sport*'s coverage of marginal events (even some that were clearly non-sports) the same on-screen gravitas, he was trying to endow them with more credibility and prestige than they deserved.

You couldn't blame him for trying. We knew there was better stuff on *Grandstand*. Dickie knew this too. And the twinkle in his eye told us he knew that we knew.

LOCAL HEROES

TV SPORT'S ability to transport the viewer, to lift him or her away from the immediate banality and boredom of real life, is irrefutable. At the very least, it offers a temporary distraction. But it can provide something much greater than that too; a warm, snuggly security blanket that offers protection from life's ills. It takes you away from home turf, depositing you in locales either glamorous (say Monaco on Grand Prix weekend) or prosaic (perhaps Castleford, for a muddy rugby league encounter with Halifax or Featherstone Rovers). But whatever the destination, TV sport takes you out of yourself.

Very occasionally, though, TV sport comes to you. It travels to your neck of the woods, to your reality. In September 1982, the BBC did just this when it broadcast the Road Cycling World Championships from Goodwood. It brought the exotic to the known, to my backyard. That particular Sunday afternoon, I perched excitedly on the edge of my bed, recognising the roads this peloton (a word learned just a few minutes before) were barrelling along. I knew every lay-by, every road sign. Here they were, taking a sharp left-hander at the crossroads where – at least before *Sunday Grandstand* landed on our screens the previous summer – I'd watch through the wire fence as Sunday afternoon amateur racing drivers buzzed around the Goodwood motor circuit.

This was too good to keep to myself. I went downstairs to where my dad was busy snoring the afternoon away on the sofa and my mum was beavering away on the sewing machine. I had to share the experience of this local race with them. But, more honestly, I had to see it in its vivid true colours.

Cycling was a breath of fresh air to someone who thought he knew most of the ways of the sporting world. It was teaching me new rules, new conventions, new tactics. And a new voice was guiding me through – the gushing tones of a commentator I'd not heard before, but one whose voice would become very familiar over the following 30-plus years: Phil Liggett. So transparently excited was Liggett that he kept describing the hill up to the racecourse as 'the mountain'. I'd ridden this hill a few times (and would do many more times in the following years, imagining myself to be participating in a world championship all of my own). I'd also been to the Lake District on a couple of occasions. Both experiences made me eminently empowered to decree that, in no uncertain terms, did this hill qualify – let alone even remotely resemble – a mountain.

But I knew what Liggett was up to. He was trying to sell a sport rarely seen on our screens to the British public. He was reimagining my backyard as the Alps, trying to add an extra veneer of glamour to an event already made infinitely sophisticated by the presence of numerous French, Italian and Spanish riders. And, with me, he pretty much succeeded.

I was instantly fascinated by these world championships. They showcased a team sport that was also an individual sport. The two shared a brittle coexistence, a fragile peace between collective duty and personal glory that could shatter at any time, as it did on the lanes of Goodwood in the last mile of that afternoon's race. In my innocence, I saw the unfolding events in pretty blunt terms. An American who had made an early bolt for the line was chased down by another American, resulting in the former being royally cheesed off by the latter's decision not to allow him the victory.

I understood the situation in ways that the cheesed-off rider seemed to have trouble comprehending. There was an easy context for me to apply it to. The scenario was surely the same as that of Coe and Ovett at the Moscow Olympics. Yes, these two sportsmen shared the same team colours, but their priority, their ultimate commitment, had to be to their personal ambitions. Why hold back and let a fellow countryman take the spoils if you felt you still had enough left in the tank to win it for yourself? You hadn't given over half of your life thus far to your sport, making too many sacrifices to mention, with the express purpose of letting someone else take the glory for themselves. It seemed pretty clear-cut to my adolescent eyes. Nearly four decades later, I still think the same.

In the end, the spoils bypassed both Americans – Greg LeMond the chaser and Jonathan Boyer the chased. As LeMond closed on his compatriot, an Italian by the name of Giuseppe Saronni flew past at a velocity the TV cameras could barely contain. The blue flash was off. Out of shot, out of sight.

I was off, too. Hooked for ever.

THE FRENCH DISCONNECTION

THE SAME bad blood that had simmered between Greg LeMond and Jonathan Boyer resurfaced in another sport three weeks after the world champs at Goodwood. Two more compatriots, two more teammates, trying to square the personal-versus-political circle. This was the story of René Arnoux and Alain Prost at the French Grand Prix.

Of the two Renault drivers, I definitely gravitated to Arnoux. With his hair sitting on his collar, he was undeniably the cooler one, a concept very important to the teenage onlooker. He also appealed to me because he was the lesser partner in the relationship, despite being at Renault two years longer than Prost, as well as being nearly seven years older. Seniority wasn't gauged by age or length of tenure, though; it was determined by results. Prost had five career Grand Prix victories under his belt, including two that season, and was better placed in the drivers' championship. Arnoux, for all his speed, especially in qualifying, had yet to break his race-winning duck. If there was a political agreement within Renault regarding race management, the stats dictated that the decision would always favour the younger man.

The last few laps of that French Grand Prix were fascinating. Arnoux was almost 20 seconds clear of Prost, but team tactics ensured it was anything but a benign procession. Intrigue was high. Could anyone second-guess what Arnoux's intentions might be? Up in the BBC commentary box, Murray Walker and James Hunt recognised how pressing the matter was becoming. The team orders – to slow and allow his teammate the victory – were clear and visible as Arnoux sped past the pit lane signs. Hunt, the former world champion, put himself in the Frenchman's seat. He understood the magnetic pull of registering a first-ever Grand Prix victory, especially at a comparatively advanced age (Arnoux's 34th birthday was the following day). The chance might never come again, mused Hunt. 'Do I pretend I didn't see it? How can I explain that I misunderstood it when I get in?'

If he was going to hand Prost an ill-deserved victory, everyone expected Arnoux to do so on the last couple of bends of the final lap, leaving it as late as possible to pointedly show that he was the moral victor who'd been denied his right of crossing the line first. But slow down he didn't. The lure of recording that maiden victory was never going to divert him; there were enough Formula One drivers who never registered a race win and Arnoux was too good behind the wheel to be consigned to that particular bracket.

As with LeMond's tilt at personal glory at Goodwood, I had no trouble with Arnoux disregarding team orders. Personal ambition and collective duty might have needed balancing, but that didn't mean that the former couldn't enjoy at least one day in the sun. Despite recording four pole positions that season prior to the French, Arnoux had only actually finished two of the first ten races. He needed something tangible and strong to help rescue a career that was beginning to stall. And he was no doubt fighting to survive at Renault and secure a drive for the following season.

Having taken the chequered flag, Arnoux soaked up the acclaim and applause of his homeland crowd. He had led home a French clean sweep of the first four places, with Prost taking second, followed by the Ferrari pair of Didier Pironi and Patrick Tambay. 'He had better enjoy his slowing-down lap,' observed Hunt rather tartly. 'It might not be so much fun when he gets back.'

A bitter row did indeed then ensue. Rather than cement his place at Renault for 1983, Arnoux's decision to drive for himself that day (he maintained that there was no agreement in place to submit to Prost) saw him thrown off the team at season's end. He had my utmost sympathy.

Arnoux might never have actually made it to Circuit Paul Ricard. At the Dutch Grand Prix in July, one of the races where he squandered pole, he suffered what could have been a very serious crash. Major injury – or worse – had been averted thanks to a sand trap and a solid tyre wall. He lived to fight another day.

Gilles Villeneuve wasn't so lucky. Earlier in the season, during practice for the Belgian Grand Prix, the French-Canadian – arguably the most scintillating driver of his generation – lost his life in a horrific accident. TV viewers knew there was something wrong; the qualification rounds of a Formula One race weren't usually the concern of the Friday night early-evening news bulletin. And when newsreader Jan Leeming formed the words 'Gilles Villeneuve' and started talking about him in the past tense, a numbness took hold.

Sport was an important facet of life. I knew that as much as, or more than, anyone. But death shouldn't be a facet of sport. The relentless pursuit of glory at all costs required some sort of curtailing. Ambition needed to stop at the water's edge.

HAFNIA AND HITACHI

BY 1982, shirt sponsorship in English football had been established for three years, but it was still a hot potato for broadcasters, especially the BBC. Indeed, during the 1981 European Cup Final, not only was Liverpool's sponsor absent from their shirts, but each player had had to wear a white tab across the small Umbro logo to satisfy the corporation's guidelines for live matches – largely in the same way that *Blue Peter* had to blank out the manufacturer's name on an empty cereal packet being used to construct a faithful reproduction of the Empire State Building.

My inner marketeer saw some issues with shirt sponsorship, with players transforming into fast-moving sandwich boards (or, in Emlyn Hughes's case, a slow-moving sandwich board). By linking your product to a particular club, you might be tapping into their substantial base of supporters, but you would also be alienating those of other clubs. For instance, from the late '70s onwards, would any true-blue Evertonian remotely consider buying a Hitachi television, redecorating their front room using Crown paints or taking even just the swiftest sip of Carlsberg? To do so would surely be to favour the red side of the city. In return, though, there was no danger of Liverpool fans even accidentally buying meat products made by Hafnia,

Everton's first shirt sponsor. This appeared to be a company whose wares weren't actually available in British supermarkets.

Pitchside advertising offered 90 minutes (plus injury time) of exposure that the public-service BBC couldn't avoid. And by advertising at most First Division grounds, the alienation by association potentially encountered by shirt sponsors was alleviated.

The regular advertisers, those who took space at Wembley and Villa Park and Maine Road and many points in between, certainly burned their names into my psyche, even if the prepubescent me had no clue what the likes of Metaxa or Rizla were. Many of those sponsors' names remain vivid to this day. Should this vegetarian ever renounce the pledge, Danepak bacon would be on my shopping list. Similarly, if I had needed to rent a TV at a wallet-friendly rate, a quick hop to Visionhire would have been all it would have taken – not that it's an industry that exists any more, but you get the (fuzzy) picture.

Most significantly, were I to ever require some industrial-strength metalwork, I'd know who to call. Rainham Steel, of course, still taking out pitchside advertising decades later. It must be a medium that works.

LETTERS FROM AMERICA

IF A solid understanding of the team politics and race tactics of road cycling had, earlier in the year, tested the analytical side of my brain (married to, of course, my continuing distance from the laws of rugby union), another sport new to me joined them by flummoxing me even further. Three letters from America: NFL.

This was a sport of quarterbacks and running backs and tight ends and linemen. Alien words, alien phrases.

Furthermore, for some reason, it was a sport that required a 30-strong brass band in the stands and a bunch of toothsome gymnasts throwing each other in the air on the touchline to keep the crowd entertained. You never got that at Deepdale or Ayresome Park.

Channel 4 had launched earlier in the year, turning its face into a blizzard of righteous anger from the Mary Whitehouse-led tutting classes for its daring, occasionally potty-mouthed programming. Mrs Whitehouse might not have approved, but it was a programming strategy that was exceedingly attractive to a teenage boy at that point unsure whether he yet knew the full lexicon of four-letter words.

The channel took a further left turn when it unexpectedly dipped its toe into sporting waters in early November. The NFL seemed a strange choice for them. I regarded it as a sport for hollering, beer-guzzling jocks, not sensitive liberal types. Despite the confusion it caused me, though, I did grasp the fundamentals: you had four attempts to gain ten yards of territory, not dissimilar to rugby league's six tackles. Unlike rugby league, though, you could chuck the ball in a forward direction.

There was a little too much whooping, hollering and chest-bumping, and too many of those suntanned cheerleaders, but – with *Sunday Grandstand* now in its annual autumn hibernation and *Ski Sunday* not returning until the snows of Europe got properly heavy into the new year – it filled the Sunday teatime void. It would do for now. It might have been a foreign sport from a foreign country, seemingly explained in a foreign tongue. But it was still a sport.

DUST TO DUST

ANOTHER PHILOSOPHICAL conundrum with which to confuse a teenager: if a tree falls in the forest and no one hears it, does it make a sound?

Similarly, if an Ashes Test takes place in Australia and no one in the UK can see it live on TV, does the result actually count?

Good. Thought not. We lost.

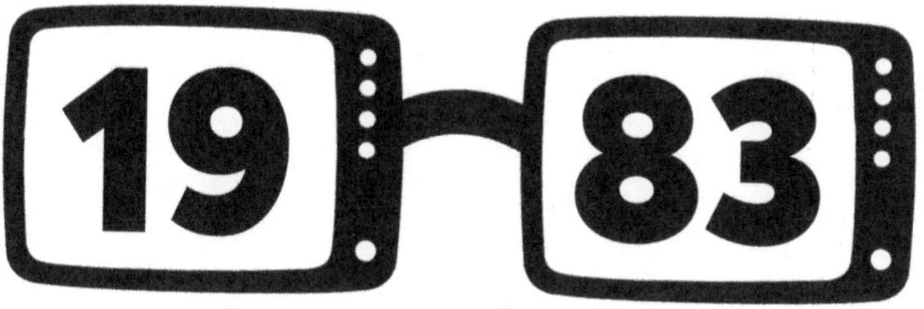
1983

THE OUTSIDERS

SOMETIMES YOU never see the headline-makers coming. You're either looking in the opposite direction or they're flying under the radar before making a sudden appearance right in the heat of the action where they've never previously belonged.

And so it was with a young man from Ipswich called Keith Deller. In the first week of 1983, he shocked the world. At least, he shocked the portion of the world that followed darts. Granted, it was a modest slice of the global population, but in the UK it equated to 10 million people tuning into the final of the 1983 Embassy World Darts Championship.

As an unseeded player who'd had to work his way through the maze of qualifying rounds before reaching the tournament proper, Deller was now stepping onto the stage of the world final. He'd been largely invisible in the opening couple of rounds, taking on and beating a couple of equally invisible opponents while the TV cameras busied themselves elsewhere, focusing their gazes on, and widening their lenses for, the sport's more heavyweight names.

Deller was different. For starters, he didn't boast the waistline of his opponents. At 23, he hadn't served quite the same lengthy apprenticeship as the lifers would have done in beer-soaked, smoke-fugged pubs and clubs up and down the country. He didn't suck deeply on a Rothmans at the end of each leg, nor take a long draw on a pint of mild to maintain some sort of equilibrium. Almost immediately, observers saw the dawn of a new, cleaner-living era of the sport.

Age was on Deller's side, and with it came the fearlessness of youth. That year, he threw his darts without the merest hint of apprehension, recruiting the nation to his cause as he knocked out two former world champions – John Lowe and Jocky Wilson – en route to this showdown in the final against a third, Eric Bristow.

Bristow was only actually a couple of years older than Deller, despite his face already resembling a Toby jug made flesh. Compared to his opponent, who still retained the bloodless pallor and sad eyes of adolescence, Bristow both looked and behaved as if he was from a different generation. His demeanour suggested he could eat Deller for breakfast and still have room for a bacon butty. The unseeded qualifier wasn't so much the underdog, quipped BBC commentator Sid Waddell, as 'the underpuppy'.

But Deller's tournament-long form didn't desert him in the final, at least not until, leading by five sets to three, seven of his darts missed the double that would have given him his sixth set and the world title. Bristow could smell the blood in the water. He drew level at five-all and started circling for the kill.

Deller didn't crumble, though. The admiration of the nation grew with each successful double. Very soon he was, again, one leg away from the ultimate anointment. And, with the forefinger of his right hand wrapped around the top of each dart he threw, he could do no wrong in that final leg. Ice-cool. Unflappable. 'He's got an arm as true as Alan-a-Dale,' noted Waddell, a man who, as a Cambridge graduate, could always be relied upon to bring literary flair or historical allusion to proceedings, all delivered in that tangy Northumbrian accent of his.

And Deller's arm was never truer than in the last three darts of that final. While Bristow hedged his bets and declined to go for the bull, believing he'd return to the oche in this leg, Deller filed a nerveless 138 checkout to lift the roof off Jollees Cabaret Club in Stoke. More than 200 miles away in Sussex, the tiles were in danger of being repositioned on our house too. 'I'm telling ya,' screamed Waddell. 'I'm telling ya. I've seen nothing like it in me life!' He was speaking for us all.

As thrilling as Deller's win was, Waddell was an equal hero that day, and for many days to come. He became the primary reason to watch televised darts for the rest of the decade and beyond. After spells in both academia and folk music, he had moved into television production in the mid '60s, putting together news and current affairs programmes for Granada and Yorkshire TV. His most quixotic creation was *The Indoor League*, a low-octane show featuring pub games – bar billiards, skittles, arm-wrestling, shove ha'penny – and hosted by a pipe-smoking, ale-supping Fred Trueman.

Shunting across to the Beeb in the mid '70s, Waddell soon found the fast-shifting sport that matched his high-peak accent and his aptitude for quick wit. The boisterousness of the oche was a dovetail fit. 'The cathedric calm of snooker ain't my bag,' he once explained, in the process adding a new word to the English language. Waddell was unlike any other BBC commentator, poles apart from the precise and frostier delivery of a David Coleman or an Alan Weeks. He wasn't a company man – nor, rather, a corporation man – one obediently toeing the party line, keeping the apple cart upright. If the Beeb hadn't had the rights to world darts, there wouldn't have been a spot for Waddell in any of their other commentary boxes. Imagine him trying to strike the right note during their more drawn-out, snail-slow broadcasts: a five-day Test match, say, or an Olympic dressage competition. He'd have been in hell.

Like Deller, Waddell appealed to me because of his outsider status, because he wasn't one of the anonymous herd. He was undoubtedly a one-off, a curious amalgam of broadsheet intellect and tabloid exclamation. I loved the way he added the odd learned flourish to his commentary. After all, why should appreciating sport and being well read be mutually exclusive? The fact that he combined them within the parameters of a working man's sport like darts made it even more pointed. And, to me, as the sports fanatic harbouring literary ambitions (if the unread volumes of Joyce and Steinbeck and Lawrence, recently bought with Christmas book tokens, were anything to go by), he was speaking what I thought was my language. Or, at least, the language I fancied speaking.

But, as honest and exuberant as that narration of Deller's greatest moment in 1983 was, Waddell unleashed his best, and most quoted, line two years later, when he drew on his days as a history undergraduate to describe Bristow's fourth world title. 'When Alexander of Macedonia was 33, he cried salt tears because there were no more worlds to conquer. Bristow's only 27 . . .'

PINNED AND MOUNTED

AS ALREADY mentioned, in our house we were late adopters of the cutting-edge technology of what had already been christened the 'video age'. Most, if not all, of my friends were already conversant with a world of top loaders and video nasties.

I had no interest in horror films. Instead, I saw our belated hiring of a video recorder from Radio Rentals as a chance to summon my inner librarian. My aim was to build up an extensive collection of sporting action culled from across the TV schedules. Once the collection reached a certain number of tapes (50? 75?), I could even call it a library. That sounded impressively high falutin, even though I would never be daft enough to allow a single volume to leave the premises.

This wasn't my first attempt at doing something like this. As an 11-year-old, I had diligently recorded the radio commentary from the 1980 FA Cup Final onto an audio cassette, believing that I'd start a back-up collection of the nation's greatest sporting moments in the event that the BBC archives ever fell victim to a catastrophic fire. I genuinely felt I was doing a national service. I even had the foresight to use a C120 cassette so that the injury time of both halves of the match wouldn't be cut off in their prime. There'd even be space for including the half-time reflections that were broadcast. I just knew how important historically these would be when they were stumbled upon in later centuries. A bit like the discovery of Sutton Hoo or the raising of the *Mary Rose*.

I was answering that distinctly male urge to collect, compile and classify. I could have chosen other routes: pinning and mounting dead butterflies or being a fastidious completist when it came to football programmes or the releases of a particular band.

My own urge to collect, compile and classify was an act of altruism that didn't last long. A lazy person can't be a completist. The archive of back-up recordings only ever had that single item on its shelves. Within a year, it had none. I taped over West Ham's Cup Final triumph with Jeff Wayne's *War of the Worlds*.

The video archive didn't last much longer. I hadn't thought it through. Either I videoed every episode of *Grandstand, Sunday Grandstand, Match of the Day, Sportsnight* etc. every week (and the outlay for the blank video tapes required for this was well beyond my means) or I simply cherry-picked and prioritised the important stuff. This was 1983. A summer without a World Cup, without an Olympic Games. There was very little really important stuff worth committing to magnetic tape.

And, besides, I had competition. The BBC had already given some thought to commemorating sporting history and heritage, and to how to refresh the public memory . . .

KILLING TIME

IN THE days when there were just four terrestrial channels, before satellite dishes and digital signals and EPGs, the timing of television programmes wasn't such a precise art. Things were a little looser. The news didn't necessarily start bang on the hour or half-hour. Indeed, it wasn't unusual for bulletins to begin at 12 past, or 23 to, the hour. It's an irregularity that's missing from today's regimented schedules.

Quite often – and sometimes, inexplicably, even if they were pre-recorded – programmes finished earlier than scheduled. The gaps these created (and we're not talking 40 seconds here or a couple of minutes there) would usually be filled by a *Tom and Jerry* cartoon. No problem: the combative pair were always welcome guests in our house. If the gap was closer to ten minutes, we'd get the thrill of a double bill.

At the tail end of 1982, a new measure had been introduced to fill these ad hoc spaces in the schedule. And it was even more welcome than the brutal misadventures of a cartoon cat and a cartoon mouse. *100 Great Sporting Moments* was the cheapest, but the most watchable, filler programme. At no cost to the BBC – because the footage was already in its possession, at the time becoming increasingly mummified under a thick crust of dust in the archives – these five- or ten-minute pockets of highlights of a particularly special sporting occasion served as brilliant history lessons. While plugging holes in the schedule, they also plugged holes in our knowledge. The matches and races and fights that had earned their permanent place in the history books well before The Sundance Kid struck up his committed relationship with TV sport, now became part of the archive in his brain. David Bedford taking more than seven seconds off the 10,000m record at Crystal Palace in '73. Arkle beating his great rival Mill House in the Cheltenham Gold Cup in '64. Those highly controversial final three seconds in the USA/USSR basketball final at the '72 Munich Olympics.

The repeated screenings of *100 Great Sporting Moments* were also how particular snippets of commentary became a permanent fixture in my memory. I can still recite some of them today without recourse to YouTube:

'There's a minute left on the clock. Brady for Arsenal . . . Right across . . . Sunderlaaaand! It's there! It's 3-2!' (John Motson at the FA Cup Final, 1979).

'This is Gareth Edwards. A dramatic start. What a score!' (Cliff Morgan describes the opening minutes of Barbarians vs the All Blacks, 1973).

'He's done it! He's done it! And my goodness, it's gone way down to Swansea . . .' (Wilf Wooller on Gary Sobers' six sixes for Nottinghamshire against Glamorgan, 1968).

These short space-fillers illuminated and informed my appreciation of TV commentary and presentation no end. Whoever's idea it was to make right and proper use of the BBC archives in this way deserves some kind of recognition for services to eager-to-learn teenagers. Perhaps they should be awarded a replica of the gold medal that was used on the programme's opening titles.

However, the rights department at Looney Tunes, to whom not insubstantial repeat fees would have previously been paid for those recurring appearances by *Tom and Jerry*, might well disagree.

STEVE DAVIS vs EBENEZER SKEET

I WAS fortunate that overfeeding on TV sport didn't come with too much parental interference. I wasn't indulging in this obsession in the face of buffeting criticism and imposed restrictions. I'd done my calculations, I'd judged it well. As long as I went outside for one half-hour in every six during the school holidays (usually to re-enact the goals from *The Big Match* the previous Sunday), or emerged from my room to play the odd frame of snooker against myself on our warped and wobbly table, there wouldn't be too much pressure bearing down on me. And as long as there were no notes coming home from school detailing a litany of missed homework and unexplained absences, the status quo went untouched.

Indeed, on the rare moments that I was forced to turn off my TV during school holidays, I simply got on my bike. Six minutes later, I was round at Gran's house for an uninterrupted afternoon back inside, out of the sun, in front of the snooker or tennis or golf and almost certainly fortified by a plate of shortbread fingers.

Had I been born into a more academically minded household (a couple of years later, I'd break new ground for the family and all its known extensions by becoming the first to enrol for A-levels), the pressure would have been more acute, more intense. Were a long line of scholarly achievement in danger of being halted by my dedication to televised sport, the obsession wouldn't have been allowed to spread and deepen as far as it had. The significance of sporting knowledge – at the expense of understanding Pythagoras's theorem or appreciating the role of the free city of Danzig in shaping the post-First World War landscape – would definitely have been a matter for parental debate. A key question would have been asked.

'What are you actually *learning* from all this sport?'

In the unlikely event that such a philosophical conundrum be directed my way, I had an example that would prove the worth of sport in my education and, at least temporarily, stymie any criticism. In the third year of secondary school, we were taught maths by a frail, spindly man called Mr Skeet. We knew the first names of a fair few of our teachers – Simon James was the easily distractible history teacher, Frank Casey the cane-wielding deputy head, and the entire PE department seemed to answer to 'Rob'. But we didn't know Mr Skeet's first name. Knowing it began with an E and taking on board his decidedly Victorian demeanour, he became – under our breath, of course – Ebenezer.

One day, Ebenezer was trying to explain the rules of geometry to our disinterested group of young teens whose appetite for trigonometry was nothing like our appetite for break-time cream doughnuts. We were hungry. But then he said something that grabbed the attention of the more sport-literate members of the class.

'Whatever angle an object hits a solid at, this will be mirrored by the angle of its exit.'

Several hands went straight up in the air, the first volunteering of information or opinion in the entire lesson.

'But, sir. That's not true. Side spin.'

Ebenezer looked confused.

'Snooker.'

The confusion remained.

'Didn't you see how Steve Davis got out of that snooker that Eddie Charlton put him in last night?'

Ebenezer's Victorian demeanour, and his now-furrowed

brow, suggested his working knowledge of professional snooker players was limited to only those prior to 1890.

I took charge of the situation, proving myself surprisingly eloquent.

'If you hit a cue ball straight at a cushion but address it to the right of its centre, it'll bounce off the cushion to the right. The angle it hits the cushion at will be different to the angle it leaves the cushion at.'

Ebenezer initially looked dismissive and then flustered. He started to deny that this could be true, but the weight of protestations from the sporting quarter in the room (joined by others who, despite little snooker knowledge, could recognise when a teacher was on the ropes) meant he could do little more than ultimately offer a shrug. Forty-odd years of teaching and accumulated knowledge had taken a dent.

We generously offered to take him on an impromptu field trip to the sixth-form building where we could prove the science using the A-level students' pool table. It was only when someone with an older brother pointed out that table tennis and darts were the only sports offered there that we abandoned the plan. Those cream doughnuts were calling anyway.

We'd made our point. When it came to televised geometry lessons, not even the Open University's boffins could explain the subject quite as directly, and in language we spoke, as an hour or two of coverage from the Crucible in Sheffield or Preston Guild Hall. As viewers, we would study the angle required to escape from a fiendish snooker with the same diligence and expertise of a Thorburn or a Meo.

An admission, though. More than 30 years on, I've still yet to find an application for the knowledge of side spin outside of a snooker hall. Just don't tell Ebenezer.

OUTSIDE INTERFERENCE

WHEN I wasn't learning some of the never-to-be-used rules of trigonometry, I was also absorbing other life lessons – and not necessarily through the filter of sport.

By the age of 14, I was also carrying on with a new love, a new obsession. Music. I didn't let it affect my relationship with TV sport, though. The pair could coexist. I'd been taking *Smash Hits'* fortnightly fix of pop shininess for a couple of years, but that was a mere gateway drug. It was 1983 when I graduated to the harder stuff: the *NME*. It was a natural evolution, one as inevitable as vinyl LPs replacing Figurine Panini stickers as the exchange currency of the classroom.

The *NME* – and others it led me to, like *The Face* – shined a light on cultural phenomena that a *Shoot!* reader wouldn't otherwise have stumbled upon. Not only did these new publications take me to exciting new musical worlds, but they engendered a growing politicisation within me. This was the year – an election year that pitched Tory hardliner Margaret Thatcher against Labour hardliner Michael Foot – when I first properly understood what left wing and right wing meant in a political context. Previously I knew them to be the difference between Man Utd pair Gordon Hill and Steve Coppell. And this grasp of politics unconsciously spilled into my mushrooming appreciation of music, as shown by a healthy accumulation of records by politically astute acts like the Redskins and Billy Bragg.

It was an unwritten rule that music had to fit around my ongoing sport-watching commitments. Music was there to complement, not to crowd out. Saturday mornings increasingly revolved around a trip to town and a couple of hours zigzagging between record shops, deciding which LP to buy with my weekly £5.50 wage from the paper round. But it would never interfere with prior engagements; I had to be back home in front of the box by the time Bob Wilson kicked off *Football Focus* at 12.20pm.

After all that day's results had been delivered and chewed over at the tail end of *Grandstand*, Saturday early evenings, like Saturday mornings, were often another dead zone for TV sport, especially so in the colder, barren months of autumn and winter. This was a gap handsomely filled by Janice Long's enlightening Radio 1 show, a 7.30–10pm treat that took me close to the start time of *Match of the Day*. While John Peel's influence on my record collection would make itself known later in the decade, his school-night shows were simply on too late for an early-rising paperboy.

In the meantime, Janice took on the mantle of broadening my musical horizons – from James Brown to the Woodentops – as well as tipping me off about records that were imminently coming out. Having heard a pre-release airing of 'Blue Monday' on her show, I was straight out of the traps on the day the record hit the local Our Price, the first person in the entire school to own a copy. Brownie points and bragging rights. Hearing the song today takes me straight back to those wet, football-free lunchtimes when, having liberated one of the mono cassette players used in French and German lessons, we'd listen to it constantly – play, rewind, play, rewind – while replicating its distinctive drum pattern on the classroom's gnarled, weather-beaten desks.

But, notice, this was only when we couldn't play football. Sport was still the boss; music was second in command. When our English teacher Mrs Clarke told us we had to compile a poetry project – dissecting someone else's verse, not creating our own – it was sport I first thought of. I mooted the idea of looking at the words of the best sport commentators; these were often poetry to my ears. This didn't hold up to Mrs

Clarke's definition of the form, but she did go for the fallback position: analysing, in an awkward and pretentious teenage way, the lyrics to The Teardrop Explodes' album *Wilder*, with its heavy themes of isolation and colonialism. (At the desk behind me, Ian Fogden took inspiration from this and chose to do his project on Marillion's just-released *Script for a Jester's Tear*. I can't attest to the literary insight he brought to Fish's lyrics, but the colourful drawings of court jesters he did to accompany his words were really good. Too good, in fact. I reckon he must have traced them.)

This first stab of mine at music criticism was far from successful. C minus. Had I been allowed to do the commentary option, I'd have been close to an A. Almost definitely, yeah. My love for the subject would have poured forth.

It had been my first choice, after all. Music was trying hard, but TV sport remained at number one in my own chart.

WEDNESDAY NIGHT LIGHTS

THERE'S A school of thought that suggests television in the '80s reached the height of glamour with the weekly instalment of *Dynasty*, that fictional world of champagne and shagging and dastardly backstabbing. It's a school of thought that's wrong. *Dynasty* wasn't the high-water mark of sophistication on the small screen at the time. For Blake Carrington, substitute Harry Carpenter; for Denver, Colorado, substitute any sporting hotspot across Europe. We're talking *Sportsnight*.

The programme was a portal into a more globetrotting life. Just the names of the destinations or the venues made you feel like a juvenile Alan Whicker, bouncing from one exotic European city to another, even though, fixed to the sofa, you weren't moving a muscle. A Cup Winners' Cup tie at the Dinamo Stadium in Tbilisi, an athletics meet in the Bislett Stadium in Oslo, international swimming from Sofia . . .

These were our ports of call, mythical stamps in a mythical passport.

When I started at secondary school, I had high hopes for my geography classes. Those expectations evaporated within the first fortnight when I realised the slow passage to the O-level exam wouldn't be five years of gazing in a fascinated fashion at maps or answering endless quizzes on capital cities. Instead, it seemed to be all about arable farming and central business districts.

Harry Carpenter was my saviour. Through him – or, at least, through the events the *Sportsnight* production team chose to broadcast – distant destinations, just dots on the page of an atlas until that point, came to life. They became impossibly alluring. Somewhere else, somewhere *other*. Zürich, Cologne, Bilbao, Split, St Etienne . . .

For a young man who didn't leave England between the ages of four and 19, not even to visit Wales or Scotland, it was like Carpenter was reading an airport departures board out loud.

I had to be content with simply paying these locations a visit every Wednesday evening through grainy televised pictures. That would do for now. Obviously, back then I fully thought that I'd be visiting them later in life to occupy the commentary gantries of their stadia. The result was that all I ended up knowing about each city in the early '80s was framed by sport. I couldn't tell you much about their histories nor their demographic breakdown nor their respective contributions to the economies of Europe. But, thanks to *Sportsnight*, I could identify their sports stadia within seconds. I knew the difference between the athletics tracks in Zürich and Koblenz; the former had a stand with a roof along the back straight, while the latter left its crowd open to the elements. At one time, I could even recognise a number of European football grounds from their dugouts alone.

By its very nature, the action on *Sportsnight* was alluring, simply because it was after dark and under lights. A Saturday afternoon at Molineux has its own qualities, but it simply can't compete with the edge and anticipation and atmosphere of a high-ranking sporting occasion played out in the beam and glare of floodlights. Even a humdrum five-a-side pitch takes on a special quality when the lights are on.

The attraction of *Sportsnight* and its bill of fare wasn't just visible. It was audible. This manifested itself in several ways. It could be the chants and cheers of a foreign crowd, and the whizz and bangs of the flares they'd let off behind the goal. It was certainly Tony Hatch's pulsing, high-tempo theme tune, one that never failed to provoke a Pavlovian response in you: to park your backside down and not move for the next hour or two. The tune excited you. It pricked your skin.

But the sound that was most evocative was that of the commentator – Davies or Sinstadt, Coleman or Weeks – down a less-than-perfect line from whichever corner of Europe they'd been dispatched to. The more brittle the line, and the more distorted the voice, the more real and visceral it all became. And it was confirmation they weren't just in a side studio at Television Centre, commentating while merely watching the same pictures as us. There are plenty of folk who believe that the moon landings were faked, but they could never fake the accelerated sound of David Coleman in the main stand in some European athletics stadium, desperately hoping that the feed taking the words and pictures back to London will hold out for the remainder of a 1500m race being run at world-record pace. We were always crossing our fingers too.

THERE ARE few sounds in sport more distinctive than the hooter at the end of a rugby league match. It is definitive and unyielding, like a piercing school bell announcing the start of lessons or the pit siren at the end of a long shift underground. On the debit side, it also sounds a little comical, as if the previous 80 minutes of bruising play have been of no greater importance than an episode of *It's a Knockout*.

Of course, there was one man who united the BBC's rugby league coverage and *It's a Knockout*: Eddie Waring, the man behind the mic at the former and the master of the scoreboard at the latter. When I was starting to appreciate league, Waring was on his way out. His departure probably helped me to learn more about the 13-man code. Until then, I could barely understand a word that trilby-hatted Eddie was saying.

In the early '80s, Ray French – a former player with St Helens and Widnes – replaced the populist Waring as the BBC's chief rugby league commentator. He might not have littered his words with the same literary flourish as someone like Sid Waddell, but I thought French was great, his commentaries full of the requisite grit and crunch, and as breathless as the game itself. Thanks to his avuncular guidance, and thanks to my ongoing grapple with the confusing nature of rugby union, I definitely preferred league. It made more sense. It was more singular, more direct. Players just charged on and the game flowed freely, reluctant to lose itself in a tangle of rules and regulations. Accordingly, I would always be riveted whenever the grey BBC Outside Broadcast vans hit the motorway, destination Castleford or Halifax or Wigan or Warrington.

On the first Saturday of May 1983, the Outside Broadcast vans stayed off the motorway, only venturing a few miles north of Television Centre. For this was league's big day out, the annual occasion when the sport packed a flask and sandwiches and made its way south to Wembley. This was Challenge Cup Final day.

The final – unhealthily sponsored by cigarette brand State Express, who received plenty of namechecks on the BBC – pitched defending champions Hull against underdogs Featherstone Rovers. Hull's ranks were packed with the cream of Antipodean oval-ball talent, while the total population of mining town Featherstone could have fitted into Wembley seven or eight times over. Naturally, I was siding with David again, although I did dig the road atlas out from the under-stairs cupboard to see exactly where Featherstone was. That was the least I could have done to show my commitment to the cause.

As we were well into the warmth of spring, someone would have inevitably called round for me to see if I was up for spending the afternoon hanging round a bus shelter or down the swings. And that same someone would have inevitably struggled to understand why that didn't appeal and why I was staying inside to pay respect and homage to a sport not played remotely close to our location in England's Deep South. The sport's epicentre was the best part of 300 miles due north, so what was my connection? Perhaps I saw a little exoticism in the industrial heartland of the M62 corridor, a landscape far removed from the flat fields of home. After all, the north was increasingly informing my cultural life, whether music (the post-punk output of both Liverpool and Manchester) or books (*A Kestrel for a Knave, Billy Liar*), so why not my sporting life too?

It goes without saying that it was the right choice to stay home. The final was as close as could be, the teams only divided by a last-minute Featherstone penalty. Combined with Keith Deller's takeover of the darts world at Jollees back in January, this was proving to be the year of the underdog. And reliable Ray French did full justice to the winning kick, confirming himself to be a master of high drama.

'Seconds ticking away,' he breathed. 'The Challenge Cup to be settled here.' A respectful silence while the ball arced up and over. And then the roar. 'And it is! It is! It is!'

THE SEAGULLS HAVE LANDED

IF FEATHERSTONE had sprung a surprise, there was another on the cards back at Wembley two Saturdays later. The surprise wasn't just that already relegated Brighton almost snatched the FA Cup from Manchester United (the infamous last-minute 'Smith must score' miss), it was the manner in which they approached the final. Literally approached it, that is. No gridlocked coach journey across London for Jimmy Melia's boys. Instead they rose above it. They arrived by helicopter.

That the BBC had both a cameraman and roving reporter Alan Parry on board was a real coup for the corporation over their rivals at ITV. 'There used to be behind-the-scenes wars going on in those days,' Parry, a man who batted for both channels in his career, later told me. 'Who could get the first interviewee? Who'd get the winning manager? Who'd get the scorer of the winning goal? All kinds of skulduggery went on. Bribes being offered and everything. It was so competitive.'

On board the helicopter, it was a scene of serenity. As victims of geography – as well as counting British Caledonian as their shirt sponsor – Brighton often flew to further-flung fixtures. Accordingly, the squad were perfectly at ease, with not a trace of nerves, as Parry made his way down the aisle to interview club officials and senior players, all of whom were dressed in their cream suit jackets, dark trousers and white shoes.

The viewer at home was familiar with Cup Final interviews with teams in transit, even though they were usually conducted aboard a luxury coach gridlocked somewhere on the North

Circular. The flight added another level to the pre-match fuss, with an accompanying helicopter offering grand views of the Brighton chopper as it gracefully crossed the London skyline. And, as with State Express at the Challenge Cup Final, those pictures gave extraordinary exposure to British Caledonian on the advertising-free BBC. Brighton might have been a team heading out of the top flight for the next 34 years, but they showed no blunt edge when it came to joining the public relations dots.

Every year, those en masse pre-match interviews were manna from heaven to the nosy TV viewer. They were a window into the soul of a team, the equivalent of a five-minute peak round the dressing-room door. They gave you a hint of the balance of power among the players, revealing (or confirming) who were the alpha males, who were the more reflective ones, who were the jokers.

On the evidence of Parry's interviews that day, it appeared that Brighton consisted exclusively of jokers. Half a decade before Wimbledon made it to Wembley and their own Cup Final appearance, the Seagulls showed they were the original Crazy Gang, the punching-above-their-weight high-flyers.

AWAY DAYS

MY SCHOOL – that all-boys comprehensive – naturally leaned towards sport, an ideal state of affairs for a TV sport obsessive and his similarly sport-obsessed chums. Our playing fields extended as far as the eye could see, seemingly into the next county. Football pitches, cricket squares, rugby posts, hockey goals, running tracks . . .

This meant, when it came to the supposedly educational trips that the school was probably legally obliged to provide, we weren't sent on a rancid, diesel-fumed coach to some dusty museum or cobweb-covered castle. Instead, we were sent on a rancid, diesel-fumed coach to some of the nation's favourite sporting venues.

In the summer of 1983, it was the turn of Wimbledon.

This was the first sporting event I had been to that was being televised. And we wanted a piece of the action, to make our debuts on the small screen, no matter how fleeting. If, to our loved ones at home, we were vaguely recognisable faces in the crowd, that counted as our first, teetering steps towards fame and recognition. At one point, a couple of us greatly improved our chances of appearing on screen by managing to squeeze into Centre Court for ten furnace-like, air-free minutes in Free-Standing Area G. Ten minutes was all we could take. I think Billie Jean King was playing, but I couldn't be sure as I was largely distracted by trying to locate the nearest exit. Our cameo could well have made the live coverage, but as Billie Jean's match wasn't part of that evening's highlights, we could never be certain that we had broken our televisual duck.

Fortunately for a group of us, though, the action on No.3 Court rarely made the live broadcast. Had it done so, the nation – including, and especially, my mum in her shop with the black-and-white portable set – would have seen the moment when play was held up while we noisily ran at speed across the top row of the stand. And we did it for no other reason than we were teenage boys and that was what teenage boys were supposed to do.

HEAVEN AND HELSINKI

AFTER FOOTBALL, athletics was probably the sport I most enjoyed watching on the box during the early '80s. There was such variety on offer over the course of just two hours of coverage, the viewer zipping back and forth around the stadium to take in all manner of running, jumping and throwing. If a televised Test match was a long lunch languidly picked over, athletics was a fill-your-plate, all-you-can-eat buffet.

Being an odd-numbered year, 1983 should have been a comparatively fallow period for keen students of track and field. The Commonwealth Games in Brisbane and the European Championships in Athens had been held the previous year, while the Los Angeles Olympics were a date on next year's calendar. But, the IAAF in their wisdom – which later years would reveal to be far from infinite – had decided to introduce and institute a new competition: the functionally titled World Athletics Championships.

Stepping outside the political tit-for-tat that ensured both the Moscow and Los Angeles Olympics suffered from boycotts by sporting superpowers, the inaugural World Championships wouldn't be depleted by the absence of the planet's best. On the western side of the Iron Curtain, but also not a member of NATO, politically neutral Finland was a particularly judicious choice of host.

It was to be a true contest between all globally significant athletes. And some genuine legends of track and field were there, scooping up the medals – Marita Koch, Jarmila Kratochvílová, Mary Decker and Grete Waitz on the women's side, and Carl Lewis, Sergey Bubka and Ed Moses on the men's.

Ongoing illness had meant that Seb Coe didn't make it to Helsinki, so – having also missed the 1500m at both the Commonwealths and Europeans the previous year – he again couldn't test himself against the Jarrow Arrow, the 22-year-old Steve Cram, who had taken those two major titles. Steve Ovett made it to Finland, but Cram's tactical superiority, as well as his talent for running away from A-class athletes like Steve Scott and Saïd Aouita, saw him home. Ovett, boxed in towards the back of the field at one point, finished outside the medals.

Aside from Cram's gold (and one for Daley Thompson too in the decathlon, as well as a silver for Fatima Whitbread in the javelin, cruelly edged back into second place on the very last throw of the competition), it was at Helsinki where I truly first appreciated the high-speed ballet that was relay running. This appreciation was lubricated by British success. The women's 4x100m squad held off the Jamaicans to take a brilliant silver, while the men's 4x400m quartet went home with the bronze. The latter squad would become a staple of medal ceremonies throughout the rest of the decade and beyond, making household names out of those who rarely shone individually, athletes like Todd Bennett and Phil Brown.

And, of course, just as a 4x400m race wasn't worth its salt if Britain's anchor leg didn't come from behind to grab a medal, it also didn't really count unless David Coleman reminded us that 'We won't get a true picture of the race until the stagger unwinds at the start of the back straight on the second lap'. Without fail. Championships after championships.

As if we could forget, David.

THE SHIPPING FORECAST

WHEN NEARLY all was done and dusted at the end of *Grandstand*, when the curtain was about to be drawn across five continuous hours of sport, there was one last short item to cling on to, one that would be squeezed in before the closing titles. The club rugby results.

I didn't care for the results themselves; I had no idea what the significance of a home win for Orrell might be, nor whether a heavy defeat for Maesteg was the continuation of a bad run of form. What I liked about the club rugby results were the names themselves. In this way, they appealed to me as the *Shipping Forecast* appeals to others, offering both a sign-off to the day and some sort of comfort to know that places like Rockall and Dogger and North Utsire exist. Their continued existence was enough; you didn't need to know their precise location, nor what 'moderate or poor, becoming good' meant to a sailor's ears. For me, hearing the names of Kelso and Sale, Moseley and Abertillery, served the same purpose. The rhythm and poetry of the names was all that was required. You didn't hear of these places anywhere else or at any other time – only on Saturday afternoons, just around five o'clock. I knew the big cities because football took care of these. Sheffield, Leeds, Nottingham, Southampton . . .

Rugby, though, ventured into the pockets in between.

If I caught *Rugby Special* on a Sunday teatime (who am I kidding to suggest there was such a concept as 'if'? It was sport, wasn't it?), I would find out where a few of these places were. Lydney, presenter Nigel Starmer-Smith would tell me ahead of a highlights package, was found in 'the depths of Gloucestershire', while Redruth saw itself as 'the rugby capital of Cornwall'.

These towns were represented on their rugby pitches by local heroes. They were folk willing to throw themselves into the line of fire every week, on Somme-like pitches, just for fun. For them, it was all about love not money, about the upholding of the amateur code. Doctors and solicitors and bank managers during the week, they'd transform into bloodthirsty, steam-spewing monsters come the weekend.

Only one thing betrayed their rapaciousness. If their exploits were given the highlights treatment on *Rugby Special* the following afternoon, the programme's theme music gave them an inadequate entrance. It was a weedy, synthesiser-led tune more suited to a kids' quiz show – one possibly that was spelling-based and presented by Richard Stilgoe – than to getting the viewers' juices going for 40 minutes of bone-crunching intensity. Give me 'Ride of the Valkyries' any day.

BRIAN MOORE KNOWS THE SCORE

IN 1983, it turned out to be a significant year for televised football, especially on ITV. Until the start of the 1983-84 season, the independent regional companies broadcast their own football highlights shows on a Sunday afternoon. A home game featuring a local First Division club would be the main match, but the producers could then cherry-pick the best highlights from their regional counterparts.

While viewers in Granadaland got *The Kick Off Match* and Midlanders sat down before *Star Soccer* on Central, southern England had London Weekend Television's *The Big Match*. Presented by Brian Moore, the main game would almost certainly be a London match from the day before, one that Moore would have commentated on. He rarely travelled far. Occasionally he might make it to Vicarage Road when Watford were in their early '80s heyday, but in the main he was a creature who seldom breached the North or South Circular in a professional capacity.

With the likes of Highbury, Stamford Bridge and Loftus Road becoming very familiar territory (although White Hart Lane seemed to be the ground the LWT cameras would visit the most), the highlights from elsewhere in the country were of particular interest to me. They offered the chance to analyse the performances, and soak up the voices and styles, of commentators on their local patches. If *The Big Match* producers hadn't taken footage from across the country, I wouldn't have been bathed in the rich, smiley tones of Hugh Johns, the voice of Midlands football. I wouldn't have revelled in the way that Gerry Harrison, Anglia TV's fixture at Carrow Road and Portman Road, announced 'Why-mark!' on a regular basis. And I wouldn't have enjoyed the gritty reportage of John Helm, the number one mic man at Yorkshire TV.

All that changed halfway through 1983 when ITV abandoned this delightful *modus operandi* and decided to centralise their coverage. Everyone in the country now saw the same highlights, the same matches, in the same order and at the same length. The regional quirks and character were washed away with the bathwater, with two main commentators – Moore and Martin Tyler – doing all the big league games.

It was a pivotal year for another reason. On 2 October – and, possibly inevitably, from White Hart Lane – ITV showed the first-ever live league match. This was an obvious yet still radical move, one that courted plenty of controversy. Newspaper columnists rose up in their dozens to denounce this as a short-term gain that would produce a long-term loss: that delivering a full live match straight to the warmth and convenience of the living room would be to the grave detriment of the national game. Attendances, already on the slide, would inevitably take the brunt, the naysayers bleated. How could they not?

While the BBC opted for a Friday night schedule slot for their live matches, ITV kept their coverage on a Sunday afternoon. And that first game, a spirited affair between Spurs and Nottingham Forest, disproved – at least temporarily – the doubters. Viewing figures were strong and the 30,000-plus crowd was the biggest attendance of the weekend. Certainly the Spurs chairman Douglas Alexiou was a content man as he joined Jim Rosenthal and Jimmy Greaves for the post-match analysis. That analysis didn't dissect any aspect of the match itself. All discussion revolved around whether the whole spectacle, and the novelty of a Sunday afternoon game, was what Rosenthal described as 'a good advertisement for live football'.

This initial success wasn't taken as a given. 'I believe it's important for the future of football on television that it is a thriller,' cautioned Brian Moore in *TV Times*. 'A number of critics are still looking to stick knives into live TV football. We started off very well with the Spurs vs Nottingham Forest game, but every time we screen a match that doesn't live up to expectations, the knockers are ready to write us off again.'

I was neither critic nor knocker. I was an evangelical. With an unsophisticated notion of how big business sustained itself and thus ignorantly unconcerned about declining crowd numbers, I was all in favour of these live games. I was especially in favour of the BBC's decision to plump for Friday nights for their transmissions. That was a time of the week that usually resembled a black hole where TV sport was concerned. And, once again, it dovetailed beautifully with my music commitments. I could watch *The Tube* until its closing credits at five to seven, scoff the quickest of dinners and be right back in place for when Jimmy Hill would appear at five past the hour.

An extra bonus was that the BBC's first live league game fell on my 15th birthday. Both teams – Manchester United and, again, Spurs – seemed to heed Brian Moore's warning and served up a cracker, a six-goal thriller in which Ossie Ardiles made his first appearance since the Falklands War 18 months earlier. His return was soundtracked by a near 360-degree chorus of boos from the Old Trafford faithful. Ardiles wasn't fazed. He had a strong sense of occasion. Just 16 seconds after coming on as a second-half sub, 16 seconds back in English football, he set up Mark Falco for Spurs' second.

The boo-boys would boo and the knockers would knock, but live league football was here to stay. This was one revolution that *would* be televised.

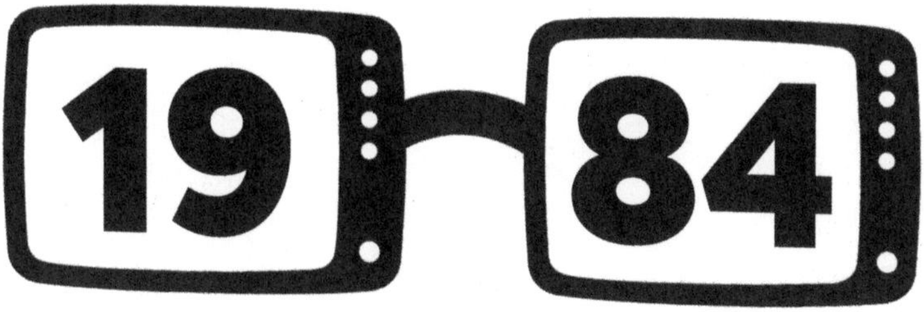
19
84

LOVE IS A WONDERFUL COLOUR

THE WRITER Andrew Collins believes that the year you turn 18 is a crucial year for absorbing music – and culture in general – 'in a way that's even more profound than your earliest love affairs with the stuff. I loved Slade and The Sweet and Alice Cooper when I was a kid but, at a young age, I couldn't do anything about it, beyond getting a poster of them, or reading about them in *Look-In*. At 18, you can go to gigs and have income from a Saturday job, and you can actually start to build your own persona around your purchases and choices.'

He's on to something here. Andrew came of age in 1983 and so the year of 'I.O.U.' by Freeez, and Wah!'s 'The Story of the Blues' looms largest for him. He's three years older than me so, as I recognise 1986 as my musical *annus mirabilis* (*The Queen Is Dead*, *Lifes Rich Pageant*, Throwing Muses' debut), I fit the bill too.

I can take Andrew's premise even further. Such is the order of things in many teenage boys' development – where a devotion to sport is often the forerunner of a devotion to music – I'd suggest that a person's favourite sporting year occurs a couple of years before then. Thus, through the application of my dubious, clinically unproven science, I can thereby declare 1984 to be sport's greatest year.

Actually, so much for sociological insight, because 1984 became such a totemic sporting year for me for one reason: a white box that might have cost in the region of 80 quid but that would beam the world in all its glorious Technicolor straight into my bedroom. It seemed like a bargain to me.

In comparison to the black-and-white TV set with the unmemorable manufacturer's name (which, of course, I diligently kept in my room as back-up), the 14-inch screen of a Ferguson TX offered the full cinematic experience. *Brookside* had been fine to watch in fuzzy monochrome; it actually gave its storylines extra kitchen-sink grit. It was just that every time the racing pigeons from one of the houses behind ours flew past the window en masse and disturbed the already weak signal, Bobby Grant's face would distort wildly as if viewed in a hall of mirrors.

Those pigeons would no longer determine the quality of my viewing experience. Instead, a cable was kindly run straight into the aerial on the roof; all I had to do was plug the Ferguson's aerial into the new socket in the wall and pin-sharp sporting action was on tap. No more did I have to adopt a strange, one-legged standing position, aerial in hand, whenever inclement weather, or the local bird life, affected the signal.

Fourteen-inch portables didn't tend to come with remote controls then, so I devised one of my own, one for which I didn't need any electrical engineering knowledge. Without needing to shift my horizontal position on the bed, I could easily operate the on/off switch with the underside of my big toe. But the eight smaller, more delicate channel buttons were a challenging proposition – if I wanted to avoid simply sitting up and reaching out my arm. I found the answer, though. I stopped cutting the nail on that big toe and, within a couple of months, it had grown to a sufficient length to prove up to the task of delicately selecting each small button. I could now channel-hop at will while barely moving a muscle. What a lazy sod.

The Ferguson had largely been financed by the tips as a paperboy from the Christmas just gone and, as such, was vindication that I had chosen the correct career path. I'd had offers for Saturday day jobs at both the butchers and the newsagents, but had turned them down as they would have interfered with my consumption of *Grandstand*. I would have been sweeping up entrails and sawdust, or weighing out Kola Kubes for ungrateful, snotty-nosed kids, when really I should have been giving myself wholeheartedly to the indoor bowls being beamed live and direct from Coatbridge near Glasgow. Thinking about it now, perhaps my flunking of the job interview at the library at the end of our street was in fact a calculated plan on the part of my subconscious to keep my Saturdays free.

The Ferguson's pictures beaming straight into my room, though, had a significance beyond the sporting action. Everything I wanted to watch was now delivered straight to me in both high quality and vivid colour. This meant I didn't need to go downstairs (or, in my more sociable moments, pop round to Gran's bungalow) to watch the snooker. And there was no longer a Five Nations colour clash between two grey-shirted teams.

It also meant I hunkered further down into my burrow at precisely the moment that I should have embraced the light and started to bloom. Instead, I only emerged for hastily scoffed meals before retreating back to the bunker. The solitary out-of-school life wasn't just continuing, it was intensifying. Perhaps this should have been the year where I felt the first flush of teenage romance. Certainly the song I most associate with that summer – The Kane Gang's 'Closest Thing to Heaven' – would have provided the ideal soundtrack ('Here they come / A lonely boy and a lonely girl . . .').

Instead, with my glasses and blackheads and dubious fashion sense, I remained a couple of years behind my contemporaries and their stories of encounters with the opposite sex. I buried myself even deeper behind those closed curtains, with my colour TV and my Smiths records for company. Morrissey wasn't one for sport, but he didn't do romance or sunlight either. As a role model, two out of three wasn't bad.

BLOODLINES

WITHOUT A devotion, without a *duty*, to blindly and blithely pin my colours to a particular football team and trail them across the train or motorway network, as a teenager I didn't attend many matches in the flesh. And when I did go (or, rather, when I was taken), quite often my dad chose potentially uncomfortable fixtures, where a sense of danger and edge hung heavily in the air. These weren't necessarily the most appropriate games to take your stick-thin, bantamweight son to.

My first-ever match had been Brighton versus Crystal Palace at the old Goldstone Ground, the so-called M23 derby. There were 50-odd miles between the clubs, which stretched the definition of a local derby somewhat, but the bad blood between the two had flowed since a particularly feisty FA Cup tie in the mid-70s when two former Spurs teammates, Alan Mullery and Terry Venables, had been in charge at Brighton and Palace respectively. In the end, this cherry-losing first game of mine was a benign affair. Or, at least, I didn't *witness* any argy-bargy. The abiding memory certainly isn't one of arbitrarily administered violence. It's of Michael Robinson scoring two goals within 40 seconds to swing the game in the home team's favour.

Portsmouth versus Southampton in the FA Cup fourth round in 1984, though, was anything but benign. This was the first competitive match between the two clubs in nearly a decade. The bad blood was far more sour and nasty than that shown by the M23 derby rivals. Twenty short miles separated

The Dell and Fratton Park. The word 'Southampton' wasn't in the vocabulary of those on the eastern side of the rivalry. Instead, they almost universally referred to the city, its people and its football club as 'Scum'.

Perhaps I was taken to Fratton Park that January afternoon as some sort of rite of passage. In the absence of national service, maybe experiencing the worst part of human nature this side of a warzone would turn boy into man. It was certainly an eye-opener. I'd never seen so many police officers; it felt like the constabulary of the entire county was present. I remember thinking that the criminals of Hampshire could all have gone on leisurely crime sprees that day without any fear of being felt by the long arm of the law.

The game had needle and antagonism in abundance. Goals, though, it didn't. And the longer it stayed scoreless, the tighter the tension drew itself. Packed onto the North Terrace, my view was far from perfect, especially when everyone went on tiptoes to see what was occurring towards the corner to our left. 'Mark Dennis just got coined!' shouted the man next to me, dissolving into laughter, delighted that someone on the North Terrace had nobbled the Southampton full back. I couldn't see Dennis's prone figure, but the sight of the Southampton physio scurrying onto the pitch suggested it might be at least a semi-serious injury. If this was what a lifelong devotion to one particular club meant – that you excused or justified physical assaults if they injured one of the opposition's players – I was glad I had plumped for non-affiliation.

The small window of the pitch that I could see clearly did at least offer up one piece of memorable action. It involved Alan Biley, the Portsmouth striker whose spiky peroxide haircut TV commentators seemed contractually obliged to compare to that of Rod Stewart. The future commentator within me wouldn't have lazily resorted to such a hoary cliché. I'd have noted how it made him look way closer to one of the knobheads in Black Lace.

Late in the game, Biley collected the ball with his back to goal before turning his marker and leathering it as if he was 25 or 30 yards out. Unfortunately, he was only six yards from Peter Shilton's goal at the time. Biley blasted his effort with such power and such inaccuracy that it could have caused serious injury to someone in the Fratton End. Or one of the police horses in the street beyond. It felt like that was the home side's last chance of victory.

'These are the kind of wankers that score in the last minute,' the guy next to me loudly declared. He turned out to be a pretty accurate soothsayer. With 89 minutes gone and a midweek replay on the cards, the prolific young striker Steve Moran ghosted in at the far post to convert a David Armstrong cross – although I would only see the goal itself on the TV highlights later. Moran had sent Southampton fans delirious. He'd also sent Portsmouth fans angry and in search of targets.

We took a serpentine route back to the station, down iffy-looking back streets and side alleys. But thankfully these were quiet back streets and side alleys. It turned out all the fighting took place up on the main road instead. There were a few bloodied casualties nursing their wounds on the train. I was fairly sure that this didn't enhance the live experience and went to very few matches for many seasons. Ever the adventurous soul, I declared that I was happiest at home in front of the telly. You didn't get the scent or sight of blood there.

MR GREY AND MR WHITE

APPEARANCES CAN be deceptive.

Steve Davis wasn't, of course, the dull, passion-free snooker player that his billing made him out to be. Yes, as a player he was the steadiest of Eddies, an automaton whose capacity for unforced errors rarely made itself known, if it existed at all. But the wry smile that occasionally appeared at the corners of his mouth, and the slight twinkle in his eye, suggested there was plenty more going on under the bonnet.

Davis's public image problem was that the unrelenting regularity and comparative caution in his play had trouble pumping the public blood, stirring their sinews. What it could do – and what was presumably most important to him – was win him titles and boost his bank balance. (Indeed, the gushing waterfall of cash coming Davis's way meant he became a happy shopper with mail-order record retailers, deepening his concurrent – and, possibly, stylistically contradictory – fascinations with jazz funk and prog rock.)

What this disciplined, outwardly easy success failed to win was an avalanche of love and devotion. Davis wasn't fussed. It didn't provoke him into sharpening the edges of his character or introducing a sense of reckless abandon to his game. Accordingly, the public continued to admire rather than adore. Caution doesn't breed heroes.

Favouring Davis as a hero ahead of an Alex Higgins would be like a football fan preferring a full back – a Mick Mills, say, or a Phil Neal – over an Arnold Mühren or a Kenny Dalglish. The latter were a select breed. Players who didn't play the percentages. Players who liked variables. Artists, not scientists. My kind of sportsmen. Teenage boys – even, or *especially*, those who've barricaded themselves in sunless back bedrooms – crave danger and peril and flair and unpredictability. And that's where James Warren White came in. Jimmy Jimmy.

Like Alex Higgins, White played the way that impulsive adolescents did, the same way that I did on the warped six-by-three table at home. As he wound back his left arm ready to unleash it, like a pinball player pulling back the launch spring, there was never 100% certainty whether the object ball would slam at high velocity into the intended pocket or the cue ball would rise up and endanger the life of someone in the front row.

'I can't play any other way,' he once confessed to BBC presenter David Icke.

'Have you tried?'

'Yeah, but I don't enjoy it, so I won't play like that.'

White had already won us teenage boys over earlier in 1984 when he pocketed his first major title in January, winning the Masters after a truly mesmerising final session against Kirk Stevens in the semi-final, one in which he eclipsed his opponent with absolute brilliance, despite the Canadian firing in a 147 earlier in the match. I'd never seen more flamboyant shots than the ones with which White dispatched pink and black in the final frame, thunderbolts of verve and swerve that defied the laws of physics. Art beating science.

In that year's World Championship, White was ready to give the sport's foundations a right royal rumble. Seeded 11 despite his Masters victory, he effortlessly brushed aside a pair of 50-somethings – Rex Williams and Eddie Charlton – in the first two rounds. Former champion Cliff Thorburn met the same fate in the quarter-final on White's 22nd birthday, before another victory over Stevens set up a showdown with Davis in the final.

The pair were both sons of south London, born just a 15-mile drive along the South Circular from each other (although, once he signed to Barry Hearn's Matchroom stable, Davis became an adopted Essex man). But the temperament, playing styles and world view were markedly different. Davis, that copper hair brushed and parted, wasn't intimidated by White's raw power, nor by the Sheffield crowd that clearly favoured the raven-headed lad from Tooting. At 26, Davis was both top seed and two-time world champion. He'd been here before and he wasn't afraid to show it, racing into a 12-4 lead at the end of the first day.

It was a dominant display that had ticket holders for the final session the following evening checking the small print to see if refunds were payable. There was a strong chance that, by the time they should be taking their seats in the auditorium, Davis would already be heading back down to Romford with the trophy in his luggage and a winner's cheque burning a hole in his waistcoat pocket.

They needn't have worried. Jimmy made sure of that. An enthralling second day was in store on that Bank Holiday Monday. White flew out of the traps, taking seven of the first eight frames and letting Davis know that retaining the title was far from a given. By the end of the afternoon session, the deficit was just two frames.

Into the evening session, Whispering Ted Lowe, the gravelly voice behind the BBC mic, still saw White's comeback as looking ultimately futile. To him, Davis's butter-smooth break-building was 'monotonous magic'. The rest of us were hoping otherwise but, by the 33rd frame, it was looking less and less likely. Davis, leading 17-15, needed just a colour and a red to leave White in search of a snooker to save the match and the tournament. But, uncharacteristically, a long blue from Davis wobbled in the pocket's jaws and stayed on the table.

His prematurely ended half-century barely received a modest smattering of applause as he returned to his seat. The roars were for White who was already prowling around the table. Less than three-and-a-half minutes and 16 balls later, the cheers were as if his immaculate clearance had secured the title itself.

The charge couldn't continue, though. The next frame was White's undoing, much, I guess, to the pleasure of his detractors who thought his style too impulsive, too impatient, too flash. Going into the colours 17 points down, he played several wild, impetuous shots, taking on balls that you might consider in a £5 wager match in a snooker club on a wet Tuesday afternoon but not in the Crucible, not in the world final, not with millions of eyes, like mine, gazing studiously – adoringly, even – at the young pretender. But, of course, to suddenly administer caution would have been too sensible, too much like Davis. Death or glory. Going down with style. That was White's way. That was how reputations were made, how cult heroes were canonised.

'Well, Jimmy had a go,' sighed Whispering Ted as Davis mopped up the colours, the frame and the title. Yes, he had a go. Our Jimmy had a go. And, at just five days into his 23rd year, we knew he'd be back. A future world title, or a trail of world titles, were surely his for the taking. He wouldn't be the eternal bridesmaid. He'd catch the bouquet one year.

Surely.

INCONTROVERTIBLE EVIDENCE

THERE WERE in the region of 1,500 kids – 1,500 boys at that – at our school, so the law of averages dictated that there would be some good names among them. Charlie Mustard and Martin Curd were two names that seemed to have escaped from the pages of a Roald Dahl tale, while Jeremy Squibb was clearly a creation of Dickens's pen. There was also Corey Divers, a pupil mainly remembered for three things: for being able to run extremely fast over a short distance; for turning up to school on most days in the uniform of the Combined Cadet Force; and for his occasional flexibility when it came to trustworthy reportage.

The ultimate example of the last one occurred in early June 1984, on another of those deeply educational school trips. This latest excursion to London was consistent with that of the previous year. Again, that tatty bus didn't take us to admire the weaponry held by the Imperial War Museum or to the National Gallery to stroke our chins in front of the works of Degas or van Dyck. Sport still ruled the school's extra-curricular agenda. NW8 was our destination this time, the occasion being that summer's third and deciding one-day international at Lord's between England and the West Indies. The tourists were in their hard-hitting, fast-scoring pomp; this was the summer of the 'Blackwash' Test series.

The match turned out to be the most leisurely of cruises for a West Indies team packed with legends, kings and gods: Lloyd, Richards, Holding, Marshall, Greenidge, Haynes, Garner . . . They had restricted England to a total of 196, conceding just three boundaries in the entire innings. Unsurprisingly, they eased to victory with 45 balls left and only two wickets down. A contest it wasn't. But while the finish failed to be remotely nail-biting, close of play did offer one last thrill for the teenage cricket fan: the charge over the boundary rope to invade the pitch.

Showing that lightning speed, Corey Divers was the first man over the top, evading the stewards' grasp and surging like a bullet towards the wicket. It would be a good 20 minutes before we saw him again, this time back on the bus parked on St John's Wood Road. But he wasn't embarrassed to be the last lad back on board, the one whose vacant seat was waiting to be filled before we could set off for home. He took the moaning and jeers in his stride. Instead, he was beaming from ear to ear and clasping a souvenir of which we were all jealous – a white plastic fielding disc, recovered from the Lord's turf.

We were all even more jealous when, as he slumped into the one empty seat on the coach, he recounted a short conversation he had out in the middle with a victorious Viv Richards.

'I went to grab a stump, but Viv said, "No, that's mine. Get yourself a fielding disc instead."'

Being in possession of a fielding disc was one thing. Having a conversation with a deity like Viv Richards was another thing entirely. We were impressed. Mightily so. There were now just two degrees of separation between us and the great man. Or so we believed.

There was nothing remotely unusual about the nature of Corey Divers' report from the batting square. I'm certainly not trying to shame him more than three decades later. Hell, if I possessed his raw speed, I'd have been first out to the wicket and last back on the bus, primed and ready to boast. Most, if not all, teenage boys embellish and exaggerate and amplify in order to seek acceptance and approval from their peers. Many still do so in adulthood. It's just that, that particular evening, it was inadvisable to embellish and exaggerate and amplify when the cameras of the BBC Outside Broadcast unit would later offer indisputable evidence to the contrary.

When the bus finally delivered us back to deepest Sussex and we put our respective keys in our respective front doors, the closing titles of *Newsnight* were playing. Perfect timing. The highlights of that day's match were about to start. And, approximately 42 minutes later, we realised we'd been strung along. We'd fallen for a tall tale.

As the winning run was struck, the highlights showed Richards – having notched up an imperious, unbeaten 84 that included 14 boundaries, more than four times the number that the entire England team had mustered – turning on his heels to sprint at full lick through the invading crowd and towards the sanctity of the Long Room. As he disappeared off the bottom of our screens, a pair of pinstripe jeans and a green Marks & Spencer carrier bag appeared at the very top. They belonged to Corey Divers. While he had certainly made his way out to the middle at a speed none of us could have managed, he was nowhere near Viv Richards. Thirty yards away at least. No conversation had been had. Definitely no conversation. Those degrees of separation returned to the long-distance state they'd been in that morning.

As well as disproving the claims of one of our cohort, the highlights offered me the chance to see something else I'd not seen that day: the dismissal of Derek Pringle by my favourite West Indian paceman. Joel Garner was both a giant in my estimation and a giant in real life, six foot eight in his stockinged size 13 feet. Pringle's was the only wicket that he'd taken that day and I had missed it. A couple of us had been ambling around the Lord's concourse – perhaps in search of one of those confectionery stalls that Richie Benaud had so memorably referred to three years previously – when a thunderous roar went up. And then I did something that showed how deeply TV sport had burrowed itself into my psyche. At a pace that Corey Divers may well have been impressed with, I belted up the steps and back into the stands. But why? Because I wanted to catch the action replay.

That afternoon, I learned something that would gain metaphorical significance in future years: real life doesn't do action replays.

THE PERFECT TEN

I NEVER saw Pelé play a full game on TV. I've only ever seen clips and highlights. At almost exactly the same time that I was saying a hearty hello to football by buying my first issue of *Shoot!*, he was saying a tearful farewell at Giants Stadium in New Jersey, having diluted his legacy with three half-paced seasons with New York Cosmos.

During the following decade, two players from different continents would stake a claim to be the natural successor to the great man. Diego Armando Maradona came closest; there are some, of course, who believe he succeeded. Maradona's moment in the brightest of suns would come two years later, but in 1984, at the European Championship, one particular number ten stood out. He wasn't a man among boys; he was a colossus among mere mortals.

As France surged irresistibly towards glory, captain Michel Platini had greedily grasped the twin roles of conductor and soloist. He scored an astonishing nine goals in France's five matches, including two hat-tricks during the group stage. But one match lingers longest: the semi-final against Portugal, when the French overturned a 2-1 deficit in the second period of extra time. The winning goal, as if you couldn't guess, was scored by their skipper.

It was a match, though, that proved France, unlike Maradona's Argentina, were more than a single man. Their midfield quartet – Platini, Alain Giresse, Jean Tigana and Luis Fernández – took complete and absolute charge, fluidly creating chance after chance and peppering the Portuguese goal with shots from all angles. No one can remember the names of the French strikers in that tournament, but with that fab four in midfield, no one needs to.

In the same way that the '81 Ashes had dragged me to Alex Cooper's back garden to smash a ball like Ian Botham, and in the same way that Keith Deller's world title had provoked me into dusting off the dartboard in the garage, I wanted to pay homage to the extraordinary French football captain, the dead-ball specialist. In the wake of each France match, and as long as the TV schedules allowed, I was outside practising free kicks, standing my bike upside down on the driveway between me and the garage door to use as an improvised defensive wall. I simply wanted to be the Sussex coast's answer to Platini. In the process, I turned into a bit of a Francophile for a while, partly also inspired by the Style Council's Paris-light *Café Bleu* album. Not only did I start to pay more attention in French lessons at school, I paid even more attention to those French-language films that Channel 4 (and hormonal teenage boys) were so smitten with.

And then I took up smoking Gauloises. For approximately eight seconds, that is.

My mum would always insist that any friends travelling across the Channel bring back a packet of the high-tar, non-filter ciggies for her. Every year, she seemed to forget that she didn't actually enjoy smoking them, ensuring that there was always a huge stockpile of abandoned packets clogging up the kitchen drawer. One afternoon, while everyone was out, I slipped a cigarette out of one of the packets and smoked it in the back garden. Well, I took a couple of puffs. It was disgusting and I threw up a little. The chickens appeared to be laughing at me, too. My first cigarette and I couldn't have chosen a better brand to put me off for life.

With my voice having dropped an octave in those few seconds, and my throat having instantly taken on the texture of sandpaper, I reasoned that I didn't need to smoke Gauloises to become an honorary Frenchman. I just needed to execute those fabulous bendy free kicks with all the poise and insouciance of Michel Platini.

Those practice sessions would continue. And the cigarettes would stay in the drawer.

THE SPRINGBOK SPEEDBALL

THE *Daily Mail* rarely ran with a sporting story on its front page. In the spring of 1984, however, one sportswoman was frequently featured. Zola Budd.

They had their reasons. The paper was evangelical in its campaign to rescue the 17-year-old South African from the sporting wilderness caused by the international community's unwillingness to compete with a country still applying the rule of apartheid. To the *Mail's* eyes, an innocent young woman's extraordinary prowess at long-distance running was being unfairly curtailed simply because of her homeland's chosen system of government. Sport and politics, its leader writers would contend, were separate entities. The purity of sporting endeavour should never be sullied by the grubbiness of political life. They should be kept apart. Never the twain and all that. (This stance, of course, conveniently forgot that the *Mail* had trumpeted its support for Britain boycotting the previous Olympics hosted by those Communist types.)

As the *Mail*-led campaign to declare Budd an English rose gathered momentum, it became a hot topic in the pubs and clubs – and, at our school, in the General Studies classrooms overseen by supply teachers. One such teacher chose to set us a task: a short essay along the lines of 'Politics and sport should be kept separate and Zola Budd should be allowed to run for Great Britain at the Olympics. Discuss.'

By this stage, a self-prescribed social conscience and political edge had been growing within me, one further empowered by the Special AKA single 'Free Nelson Mandela', which had been released just a week or two before. My essay argued that sport and politics were as inextricably linked as, rather neatly I thought at the time, two intertwining strands of spaghetti. Sport requires fairness, a level playing field. No matter what angle you viewed it from, white minority rule didn't remotely offer such a virtue. The supply teacher, her cheeks scarlet with indignation at my argument (and seemingly oblivious to the genius of the spaghetti analogy), was obviously the *Daily Mail* reader in the staff room. Zola Budd, she huffed, had every right to expect to run in the Olympics.

When I then suggested that were it a supremely talented black South African athlete who was being denied the opportunity to compete on the world stage, there'd be no such campaign whatsoever, the supply teacher's cheeks darkened even more. In one fell swoop, I felt like I was my school's leading anti-apartheid campaigner, while she was becoming increasingly, and inordinately, perturbed by my logic. I survived the blast, though. Supply teachers didn't have the power to issue detentions. Unlike my new hero Nelson Mandela, I had avoided captivity.

Having taken her first-ever breath of British air in the final week of March, it took just a fortnight for Budd's citizenship to be granted and a passport to be issued. This was surely some kind of British all-comers' record. And all without setting those bare feet of hers on the cinders of an athletics track. The teenager's debut race in the UK came little more than a week later in what would, under normal circumstances, have been an unremarkable club meeting in Dartford.

Budd's presence made it anything but unremarkable. Not only had 5,000 spectators squeezed into the modest arena attached to a public park, but the BBC's cameras had also made the trip across to north Kent that Saturday afternoon. This was the hot ticket, both for those who'd travelled and for those in repose on their sofas: the first glimpse of the Springbok speedball, the new darling of middle England. Wearing the white and green of her new club Aldershot, Farnham & District, Budd – without fuss and fanfare – won easily and comfortably within the Olympic qualifying time. The hype was holding up. Disappointingly, Budd didn't uphold her unique selling point. A pair of running spikes were on her feet.

Lining up for the final of the Olympic 3,000m less than four months later against her main rival, the all-American Mary Decker, the small, angular Budd looked like a waif. Without shoes, she looked like a stray, too. With the vivid Californian colours of the transmission beaming bright and gawdy, there seemed to be an edge in the air in the LA Coliseum, a sense of something dramatic just about to occur.

Five minutes later and with three laps left, the sight of one of the pre-race favourites lying in pain on the inside of the track, screaming in agony, was certainly dramatic. That Decker had been put there by a tangle involving Budd made it even more so. A screenwriter couldn't have traced a more explosive narrative arc. Within seconds of it happening ('Decker's down!' yelled both David Coleman and several million households), it was clear that this was the story of this particular Olympics, at least from the British perspective. It was also instantly clear that this was one of the most controversial moments of the modern Games, that books would be written, and documentaries filmed, about it in years to come.

Poor Wendy Sly – the other British runner who kept her head to take silver while Budd, perhaps voluntarily, slipped down the field – never got a look-in when it came to the following day's back (and front) pages, despite her becoming the first British woman to win a long-distance Olympic medal. I was starting to learn about the sensibilities of newspaper editors, of how a good-news story was rarely top priority.

Aside from the shock of what had happened, I didn't quite know how to feel about the incident. As a young woman, one little more than a couple of years older than me, Budd was indisputably a victim of the circus that had engulfed her. Vulnerable. Out of her depth. Too much, too young.

My overwhelming emotion though was one of – once I'd looked it up in my pocket German-English dictionary as I only had a faint grasp of its meaning – *schadenfreude*. Tomorrow's *Daily Mail* wouldn't now be full of backslapping, self-congratulatory nonsense about how the paper had won gold for Britain. That offered a little comfort. I also took some sort of pleasure in imagining how, in front of her own TV set in her own house, that supply teacher would be frustrated with the outcome too, her cheeks undoubtedly returning to their default shade of crimson.

ALPHA MALES

WE ALL remember them. Perhaps you were one yourself.

The vast majority of schoolkids struggle to get anywhere close to mastering a single sport. There are, though, undoubtedly one or two within their peer group who excel at each and every sport they tackle. They waltz into the glamour spots in the school team: centre forward, opening batsman, scrum half. Hand them a javelin for the first time and they'll chuck it into the next postcode. Asked by the PE teacher to demonstrate a particular gymnastics move and they'd nail it with a precision that would have earned them straight tens from a panel of Olympic judges.

Normally – and quite correctly – these freaks are viewed with disdain by the rest of us for making so clear our deficiencies. There was one such specimen, though, for whom we largely reserved admiration. He was an alpha male who still remembered to smile, the all-round sportsman who was better than every other all-round sportsman. Francis Morgan Ayodélé Thompson.

We knew him as Daley.

While he carried around a reputation for on occasion being rude and difficult in normal life (a trait possibly explained by a troubled childhood: his taxi-driver father was murdered when Thompson was 12), in an athletics stadium, he was near-faultless. Taking decathlon gold in both Moscow and Los Angeles, along with breaking the world record on multiple occasions, Thompson's performances seemed so effortless. It never felt like he had excessively exerted himself. Running, jumping and throwing. All came to him so naturally.

What also marked Thompson out was his unwillingness to surrender to the established way of doing things. He refused to carry the English flag at the opening ceremony of the 1982 Commonwealth Games. Later, at that year's Sports Personality of the Year awards, which he won, he turned up in his tracksuit and swore on receiving the trophy. Two years later came the biggest crime of all: whistling his way through the national anthem while on the Olympic podium in Los Angeles. 'Maybe he can't be taught how to behave,' railed the *Daily Mirror*, 'but he needs to be told.'

Whether iconoclastic or irreverent, there was an element to his behaviour that certainly appealed to the status quo-questioning, could-be-difficult-himself teenager.

The pictures beaming back from Los Angeles in '84 did reveal one slight flaw in his otherwise impeccable sporting achievements. After a successful attempt in the pole vault, he broke into a celebratory somersault on the purple crash mat, but landed on his belly, not his feet. A chink in the armour had been spotted. Perhaps he was mortal after all.

FOOLS' GOLD

NO ONE did the Olympics like the BBC. The corporation didn't go into it by halves, with commentators sent to exotic capital cities for weeks on end for an extended embedding. There was a catch, though: in return, they were often forced to commentate on sports that were largely alien to them at the point they stepped aboard the plane – judo, for instance, or hockey or modern pentathlon. By the time they landed in the host city, it was generally understood that they had become instant experts while in the air, able to paper over any deficiencies in their knowledge with bluff and bluster of the highest quality.

You could ensure that, for the duration of the Games, the BBC would leave no stone unturned, no sport untransmitted. The event was a monolith that hit the schedules like no other, squeezing and compressing everything else that was trying to get a look-in. Regular staples of the schedule were forced to move, to shift to other time slots. Or they were just taken off air for the fortnight that the biggest sporting show on earth was in town. The corporation's motivation was clear: for two weeks every four years, nothing but nothing could obstruct or interrupt the Olympics.

The BBC didn't always get it right, though.

In 1984, they insisted on soundtracking every highlights package from the Los Angeles Olympics with Spandau Ballet's 'Gold', a turgid song that pulled off the difficult trick of simultaneously sounding both bombastic and wafer-thin. To be fair, it was an obvious choice. Released the year before, its lyrics were perfectly applicable to images of sporting endeavour: 'Always believe in your soul / You've got the power to know / You're indestructible'. Whenever there was footage of someone showing their indestructibility in LA – whether it was Carl Lewis and his four golds, or minuscule gymnast Mary Lou

Retton – the BBC producer hit 'play' on Spandau's second-biggest single (second only to the even more anaemic 'True').

Like Robbie Williams later releasing 'Millennium' with just a year of the twentieth century left, Spandau probably deserve some credit for their admirable foresight: recording a song called 'Gold' the year before an Olympics. With each airing during that fortnight, the royalties kept flowing, allowing these Islington lads to continue living in a manner to which they'd become accustomed. Contrary to what Tony Hadley honked, it wasn't luck that left them standing so tall.

THE MUSIC IN MY HEAD

SPANDAU BALLET'S 'Gold' might have done it for some people, but it was just too clunky and obvious for me as a sporting soundtrack.

There were TV theme tunes and there were soul-stirring TV theme tunes. The latter didn't just go through the motions, a mere adornment to the main act. They were part of the package, an aural embodiment of the drama that was about to unfold.

I'd heard the themes to *Grandstand* and *Match of the Day* too many times to be able to judge them as stand-alone pieces of music. They were inextricably bound up in a tangle of meaning and memories. Both of these were the product of horn-heavy big bands, as was the *World of Sport* signature tune. The latter was just too bouncy and too comical – not unlike the programme itself.

In 1984, and in reverse order, this was my top five of TV sport theme tunes:

5. Ski Sunday (BBC)
This felt like it was the sound of Mittel-Europe – of Austria

or Switzerland. The weaving lines of its lithe, fast-paced strings replicated the weaving lines of a skier moving through Alpine forests with gathering pace. It wasn't all super-swift and smooth, though. The thunder of the timpani warned about the inherent danger, about the thrills and spills that we all secretly enjoyed watching.

4. Test Match Special (BBC)

In 1976, back before I had an inkling what music from the Caribbean sounded like, I presumed that 'Soul Limbo' by Booker T and the MGs was it. I first heard it introducing the action from the West Indies' Test series against England. This, coupled with the opening percussion sounding like a tin can being repeatedly struck with a stick in the crowd, fixed its place of origin being a sun-kissed isle in the Windward archipelago, and not the creation of the esteemed Memphis soul quartet that it is. It will never lose that thrill that it emits, even if Boris Johnson picked it as one of his Desert Island Discs.

3. Darts (BBC)

Where the BBC usually opted for a big band or an orchestra to deliver a theme tune that would set the high-action sporting tenor, its coverage of darts was introduced by a piece of music decidedly low-key and lo-fi. A brooding bass guitar is dominant, accompanied by drums and occasional piano stabs. Those piano stabs neatly echo darts plunging into a dartboard, but this wasn't necessarily deliberate. It was a piece of music – 'Cranes' by the Doug Wood Group – that had been bought in, not specially commissioned. And it isn't even the Doug Wood Group's best-known theme tune; that'll be the twangy guitars of 'Drag Racer', the music used for the BBC's snooker coverage. Even further, there is no such band as the Doug Wood Group. Just one man played all the instruments on these tunes: a multi-instrumentalist from New York State called, yes, Doug Wood.

2. Sportsnight (BBC)

This has already been mentioned in dispatches, but the raw excitement this tune induced was incalculable, its urgency stressing the importance of what was contained therein. This was that evening's action, hot off the press. Don't you dare go to bed instead.

1. The Big Match (ITV, 1980–1986)

Just one in the top five for ITV, but it takes the top spot. *The Big Match* had already had several theme tunes by then (usually big, bold and brassy), but its music for the first part of the 1980s dispensed with that approach. Jeff Wayne's 'Jubilation' took a more modern slant – its thick melody delivered by strong synths and enhanced by jangly guitars. It made the perfect accompaniment to the clips shown on the opening titles, whether a vigorous tackle being made on Ronnie Whelan or a grinning Tony Cottee celebration. It's never been bettered. Never.

TUNNEL VISION

ASIDE FROM an episode or two of *Match of the Day* slipped into the schedules somewhere, Christmas was usually a dead zone for sport on the box. In contrast, the pickings were rich for those who enjoyed a post-blowout war movie. On Boxing Day 1984, both parties were satisfied, thanks to the TV premiere of the three-year-old John Huston film, *Escape to Victory*. With our local cinema having been rebadged as a McDonald's, I had never got to see the film when it came out in 1981, but had read plenty about it at the time in *Shoot!* and *Match Weekly*. Both Boxing

Day constituencies were well served. For the war film buffs, it had Michael Caine as the alpha-male English officer, Max von Sydow as a German major and Sylvester Stallone as the token loudmouth US Army captain. For the sport fans, it had roles for Pelé, Bobby Moore and Ossie Ardiles – as well as, curiously, speaking parts for a fair proportion of the Ipswich Town first-team squad.

It was effectively *The Great Escape*, but with the POWs planning to flee their German captors during a football match instead, not unlike the attempt to escape from HMP Slade in the *Porridge* film. I can't attest to the veracity and realism of the POW camp scenes. I've never been an expert on the subject; *Escape to Victory* remains one of only five war films I've seen in their entirety (and that includes *Chicken Run*). But the football portions weren't too bad. Well, those that didn't involve Stallone's gobby goalkeeper Hatch, that is.

As has already been declared, Ipswich were everyone's second-favourite team at the time. This meant that for those football fans actually paying attention to the plot and not just salivating over the trickery of Pelé and Ardiles, there was an element of rooting for them to successfully flee from the Nazis' clutches. Had it been, say, Aston Villa players who'd been invited to make their movie debuts, I dare say supporters of every other Midlands club would have delighted in seeing several of them perish under German sniper fire.

While the recruitment of top-flight players gave a vaguely credible sheen to the match scenes (Caine and Stallone excepted), the reverse was true when it came to the players' acting skills. Towards the film's climax, during the half-time break in the big match in Paris, the players begin their escape down into the city's sewers, via a hole drilled into the bottom of the dressing-room bath. But there's a minor protest among their ranks. Despite being 4-1 down, some of them reject the idea of escape and opt to carry on playing, wanting to beat the Nazis on the pitch. Ipswich central defence stalwart Russell Osman leads the dissent, delivering his line – 'Let's go back. We can win this' – with all the sparkle and *joie de vivre* that he later brought to the HTV pundits' sofa.

Earlier that year, we'd been witness to more footballers showcasing their acting skills. The Channel 4 comedy drama *Scully* ticked plenty of my boxes: another gritty creation of the pen of Alan Bleasdale, a theme tune from Elvis Costello, and plenty of behind-the-dressing-room-door scenes at both Anfield and the Melwood training ground. Most of the then-current Liverpool team made non-speaking cameos during the main character's frequent dream sequences (as did Bob Paisley and Ian St John), but it was Kenny Dalglish who appeared in more scenes than anyone else. In the process, he was granted a brief speaking role ('Oh, wait a minute, wee man'), as well as having red paint thrown over him in the final scene.

He wasn't the most natural performer in front of the camera, nor was he helped by that famously impenetrable Glaswegian accent. Fortunately for Liverpool fans, though, Kenny did all his talking on the pitch.

LAW AND DISORDER

BEARING IN mind there were 1,500 hormonal boys crowding the corridors and prowling the playgrounds, good old-fashioned scraps were pretty rare at my school. I remember one clash of the titans during the third year when the two heavyweights of our class had a set-to that had been simmering for a good long while. Even when they finally got it on, though, the action comprised of little more than a desk and a couple of chairs getting upended. It was less Rumble In The Jungle and more Mild Scuffle In An Old World War II Hut That Was Now A French Classroom. And, unlike that classic fight in Kinshasa, it cruelly never received the full Norman Mailer or George Plimpton literary treatment.

Accordingly, I wasn't witness to much violence as a kid. Remember, I had only seen the bruised and battered aftermath of Portsmouth fans vs Southampton fans the previous year, not the beatings themselves.

Scenes of violence, however, were in plentiful supply on the nightly news. Inner-city riots were a recurring feature of British society throughout the decade, while the year-long miners' strike often led to physical confrontations between pickets and police, most infamously at the Battle of Orgreave in June 1984. Here, at a coking plant in South Yorkshire, ten hours of extreme and brutal conflict ensued, since described by the historian and former MP Tristram Hunt as 'almost medieval in its choreography' and 'a brutal example of legalised state violence'.

The strike officially ended on 3 March 1985, but that wasn't the end of seeing violent clashes in news bulletins. The very next evening saw more disorder, this time not in the South Yorkshire mining heartland but at a football stadium in West London. The second leg of the Milk Cup semi-final between Chelsea and Sunderland descended into thuggery and hooliganism after the home side had slid to defeat.

An even more notorious confrontation occurred nine days later at Kenilworth Road in Luton. Aggrieved at the exit of their team from the FA Cup at the sixth-round stage, Millwall fans took to the pitch at the final whistle to chase down the local constabulary while ripping out the seats and raining these down on the beleaguered police. It hadn't been saved for the end of the match. The match had already been held up for 24 minutes in the first half because of fans encroaching onto the playing surface in their dozens. This night would be the worst example of domestic football hooliganism of the entire decade.

The following morning, when I arrived home after my paper round, I watched the reactions being aired from the BBC *Breakfast Time* leather sofa. As the programme's sports reporter (and a former semi-pro keeper with Hereford United), David Icke offered something more than the usual 'What can be done with it?' chin-stroking. He revealed, quite casually, that during his playing days, he 'had lumps of concrete thrown at me and things like that. But very, very rarely . . .'

'Rarely' was becoming a less relevant word in the context of hooliganism. The Kenilworth Road riot was but one episode that defined the national game in 1985, English football's *annus horribilis*.

'ROUND MIDNIGHT

THE 1960s had several 'Where were you when. . ?' moments. John F Kennedy's assassination is arguably the chief example. Six years later, Armstrong and Aldrin's footsteps on the Moon became another.

For the class of '85, one date in particular qualified as epic, historic, defining. Sunday 28 April. This was the day that the planet wobbled on its axis, when a new world order threatened to be established. A new order in the snooker world, that is. And we all knew exactly where we were when it came about. The same answer could be given by 18.5 million Britons. We were right at home, glued to the telly.

Actually, to be historically watertight, the key moment – the equivalent of the fatal gunshot, or of the flag being planted into the lunar surface – came at 23 minutes into the following day, as a black snooker ball dropped into a corner pocket.

The protagonists were a contrast of looks and character: Steve Davis – slim, elegant and inscrutable; Dennis Taylor – portly, unathletic and all too willing to dissolve into a smile. He just seemed happy to be there. A runner-up to Cliff Thorburn in 1979, at 36 Taylor was outside the world's top ten and a 33/1 shot for the title at the tournament's start. Across the table was the game's current number one, the 20-something who'd taken the world title three times in the previous four years. And there was no doubt he was after a fourth crown, his clinical potting catapulting him into an 8-0 lead in this best-of-35-frames final. Taylor was left in his seat, thumbs twiddling, muttering to himself.

After the first session on the Saturday, it looked like the whole affair might be over midway through the following afternoon. BBC producers were no doubt digging out any number of movies from the archives with which to plug what would be a gaping hole in the schedule.

Taylor had other ideas. By the end of Saturday, he had, rather extraordinarily, closed the deficit to two frames, retiring to his Sheffield hotel room at just 9-7 down. It boded well for everyone but Davis. The next day was brimful of promise. The Sundance Kid looked forward to two full sessions of snooker, for the final to go as close to the wire as possible. I couldn't have guessed how late it would be, how thin that wire would end up being. Outside of the night sweats of a debilitating childhood illness, it was almost certainly the first time I'd seen midnight – and the first time I'd heard it struck out on a distant church bell. The Moondance Kid, in fact.

I can't quite remember, but I must have been rooting for Taylor. It was – again – my natural instinct, my default, to plump for the underdog, to side with romance. Davis had had his share of glory. Only the partisan followers of a super-successful team or individual are in favour of lengthy, impenetrable sporting dynasties.

To back Taylor was to ensure that the final would be on the screen for as long as possible, which would, of course, be what any TV sport addict would be looking for. A BBC adaptation of *Bleak House* was supposed to follow the estimated end of the snooker. I had no issue with keeping Dickens off the screen for longer.

You had to salute Taylor's pluck. He won the final three frames, out-nerving the usually Arctic-cool Davis. And you also had to salute Taylor's kamikaze tendencies. Having scrapped and scraped back to that final black, he then forgot all about the percentages, attempting not one but two extravagant doubles.

And when, at 12.23am, he dropped that final black into the pocket, it was the first time he had been in front in the entire final. Taylor had taken the lead with the very last ball of the full 35 frames. Immaculate timing – even if it had taken him all day and all of the night.

BRADFORD

THERE ARE some things you never want to see.

On 11 May, the final Saturday of the 1984-85 league season, ITV showed the most graphic, most shocking live footage I'd ever seen: the rapid escalation of a small fire in the main stand of Valley Parade in Bradford into a raging inferno that claimed dozens of lives.

The commentator, Yorkshire TV stalwart John Helm, was supposed to be describing the final game of a triumphant season for Bradford City, one which had seen them become Third Division champions, their first trophy in more than half a century. Instead, he was describing a horrific catastrophe. Fifty-six football fans didn't go home that afternoon.

The scenes were deeply upsetting. At several points, we saw the desperate attempts of fellow fans and the police to save the lives of people on fire, people engulfed in flames. The pity and pathos were all too audible in Helm's voice. There was a quandary, too. In continuing to broadcast live from Valley Parade, would ITV be accused of peeping and prying into the tragedy, of showing little respect?

As it was, Helm's commentary was the human voice, the emotionally measured voice, that viewers needed to hear. 'Words hopefully came out in the right order,' he later reflected. 'I like to think we handled it sensitively.'

Families were irrevocably reshaped that afternoon, an afternoon of tragedy upon which doubts would later be cast about the extent to which it was an accident. Not only was the main stand due to be demolished and rebuilt that summer, but the club chairman, Stafford Heginbotham, who died in 1995, has since been linked to nine other fires from which, it's claimed, he received millions in insurance payouts.

BEND IT LIKE NORMAN

'AND HERE'S Whiteside . . . Strachan is following up, Olsen on this side. That's all he's got . . . Whiteside shoots . . . It's there! Norman Whiteside has done it again!'

Norman Whiteside packed plenty into his early career. He played in the World Cup Finals at just 17 and, three years later, scored the winner in the FA Cup Final. Where do you go from there?

Sadly, retiring through injury at just 26, that's where. That extraordinary goal at Wembley, where he bent the ball into the far corner of Neville Southall's net from a seemingly impossible angle, was his career highlight, the goal that edged ten-man Manchester United past Everton and denied the Merseysiders their first domestic Double.

At 20, Whiteside had the physical presence and lived-in stature of someone a good decade older. He was less than four years my senior and yet he was a way finer physical specimen. I was ungainly and awkward. A foal to Whiteside's thoroughbred, a sapling to his Californian redwood. Just when was my charge to physical maturity going to gather pace? I still needed a belt to hold up my size 28-waist jeans and had only infrequent need of a razor. Maybe, I thought, physical presence could be found through the prodigious consumption of custard creams? As Norman was mobbed for his superlative goal by a gaggle of incredulous teammates in front of 100,000 spectators, I lay on my bed alone and opened another packet.

Aside from Whiteside's superb goal, the other pivotal point of the match was the sending-off of United's Kevin Moran for a challenge on Peter Reid. John Motson spotted the severity of it at the time: 'That has to be a booking, at the very least.' Over on ITV, Jimmy Greaves saw otherwise – and didn't hold back: 'I think the referee wanted to get his name in history before he retired, Dickie. And he's gone and done it.'

The referee, a former policeman called Peter Willis, successfully sued Greaves and donated the payout to a referees' charity. 'It was dirty money and I didn't want it,' he later explained. 'It was just the principle that mattered.'

Three days earlier, Everton had enjoyed the kind of cup success that eluded them at Wembley. In Rotterdam, in the final of the Cup Winners' Cup against Rapid Vienna, Howard Kendall's side completed a march through the qualifying rounds that had seen them play both Bayern Munich and University College Dublin.

Their exuberant display was matched by the exuberance of Brian Moore's commentary. This was a mic man who was always in the moment, whose rising cadences paralleled the action beautifully. And his commentaries always looked to the bright side; they always extolled the joy of watching football. He clearly loved his work. You suspected he would still turn up even if they didn't pay him.

HEYSEL

EVERTON'S TRIUMPH in Rotterdam was to be English football's last hurrah in Europe for a good few years, the end of a very successful era. In addition to the Toffees' win, the previous ten seasons had seen seven English triumphs in the European Cup and three in the UEFA Cup – 11 glorious nights for both travelling supporters and housebound viewers back home.

The events of 29 May 1985 brought all that crashing down. It was the European Cup Final at the Heysel Stadium in Brussels between Juventus and holders Liverpool. It promised to be a compelling affair, with Liverpool's pedigree in the competition matched by the Italians' attacking force that included Paolo Rossi, the Pole Zbigniew Boniek and my boy Michel Platini. Before the programme started properly, we had no inkling that anything was untoward, with presenter Jimmy Hill swapping chummy banter with Terry Wogan, who was handing over from his chat show. But once the opening titles had run, it was clear that a very different tone was in order. 'I'm afraid the news is very bad from Brussels,' Hill announced sombrely. 'Hooliganism has struck again . . . The scenes are as bad as anything we've seen for a long, long time.' Liverpool fans had infiltrated a section of the stadium occupied by Juventus supporters and, in the stampede that followed, a wall collapsed and dozens of Italians – fathers and sons, sisters and brothers – had been crushed. The scale of the catastrophe was immense and, like the Bradford fire, was being beamed live into our homes.

I went downstairs, perhaps subconsciously trying to get answers from my parents. But there were no explanations for what had occurred. We were all shocked at what Barry Davies described as the 'sickening and bewildering sight'. Davies was on sterling duty that evening in Brussels. For at least an hour, he described the scenes of the disaster and reached for an analysis that made sense of it all. His words were both soliloquy and newspaper editorial in one, and pulled no punches. 'Those of us in this commentary box felt once again an embarrassment to be British.' This was coming from the heart. 'What we've seen has saddened the eye and really made us feel quite wretched.'

The match itself – delayed but still played that night in an attempt to safeguard against any further violence that a postponement might have provoked – was inconsequential. By the time it kicked off, it was known that there had been heavy casualties. Twenty-eight football fans had been killed. I spent the first half not engaging with the actual play, instead just wondering how the players, almost certainly under great pressure to fulfil the match, could even think about kicking a ball around for 90 minutes. Nothing mattered that much.

Although John Humphrys had issued a warning about the upsetting nature of the footage about to be shown on the half-time news report, what we saw was brutal and distressing – even worse than the scenes at Bradford earlier in the month. Dead bodies were strewn across the concrete terraces, awaiting removal, the life taken out of them. The death toll had now reached 36, a figure that would later rise to 39. I couldn't take any more and headed off to bed and a fitful sleep.

The reality of the English football experience had reached the point of no return. It could be ignored no longer.

The consequences were severe on all English clubs, even those without a hooligan problem, with UEFA declaring a five-year ban from European competition (six years for Liverpool). There would be no more of those atmospheric nights of European football in my youth. I so loved those games. They were what *Sportsnight* was built on, a programme that now had to absorb a big dent in its content. I would be a tax-paying adult before English clubs would be readmitted after Italia '90.

HAND IN GLOVES

SCHOOL ASSEMBLIES had little point or purpose for a hall full of indifferent, adolescent boys. These were largely occasions for the rugby team to be congratulated on their latest graceless defeat, rather than the football team for their annual retention of the county cup, such were the sporting priorities of the head of PE. There might have been a hymn or two in there, grunted through by cracked-voice lads trying to see how out of tune they could go before attracting the attention of the nearest scowling teacher. Generally, though, time has erased these assemblies from memory. Their impact barely lasted half an hour into the day's first lesson.

Over the five years up to my O-levels, though, three assemblies did linger longer. There was the time when Mr Forrest, the recently appointed, ex-RAF chemistry teacher decided to impress upon everyone his credentials for his new vocation. It was a sort of audition, albeit one instigated *after* his appointment. The party piece of his presentation turned the school hall into something approximating Beirut with the use of a metal waste bin, a lit match and some unidentified but flammable substance. The headmaster's glare cut through the fug of noxious smoke. Mr Forrest never took an assembly again.

There was the time when the head of year quizzed a hall of around 400 teenage boys – while showing an enthusiasm that bordered uncomfortably close to lasciviousness – whether they were currently the victims of 'a bondage to masturbation'. One lad in the row behind me, much to the ridicule of those sitting around him, chose to audibly admit that indeed he was.

But the assembly with the most conspicuous overarching moral message (and while it stuck like glue to my brain for the next few decades, the name of the teacher delivering it has been erased over the years) simply asked whether you were a constructive or destructive force in life, in society. Basically, whether you were a good egg or a bad seed. It was a clear choice, a line you fell either side of. At a more religious school, the conundrum might have been rebadged as saint or sinner, but the message in its secular form still made an impression.

I believed I fell on the constructive side of the divide because my obsession – sport – was undeniably a force for good. Played by the right people. Watched by the right people. Understood by the right people. It enhanced life. There was poetry and positivity to be found in a cricket ball in its spinning flight, in a cross-court volley leaving an opponent flat-footed, in a cue ball coming to rest in the safe harbour of the baulk end.

But one sport seemed devoid of poetry, of positivity, of constructiveness. Instead, it was keen to snub its bent and broken nose at the light. One sport that inhabited the dark side of the line. The destructive side. The side that exerted damage – occasionally fatal damage – onto a fellow human being.

Boxing.

(I wasn't alone in my pubescent discomfort that this was a legitimate trade in which fortunes could be made. In later life, I interviewed the boxer Chris Eubank Jr, who had, earlier that week, been crowned world champion. He told me how, as a young kid, he only discovered his dad's profession through the VHS collection of a friend's father. Then came the confrontation. 'So when you go out, you're going off to punch people, to beat them up?')

On a warm, dry night in the late spring of 1985, though, my protestations were temporarily dry-docked. Put on hold. Swept under the lounge carpet. My mind was, for an hour or so that June evening, able to see some sort of poetry in and around a boxing ring. The occasion was Barry McGuigan's first tilt at the world featherweight title, an attempt to steal it away from the holder, Eusebio Pedroza.

Perhaps it was the setting: the ring in the centre of QPR's plastic pitch; a candy-striped marquee roof over the top of it; 25,000 singing with all the faith and devotion of a football crowd out under the stars. The aerial shots on the TV enhanced the sense of occasion – the bright, white light of the ring bordered by the pitch darkness of the crowd, only their disembodied voices confirming they were there.

It wasn't as if the pre-fight sideshows appealed. They were pure cornball, further evidence that boxing occasionally strayed – like its much more ridiculous stepbrother, wrestling – dangerously close to show business. That night, we got a green-clad leprechaun doing laps of the ring beforehand and the insistence of McGuigan's dad Pat on belting out 'Danny Boy' to wring sentimental tears from the crowd's eyes. McGuigan Sr, we kept being told, had represented his country at the Eurovision Song Contest. This was no badge of honour in my eyes. Brotherhood of Man had also done so. They'd won too, suggesting them to be in possession of superior sets of pipes to Pat. As his warbling tones wobbled and wafted into the west London air, I was in agreement with the verdict of the underwhelmed Eurovision jury.

But there was something about the event, about the occasion, that kept me watching. It was probably the poetry of these two dancers, shimmering around the ring with lightness and grace, not lumbering around like punch-drunk heavyweight bashers. They were skinny, like me. They were my kind of weight. Nine stone each, ounces separating them.

McGuigan's birth certificate said 24, but this was the scrawny, hairless body of an undernourished 15-year-old. The pale, unweathered skin. The whisper of bum-fluff on his top lip. The Panamanian Pedroza was older, but looked too much like kids' TV hero Derek Griffiths for me not to care about his condition, to blindly cheer for McGuigan. McGuigan, the English speaker. McGuigan, who was one of us. Kind of.

Pedroza was at that point, so Harry Carpenter explained, the world's longest reigning champion. Nineteen successful defences in seven years. I should really have known more about him. All the 15-year-old me knew was that he came from a country that existed merely for its hats (even though I now know they come from Ecuador), its canal and the cigars my dad would smoke at Christmas.

After the 15-round bout, I also knew him to be a champion of honour and pride. He gamely stuck it out for the full distance, despite McGuigan's clear superiority. The decision was unanimous. The pivotal moment had come halfway through the contest, when Pedroza hit the canvas, felled by a right hook. It was a punch undoubtedly precipitated by Carpenter's fate-tempting words ringside: 'McGuigan's work has not been so effective in this round. He hasn't found the range. Yes, he did! He's got him with a right! The champion's over in the seventh!'

On that night in west London, McGuigan proved to be a charming champion, and a few months later, he'd also win the BBC Sports Personality of the Year. Perhaps, with the blood and fire of the Troubles very much still dominating life in Ulster, he unconsciously represented something else to me and others: the Catholic from a border town who married a Protestant. Perhaps there was a glint of hope for the future.

McGuigan was certainly aware of how his cultural significance was framed by the often-violent political situation. 'Shadows run deep,' he once said after his retirement. 'My fights felt a little like sunshine.'

LIGHTNING STRIKE

WIMBLEDON 1985 was the first time, at least since all those sickbed weeks four years earlier, that I had licence to watch the entirety of the championships, every day from lunchtime through to dusk. The O-levels were in the rear-view mirror, at least until the results popped through the letterbox in August.

It wasn't the blissed-out, demob-happy experience I'd hoped for though, at least not at the start. The tournament began on Midsummer's Day, but the tone of Harry Carpenter's voice, when he opened proceedings on that first lunchtime, wasn't as cheery as it had been when McGuigan had downed Pedroza earlier in the month. The pictures were even worse – forks of lightning hitting the skyline of SW19, accompanied by rumbles of thunder that sounded like they were coming from the centre of the earth.

It was a symbol of what was to come that fortnight: the prolonged, metaphorical lightning strike that was Boris Becker.

If Becker looked like an overgrown schoolboy, that's because – wearing a kit he looked right on the cusp of growing out of – he essentially was. While he was no longer enrolled at an educational institution when he came to Wimbledon for the first time in 1985, he was the same age as those in the lower-sixth, boys just a year older than me. It would have been expected that, despite his victory on the lawns of Queen's Club a week earlier, the 17-year-old would be put in his place, especially when looking up at the heavyweights who awaited him. But, exuberant and athletic, he just kept winning.

Admittedly, circumstances opened up nicely for him. In his half of the draw, the two biggest names – second seed Ivan Lendl and fourth seed Mats Wilander – were dumped out of the competition before he was due to play them. In the end, the fifth seed, Sweden's Anders Järryd, was the highest-ranked player he faced. At the quarter-final stage, Becker even found himself up against another unseeded challenger in Henri Leconte. In the upper half of the draw, defending champ McEnroe and third seed Connors were both felled in straight sets by the South African Kevin Curren, the man the young German would face in the final.

But no matter how smooth that passage through the competition, he was a thrill to watch, throwing himself left, right and centre acrobatically, all underscored by the can-do optimism of youth. Although he would later regret winning a Grand Slam at such a tender age, at the time he offered a salutary reminder to me that adulthood wasn't far around the corner. That my time was imminent.

If the men's competition allowed such a fairy tale to blossom, over in the women's singles the ongoing duel between Navratilova and Evert was still in its highly competitive throes. They lined up opposite each other again, the sixth consecutive Grand Slam final duked out by the two, with Martina taking revenge for a French Open defeat the previous month. It wasn't that the rivalry was becoming stale – each was still perfectly capable of beating the other, meaning the finals themselves were always intriguing affairs. It was just that the passage to get to this point was far from unpredictable. Fortunately, for the post-O-level student, the concurrent Ashes series could offer alternative delights.

The BBC knew how to deliver major sporting events. No glitz, no glamour, no razzmatazz. Core values were always to the fore, the most fundamental being that the action itself was king. And they could cover two events at the same time. Despite Wimbledon entering its second week, with its action presided over by the doubles pairing of Des Lynam and Gerald Williams, the coverage of the second Test was as high quality as ever, not a beat missed and all in the safe hands of the trusted opening partnership of presenters Peter West and Richie Benaud.

It was a belting Test series. England retained the Ashes, with captain David Gower in imperious form with the bat (as was his

Australian counterpart Allan Border), and Richard Ellison and a peroxide Ian Botham gathering wickets galore. The summer filled itself nicely. It was anything but a fallow period, offering plenty of distraction while stuck in post-exam purgatory. Two sport-filled months spent occupying the waiting room of life.

TOUR DE FORCE

WHEN I was younger, I'm sure my mind conflated the Tour de France and the Milk Race. Despite their respective, and very different, levels of glamour, they were both distant, near-mythical events. Without a dedicated place in the established sporting calendar of British television, both rarely got anywhere close to the front of the consciousness, either my own or that of the nation.

I remember occasionally stumbling across highlights packages of the Tour on *World of Sport* in the early '80s, when I'd have been switching over from the racing on *Grandstand*. Often introduced by Fred Dinenage (Dickie Davies's holiday cover while he spent July in hotter, more glamorous climes than the London Weekend Television studios), these highlights seemed to merely confuse the viewer, condensing an entire week's racing into short chunks that left no room to get to know the riders, nor for an explanation of matters both technical and tactical. ITV, usually so esoteric in what rights it took possession of, didn't trumpet their coverage of the race enough. They didn't seem to appreciate the jewels they had. Accordingly, what I would later acknowledge as the world's greatest sporting spectacle eluded me – and many others – for a couple more years.

The 1982 World Championships at Goodwood had piqued my interest, but then largely silence. Until July 1985, that is, when Channel 4 took a truly momentous decision. It was a game-changer for the sport in this country, providing daily half-hour highlights, with a double-length show on Sundays. They understood the race, that every day meant a new chapter in an unfolding narrative. Weekly highlights packages didn't – *couldn't* – do it justice. And, most brilliantly, they didn't stick the race in the midnight hour, under the cover of darkness, deep in the graveyard shift. They put it on at 6.30pm. Properly prime time.

Because of the scheduling, and because of the commitment to daily programming, an entire generation who had, until then, little or no grasp of the ways of the peloton, suddenly had a new sport to immerse themselves in. I was one of them. It was a world of *domestiques* and *maillots jaune* and *directeurs sportif* – a whole new language that had to be learnt (although, admittedly, it did just seem to be French). Plus, a whole brigade of new sporting heroes were up for your approval, all sounding effortlessly exotic and *other* – Bernard Hinault, Laurent Fignon, Greg LeMond, Pedro Delgado, Luis Herrera, Fabio Parra . . . The names just kept rolling out. I had to find out all about them, to hear their stories, to learn the history of their sport.

It was perfect timing for me and, I guess, many others. While football continued to show signs of sinking into the swamps as the year progressed, becoming obsessed by a new sport seemed utterly appropriate. A new optimism was in order and I didn't need a second invitation. I dived straight in.

Just in case mystery and confusion lingered, the commentary of Phil Liggett – the voice of the BBC's coverage of those world champs in '82 – combined in-depth knowledge with an understanding of both what the layperson would want to know and how to communicate that. He would be our companion for many, many Tours to come, having, within a couple of years, been joined in the commentary box by the just-retired pro rider Paul Sherwen. The pair became another vital double act of summer television, every bit as essential as Lynam and Williams or Benaud and West.

Once that '85 Tour reached the Alps and its astonishing peaks and passes, I understood the appeal of this grand race. Its drama and its epicness made themselves immediately apparent. Everything just crystallised: the guts, the glory, the team politics, the individual endeavour. I couldn't believe something of this scale hadn't forced itself on me before now. It was like suddenly discovering a new family member, a really exciting, really fascinating new family member. And I wasn't going to let go of them.

JUST ANOTHER SATURDAY NIGHT

STEVE CRAM never got the true credit his – to borrow a pro cycling term – palmarès deserved. Had his career not been preceded by, nor overlapped with, those of Coe and Ovett, Cram's list of achievements would have given him the keys of the city and the freedom of the land. Possibly even a knighthood or a lordship. As he lined up on the track in Oslo on 27 July 1985 ahead of the Bislett Stadium's sainted Dream Mile, Cram was the current king of the 1500m: world, European and Commonwealth champion, Olympic silver medallist and world record holder, having eclipsed Ovett's time less than a fortnight earlier. But still the spotlight favoured those who'd gone before him, Coe in particular.

This was possibly because Cram's running style didn't necessarily excite people in the way that that of Coe and Ovett did. There was jeopardy in the way they raced, in the way they only revealed their hand as they came off the final bend. Cram wasn't someone who reserved a demon kick for the last 80 or 90 metres. He was an athlete who was much more likely to have made his move a couple of hundred metres before then, a move almost certainly accompanied by David Coleman's trademark caution: 'Has he gone too soon?' This proved a great tactic, as long as you had the legs to keep you out front. No one could come off your shoulder in the home straight if they weren't remotely close to your shoulder in the preceding 300 metres.

Coe was there in Oslo that night, manoeuvring himself in next to Cram as they came under starter's orders. As ever, the late-July conditions in Norway were perfect for a world record attempt. It was just another Saturday night, here at the track where so many records had tumbled, where so many athletes had run faster than anyone else in history.

In his commentary during the race's early stages, Ron Pickering insisted to us at home that 'the race is more important than the record. That's absolutely true of the two British contenders.' If this was merely a head-to-head to see who was top dog in British middle-distance running, Coe, no stranger to posting world-best times at this track, knew full well he may well also have to defend his mile record.

I'd been witness to – in fact, I'd become thoroughly familiar with – successful world-record attempts by British middle-distancers all decade, but Cram's performance that night was probably the finest I'd seen. With 200 metres to go, he simply ran off the front of Coe, turning the screw with his longer stride. As they came into the home straight, Coe visibly relaxed. The realisation was that this moment could be the baton change, the point at which he knew he was on his way back down from the mountain and that Cram, more than four years younger, still had many more peaks in front of him.

All Coe, by now in third, could hope for was that his mile record remained intact, that the clock would defeat Cram.

It didn't. He broke the tape more than a second faster than anyone had ever run a mile. It was simply scintillating, and I was punching the air. Finally, *finally*, Cram was the undisputed king.

Coleman was in agreement, his cracking voice delivering one of his most emotional post-race summaries. 'It has been said that this man is predictable, but could you really predict he'd be brave enough and bold enough to go away from a field of this class so early and run right away from them?' We both knew – Coleman in the stadium, me on my bed – that this was the changing of the guard.

THE OFF SWITCH

ENGLISH FOOTBALL'S *annus horribilis* continued into the new season. After Kenilworth Road and Bradford and Heysel and the European ban, the next bad news story to befall the national game directly affected the TV sport addict.

For the first four months of the 1985-86 season, there was an impasse between the Football League and the television companies. With opening-day attendances down across the four divisions (an unsurprising turn of events bearing in mind the catalogue of grave incidents during the latter half of the previous season), the Football League saw televised football – especially the live variety – as potentially exacerbating the decline, forcing crowd numbers to drop further still. A four-year, £19 million deal was on the table from television, but it was flatly refused.

A four-month stand-off then paralysed the game, at least as far as the armchair fans were concerned. There were no live games, no highlights packages, not even any goals to show on *Football Focus*. It was hell, a sizeable hole in both your life and your viewing schedule (which, of course, could be one and the same thing). All you could do was imagine what the goals looked like from photos and descriptions in the paper.

The Football League blinked first and a modest £1.3 million deal was thrashed out for a total of nine live games – six First Division matches and three League Cup ties. A separate deal was already in place with the FA, so – bolstered by four FA Cup games, the European Cup Final and England versus Scotland – the television companies had a grand total of 15 live games to show in the remaining five months.

After such an abject year, 1986 had to be a better one for football. The fact that it was to be a World Cup year gave grounds for optimism. It couldn't get any worse.

THE GREAT ESCAPE

FAULTLESSNESS DOESN'T teach us too much. Infallibility is an impenetrable shell. We can't get under its skin. It's the imperfections – and, more importantly, how we react to them – that reveal the person.

Just ask Randy Mamola. In the final race of the 1985 500cc motorcycling Grand Prix season, in the landlocked republic of San Marino, the Californian experienced the most blood-pumping 11 seconds of his career when he evaded what could have been a serious, life-changing – possibly even life-threatening – high-speed smash. But it was in slow motion that Mamola revealed his true brilliance.

Watching it frame by frame, like motorsport's version of the Zapruder movie, the escape remains extraordinary. Mamola loses his rear wheel and is thrown over the handlebars as the bike heads for the horizontal. But then, in an amazing show of strength and with his legs flying in every direction, he rights the bike and is able to assume some sort of side-saddle position while also appearing to almost run alongside the bike. All the while, the bike continues to move at a mind-boggling speed. And Mamola didn't have a single bruise to show for what he'd gone through.

His name marked him out when he first appeared on British screens as a teenager in 1979. Randy Mamola: a ridiculously exotic name, a ridiculously American name. I was used to more prosaic sporting nomenclatures: John Richards, Alan Minter, Kathy Smallwood . . .

But I also liked Mamola because, despite the similarities in geography and background and riding style, he wasn't Kenny Roberts. Roberts had been the nemesis of Barry Sheene, our Barry Sheene, the sand in the ointment that had denied the Londoner a smooth path to a long line of world titles.

No, Mamola would do for me. Any man whose brilliance and balance avoided serious, if not fatal, injury that afternoon in San Marino was deserving of being everyone's favourite rider. Perhaps even more so than Barry.

FACTORY SETTING

NOW A few years on from that Volvo vs ambulance sideshow at the '81 Derby, I remained desperately perplexed over the appeal of horse racing. But I did try to stick with it. Although mildly intrigued by the sudden fluctuations in pre-race odds (Ebenezer Skeet had taught probability with more authority than he did trigonometry), I still needed to find a way to care about who won. It wasn't like I could favour a particular style or character type, as I could with athletics or snooker or darts. These were horses, after all. I couldn't discern one from another.

So, in a vain attempt to make the whole endeavour remotely interesting, I devised a system to favour one particular horse in each race. As racing normally meant the point in *Grandstand* or *World of Sport* where I'd turn the volume down on the TV and stick a record on for ten minutes, it seemed apt that I'd seek musical inspiration. At this stage of teenagehood, I was increasingly captivated by the music of Manchester; by The Smiths, of course, but also by plenty of signings to Tony Wilson's Factory Records label, not just Joy Division and New Order.

Accordingly, I attempted to select winners who could, in whatever way possible, be connected with Factory's roster – a band name, an album title and so on. So, for instance, if a horse had either 'blue' or 'Monday' in its name, that'd be the one I'd back, thus forcing myself to watch the race.

If the horses themselves failed to produce a connection, the next option was to see what jockeys or trainers or owners shared surnames with key Factory personnel. Take New Order, again. While the names 'Sumner' or 'Hook' were unlikely to crop up on the race card, there was half a chance that 'Gilbert' (keyboard player Gillian) or 'Morris' (drummer Stephen) might. Equally common names like 'Wilson' (Factory boss Tony) or 'Curtis' (Joy Division singer Ian) also represented pay dirt in this cash-free parlour game.

Nonetheless, such a deeply scientific methodology still didn't guarantee a match (although if someone in The Durutti Column or Crispy Ambulance had the surname Piggott or Eddery, it would have done every single time). So a foolproof bottom-line plan was invoked. I'd simply back one of the race's 25/1 shots, based on nothing more than the existence of Factory-signed, Blackpool-based Kraftwerk enthusiasts Section 25.

On a good day, I'd be able to find a connection, however

thin, however tenuous, across all the races in the ITV Seven (and ideally not having to invoke the Section 25 rule). That to me was success, regardless of how the actual horses performed. It was the equivalent of backing the seven-race accumulator. It was my jackpot.

Jesus Christ, I must have been bored.

DEAD AIR

THIS NEWLY devised method of making racing interesting didn't last long, at least not when applied to the ITV Seven. It disappeared from *World of Sport* in September 1985. Three weeks later, *World of Sport* itself fell silent and vanished from the schedules.

Saturday's races went across to Channel 4, which had been broadcasting midweek racing for more than a year at that point, while wrestling – that *World of Sport* staple – was retained by the network, now to be presented as a stand-alone show.

Hand on heart, I can't say that I went into deep mourning over *World of Sport*'s loss. Yes, it had alerted us over the years to the likes of hovercraft racing and ice speedway and target diving, but this wasn't real enlightenment. They were humorous diversions, at best. Nothing more. *World of Sport* didn't last simply because it couldn't get (or didn't try to get) the big-hitters: Test matches, Wimbledon, Formula One and the like.

The show – and I use the word advisedly, rather than 'programme' – had to go down the esoteric, tongue-in-cheek path because that was all that was left at the buffet. The BBC had filled its plate and ITV had to make best with the crumbs that remained. And even when it had a share of the prime cuts, such as the Cup Final, ITV felt the need to differentiate the nature of their output from that of the Beeb, despite having, in Brian Moore, someone who was the equal of Motson or Davies.

ITV put distance between themselves and those on the other side by relying too often on celebrity. While the most light-hearted Coleman et al would get would be a one-off Cup Final edition of *A Question of Sport*, ITV would fill those pre-match hours with input from the likes of Jimmy Tarbuck and Freddie Starr. Any input from either was too much.

In turning sport into a clear branch of light entertainment, ITV could never hope to retrieve the attention of the sportaholics. We were serious about our sport and didn't like it tossed about so gaily by ITV. The BBC's hands, in contrast, were the safest hands around. They were the ones to be trusted with the sporting crown jewels.

When *World of Sport* spun off into oblivion, Ian St John and Jimmy Greaves took centre stage. The timing meant that, shorn of actual footage to show because of the football blackout, the pair's joshing and jocularity came to the fore on the rebadged *Saint & Greavsie*. Yes, the football pedigree of both ran deep into their respective bone marrow, but they knew – in that particular climate – some light relief was called for.

Their delivery, so much looser than that of starchy Bob Wilson on *Football Focus*, served a purpose, leavening the shadow-laden landscape for those grown disillusioned with the game since the turn of the year. It also set the template for the less formal coverage of football on the box that came along in its wake; echoes of its irreverence and humour are most definitely still heard today on *Gillette Soccer Saturday*.

They were game-changers, for sure. After all, Wilson would never have invited Donald Trump to assist in the live draw for the Rumbelows Cup. St John and Greaves did. He accepted, too.

THE COLOUR OF MONEY

AT THE age of 17, a continuing appreciation of *A Question of Sport* was, for a young man with an increasingly discerning taste at the sharper end of the arts (the records of The Go-Betweens, the films of Wim Wenders), a circle that was hard to square. The show was unrepentantly *mainstream*, a cultural position diametrically opposed to that of those of us who fancied ourselves as the epitome of precocious cool. It was bright. It was brash. It was chummy back-slapping in lemon Lacoste and Pringle pink. The very definition of sports casual.

In short, *A Question of Sport* was what, in years to come, would be dubbed a guilty pleasure. In the sixth-form building the following day, you couldn't discuss it with the cooler set. Instead, you kept talk of television to a dissection of the latest misfortune to befall the residents of Brookside Close, or to reporting who was playing live on *The Tube* that night. For those of us who wanted to retain any credibility, raising the subject of a light-hearted-but-not-as-funny-as-it-thought-it-was sport quiz was a no-no. But, on the QT, on the hush-hush, I still enjoyed it as much as I did witnessing the travails of Billy Corkhill or enduring the onstage wobbly camerawork of Tyne Tees' finest.

The appeal of *A Question of Sport* was that it offered the chance to see sporting heroes off duty, to find the real person behind the grit, to glimpse into their souls, no matter how shallow and charisma-free these might be. It was also a chance to test my *Rain Man*-like retention of facts, figures and, in the mystery guest round, faces.

During the latter, I would scrutinise – with all the due diligence of a forensic detective – not just the mystery guest's skin complexion, hair colour and clothing choice, but also the setting in which they'd been filmed. If I'd videoed an episode, the pause button acted as my assistant. My crowning glory was once recognising the emblem of the Belfry on some headed notepaper in the room in which one guest had been filmed. Even though I still couldn't precisely identify the mystery man, I could at least whittle it down to a golfer. Although, to be fair, his comfortable trouserwear had already marked out his profession.

During the course of a series, the programme's producers would extend an invitation for viewers to participate in their own mystery guest round. Each week, they'd show a clip and, after six weeks or so, viewers would hungrily send in a complete list of the sporting personalities they believed they had correctly identified.

One year, they threw a curveball. The mystery guests were always contemporary sportsmen or sportswomen, but one particular week it appeared that the long-retired pentathlete Mary Peters was the person being filmed from curious angles.

At least that's what I thought that Thursday night, an instinct I discovered was shared by several others (of the less cool sporty bunch) as we slumped into the rotting armchairs of the sixth-form building the following morning. But one kid, Stephens the Bookie, wasn't having it. Why would the BBC have, for one week only, changed its policy and moved away from filming contemporary figures? He had a point, definitely, but it sure as hell looked like Mary Peters.

As was his nature – and he was the most mathematically literate lad in the whole year – Stephens immediately opened a book on it, happily taking bets as a succession of sixth-formers queued to hand over their dinner money. They were willing to go hungry in return for a generous payday a month or two down the line, especially as the in-house bookie was offering up an altruistically generous 10/1 on it being Mary Peters, despite the collective certainty of the lengthening queue. I recklessly surrendered a whole pound (my emergency bus fare home) and began to dream about which two albums I was going to buy with the winnings.

It wasn't until the final show of the series that David Coleman revealed the results. And these were results that Stephens the Bookie, due to pay out a sum that was pretty sizeable to lads with modestly paying Saturday jobs, did not want to hear. The words 'Mary' and 'Peters' were a hammer blow to both his soul and the balance of his Post Office savings account.

Everyone's first instinct was to call his house and jeer loudly down the line. On the first attempt, the phone rang and rang and rang. He was avoiding the truth, in denial. Or perhaps he was en route to the cashpoint to prepare for that bumper payout. On the second attempt, the phone was engaged. And it stayed off the hook for the rest of the evening and into the next morning.

Even the cool kids took an interest that Friday. Nothing unites and excites teenage boys more than ripping the piss out of someone else's misfortune. You had never heard a cheer like it when Stephens the Bookie – soon to be Stephens the Bankrupt Bookie – sheepishly stuck his head round the door. Unintentionally, he had brought the whole lower-sixth, previously quartered into their own distinct tribes, together. For one morning, at least.

THE VOICE IS SILENCED

THE GUARDIAN'S Michael Hann, writing about why we are so affected by celebrity deaths, has explained how popular culture acted as co-parents to the generations who came of age in the late twentieth century. 'They drew life lessons not from fireside chats with parents, but from David Bowie and Bob Dylan and Joni Mitchell. They were entertained not by parlour games but by *The Generation Game*. When they wanted to understand why they felt as they did during adolescence, they didn't speak to their families, they listened to The Smiths, or whomever answered their particular need.' And when these 'co-parents' move on to whatever final destination, Hann observes that their admirers 'have lost part of their family'.

And so it was with Jim Laker. His voice – one that, more than 30 years later, I can far more easily recall compared to that of my own grandad – was redolent of early '80s Britain, his flat vowels and occasional sardonic barbs perfectly suited to the sight of the Old Trafford ground staff dragging the covers back towards the wicket as umbrellas went up in the stands. His was a voice not known for its high levels of excitement or hyperbole. It was measured, reasoned, reassuring. When Jim Laker slipped into the commentator's seat and slowly lifted microphone to mouth, all was well with the world – regardless of any calamity spelled out by the scorecard.

The anchormen and commentators of TV sport became surrogate uncles to me, familiar and comforting presences in equally comfortable knitwear. Aside from my dad, there was no male role model in my life after my grandad died at the turn of the decade. There were uncles within the family tree, but none I had a relationship with – or even remembered meeting. Even my football coach was my dad. So these avuncular anchormen filled a void, their calming and reliable tones reassuring an uncertain, angsty-at-the-edges teen that everything was going to be all right. As long as 22 men took to a field to hoof a synthetic bladder around, as long as Seve Ballesteros struck a golf ball with charming insouciance, and as long as a male voice choir retained the ability to supercharge the crowd at Cardiff Arms Park, life would go on. The planet would turn. In sport, we could trust.

DOUBT, DESPAIR AND DOUBLE-DECKER BUSES

BY NOW, a good half of the lower-sixth were members of the local snooker club and, with the arrival of 'study periods' in our timetables (following the packed schedule of the previous year's O-levels), more daylight hours that were good for our serotonin levels were spent in the club's smoky, murky gloom, the clink of snooker balls only punctuated by boyish, cross-table banter.

There is one particular volley of banter that has never dulled nor disappeared in the intervening years. I can still hear each syllable and the broken, teenage voice that said them. They are the words that denied me my one moment in the sporting sun.

'You can fit a double-decker bus through that gap.'

It was the school snooker tournament – the *unofficial* school snooker tournament, that is – held during those study periods, in particular those study periods that bled into the lunch break, and gave us two clear hours of play. Possibly in order to clear his debts, Stephens the Bookie was back running odds on the whole affair. I was a 12/1 shot for the 16-competitor knockout. These seemed perfectly fair odds (and attracted no bets whatsoever, not even from myself), seeing as how I'd been drawn in the first round against second seed Nick Stride. But then something happened. I managed to take the first frame of the best-of-three encounter to tee up a potential giant-killing. It was a first frame that potentially carried as much significance as the Ronnie Radford thunderbolt that opened the scoring for Hereford against Newcastle in 1972. I was on the threshold of sporting history.

And I didn't rest there. Confounding Stephens' grasp of probability, I took a healthy lead in the second frame too. Reds disappeared with both unnerving efficiency and a style that I'd never previously showcased. In the blink of an eye, Nick Stride needed a snooker to stay in the competition. Murmurs of a monumental upset filtered around the club and a modest crowd now gathered around table number six. Having put my opponent in this position, I was Ricky George who, having rounded the Newcastle keeper, simply needed to slot the second decisive Hereford goal into the empty net. An indelible entry in the history books was mine for the taking.

True to his seeding, Nick Stride confidently laid that required snooker, but I wasn't unduly worried. An unfamiliar inner calm took over me. I even played to the growing gallery by turning my glasses upside down to mimic Dennis Taylor. Whichever way I looked at it, there was definitely space to slip the cue ball off the cushion to bypass the brown and reach the yellow. Those around me agreed. A double-decker bus could make that manoeuvre. That was the consensus around the table. Sadly, though, it was a double-decker bus with me at the wheel. I clipped the brown, reducing the deficit to a manageable amount if Nick Stride simply potted the six remaining balls. And he did just that in two visits to the table. And then, in nine blink-and-you'll-miss-them minutes – and to the mirth of the bystanders whose encouragement had now turned to scorn and ridicule – he ruthlessly sent me packing in the deciding frame and glided into the next round. The laws of probability had been proved correct. In a parallel universe, Newcastle had reined back plucky Hereford after all.

A little bit more than a week later, Joe Johnson held his nerve in a way that I had singularly failed to do. In snooker's own version of Keith Deller's darts miracle three years before, the unseeded Yorkshireman came from nowhere (actually it was Bradford) to take the world title, the sport's most prestigious crown. Well, the sport's second-most prestigious crown, after the epic contest that was drawing to a close in our local snooker club.

Again, as 12 months before, Steve Davis was the vanquished party in the final. This time, Johnson was a serious outsider, a player who'd never won a professional tournament and who was no stranger to the qualifying rounds. At least Dennis Taylor had seen the inside of a world final before. At 150/1 before the fortnight began, Johnson was a way less credible candidate than I'd been in our little tournament. But he'd gone all the way. I'd not made it out of the first round.

Johnson wasn't overly blessed with star quality; he had the demeanour of a small-hours hotel bar steward. But throughout the tournament, and throughout the final, his dead-eyed potting was an absolute dream. He struck the cue ball like the champion he became. His 64 break in the final frame was the most enjoyable to watch. With every crisp pot, he was striding imperiously towards the title. Coming to the final blue with a lead of 48, a smile broke out across his lips and his head gave a slight, disbelieving shake. With five frames to spare, he was a comfortable winner. 'The most remarkable final I've ever seen!' exclaimed Ted Lowe as the players moved in for the handshakes. Ted had clearly forgotten the midnight marathon from the previous April.

Before the presentations came the customary post-match interviews with David Vine. In trying to make sense of the previous 17 days, Johnson proved a modest and generous champion. In his interview, Davis showed another example of his quick wit, one that was even on tap in the immediate aftermath of a second consecutive world final defeat.

'We can't really go on meeting like this, can we David?'

SOUTH OF THE BORDER

TO MY increasing embarrassment – albeit embarrassment that could be easily obscured at six in the morning when almost every other teenager worth their coolness was still under the duvet – at the age of 17 I still had that paper round. I was now old enough to drive a car, but I remained content with a cherry-red, drop-handlebar Raleigh racer being my vehicle of choice, wobbling along the dark, unmade roads of my village, a hundredweight of Sunday newspapers lumped over my shoulder.

I could have considered much cooler part-time employment on the weekends, a job more befitting someone with only a couple of years of teenagehood left in the tank. An assistant in a clothes shop, perhaps, or the Saturday boy in a back-street record shop, sneering at well-meaning customers on the other side of the counter simply because they wanted Bon Jovi's *Slippery When Wet* rather than any selection from the Rough Trade back catalogue.

But there was one reason I kept on with the paper round into 1986. One reason I needed to keep as many daylight hours free as possible.

It was a World Cup year.

For me, a World Cup didn't start with the opening ceremony, nor the inevitable low-score – or no-score – draw involving the holders and whoever had had the misfortune of being drawn against them. The contest started before then, in the battle of whether the BBC or ITV had the better theme tune. This would be the music to induce Pavlovian responses in football fans for the next month. It would become their call to prayer.

The BBC had the first live match of Mexico '86, the inevitable 1-1 draw between holders Italy and Bulgaria. Their theme tune wasn't terrible, but it was overly dramatic and austere with strident trumpets that got tiresome rather quickly. Introducing that night's highlights, ITV's synth-led theme – 'Aztec Gold' – was warmer, with its subtle use of maracas not overdoing the Mexican motif. Over the course of the next few weeks, 'Aztec Gold' proved the more durable. So durable, in fact, that after the tournament, the network adopted it as the catch-all music for all its football output, including *Saint & Greavsie* and *The Big Match*. Its use on the latter meant that Jeff Wayne's 'Jubilation' was jettisoned, though. A step too far in my book. A heretical act, in fact.

The BBC's defeat on this front, combined with the relentless use of Spandau Ballet at the Olympics two years previously, suggested the corporation's sport department needed someone with better ears to select their music. I made a vow to send off a letter on spec, offering my services as a consultant. (That said, the person at the corporation's Pebble Mill outpost who suggested using Propaganda's 'Duel' – THE greatest pop tune of the entire '80s – as the theme music to the William Woollard-fronted *Rally Report* most definitely deserves every last penny of their full-salary pension.)

For the England team, Mexico '86 didn't start as smartly as it had done for ITV. A defeat to Portugal in their opening match was followed by a scoreless draw against Morocco, a game memorable for two incidents in the last five minutes of the first half. First, Bryan Robson left the pitch with his arm in a sling, his tournament over. A minute later, Ray Wilkins, the scorer of *that* goal in Turin six summers previously, made another contribution to the history of the England team. After a decision hadn't gone his way in the far corner, he tossed the ball in the direction of the Paraguayan referee. It wasn't thrown with any degree of venom or vitriol; school PE lessons featured more extreme acts of dissent every week. But, having earned a yellow just two minutes before, Wilkins was off, the first-ever England player to be dismissed in tournament football. 'An extraordinary lapse from a very experienced player,' tutted ITV's Martin Tyler. 'He's let his teammates down at a critical time. He should have known better.'

A defeat and a draw. And no goals scored. The wheels were coming off the charabanc.

It was up to one man, a player whose plaster-cast-wrapped broken wrist nearly prevented him from taking part in the tournament, to save the day. Having scored 30 league goals for Everton that season, Gary Lineker belatedly found his shooting boots in Mexico and, in the final win-or-go-home group game against Poland, helped himself to a first-half hat-trick. The sense of relief was not only palpable across the land, it was audible in the BBC commentary box. Each time the ball hit the net, you could hear Jimmy Hill letting out a not entirely impartial cheer in the background.

Lineker pretty much repeated the trick in the last 16 match against Paraguay, bagging two more in another 3-0 victory. In a matter of days, he'd turned England's fortunes around and become a national hero himself. His new status was reflected in the school playground the morning after the Poland game. While his pals took the roles of Steve Hodge and Gary Stevens, delivering a series of inch-perfect crosses into the danger zone, the lad playing Lineker had even put a white sock over his left wrist, replicating the plaster cast. A bonus point for detail and authenticity.

But England's revival turned out to be a fleeting fairy tale.

The pantomime villain would make his appearance earlier than was hoped.

SUCKER PUNCH

THEY SAY you shouldn't meet your heroes. I say you should definitely at least chat with them over the phone for half an hour.

Nearly 30 years after the England/Argentina quarter-final of '86, I had the distinct pleasure of a very amiable conversation with the mighty Barry Davies. I was in journalist mode, having asked Barry to select his all-time England World Cup XI and to explain just why he'd picked the players he had. The first name on his team sheet, number one on the back of the shirt, was Peter Shilton. As he sang his praises, a post-retirement Davies also shared an opinion that he wouldn't have been able to say out loud while in the service of the BBC. It concerned Maradona's 'Hand of God' goal. 'Shilton should have left him flat on his back wondering what day it was,' he confided. 'He should have clattered him.'

That, the best part of three decades on, Davies still felt the rawness of injustice over the incident suggests he was more than simmering in the commentary box that hot afternoon. But, being the consummate professional, he kept his indignation largely under wraps. (I've also since spoken to Shilton about the affair. With the passage of time, he had grown a little more sanguine. 'I was going to get the ball, that's why he put it in with his hand and not his head. And he did it well, to be fair. He flicked his head at the same time that he punched it.')

I was glad that Davies had been given this match. With the political dimension hanging heavy over the game (despite near-universal protestations from the England camp that it was just a game of football), it needed someone of Davies's gravitas to oversee things. For such a potentially epic and significant encounter, it needed to be in the care of someone a little weightier than Motson.

The first half gave little inkling of the explosive way the game would come alive six minutes after the break. During their half-time reflections back in the BBC studio, presenter Lynam and his two-man panel of Emlyn Hughes and Terry Venables admitted they had blank paper in front of them with no notes jotted down, such were the limited highlights of the opening 45 minutes. 'Argentina are nothing special,' squeaked Hughes.

'What do you reckon?' asked Des, just before handing back to Davies in the Azteca Stadium. 'Argentina's half on points?'

'It's not about points,' was Venables' tart response. 'It's about knockouts.' Little did he realise his analogy was prophetic, that a punch was just about to change the game's complexion.

At our house, and at houses and pubs and clubs across the nation, the benefit of slow-motion confirmed the injustice of Maradona's first goal. Frustration was the immediate response; this quickly morphed into anger when the realisation kicked in that this blatant act of cheating might be the way that England missed out on reaching a World Cup semi-final once again.

Within four further minutes, Maradona put us back in our collective box with that sublime, snaking, twisting run that dizzied and dazzled the English midfield and defence over more than half the length of the pitch. There was no argument about that one. It was simply the most brilliant individual goal that anyone had ever scored, or that anyone had ever seen. Barry Davies instantly articulated it perfectly for us. For all our indignation about what had just happened, that second goal had us conceding that Maradona was operating – or, at least, could operate – on a higher plane to the rest of us whenever he felt the urge. 'You have to say that's magnificent,' reasoned

Davies. 'There is no debate about that goal. That was just pure football genius.'

While I couldn't have predicted the drama of that four-minute spell (and the closeness to which England almost retrieved the match in the last ten minutes), I nonetheless was hopeful of it being something of a classic and so had devoted a box-fresh blank videocassette to the entire proceedings: the pre-match hopefulness, the match itself, the post-mortem. I also decided – six years after abandoning that radio archive that began and ended with West Ham's Cup triumph – to stick a C120 tape in the radio-cassette player to record just how the radio guys were calling it.

Afterwards, I only listened back to the pivotal moments on the tape. I had no need to relive the dullness of the first half, of hearing Radio 2's Bryon Butler trying desperately to avoid dead air when there was actually very little of any note to describe. However, he came into his own after the break. As spot-on as I thought Barry Davies's reaction to that second goal had been, his radio colleague had actually eclipsed him. Butler's commentary was poetic both in its imagery and in the way that his words gained momentum and velocity with each stride of the Argentinian captain.

'Maradona . . . turns like a little eel and comes away from trouble . . . little squat man . . . comes inside Butcher, leaves him for dead . . . outside Fenwick, leaves him for dead . . . and puts the ball away . . . and that is why Maradona is the greatest player in the world!' It was a commentary that was every inch the equal of the goal itself.

Those in the BBC studio were, somewhat surprisingly, decidedly philosophical after the match. Nowadays, in the age of the headline-seeking pundit, witnessing such an ungentlemanly act as Maradona's would provoke a cacophony of angry voices and motormouths calling for bans to be imposed, for referees to be struck off, for heads to roll. Instead, Des, Terry and Emlyn were reflective and largely accepting. Regardless of Maradona's seismic misdemeanour, England should have done better. That was the take-home moral. Venables persisted with his boxing motif when bemoaning their inability to take the game to the Argentinians until close to the death. 'We played when we were two down. It's like the boxer who waits to get it on the chin before he fights back. And if the guy can fight better than him, he doesn't get back.'

A couple of months later, my video recording of the quarter-final would be wiped in favour of that summer's edition of *Rock Around the Clock*, the BBC's annual all-night music marathon presented by the *Whistle Test* team. While I couldn't erase the memory of the crime committed in the Azteca Stadium, I could at least get rid of the evidence from my own home. Plus, a documentary on The Housemartins and a Billy Bragg live set were far more worthy of being immortalised on magnetic tape than the left hand of dishonest Diego Armando Maradona.

THE SULTAN OF SWING

WHEN YOU'RE a kid, you're oblivious to the cogs and chains and switches and levers of the adult world, the parts of the machine that work together to create a functioning society. But in 1986, I finally got an inkling that the world as we knew it didn't just happily fall together, that there was actually some design to life. That summer, I realised that the person responsible for scheduling England's Test matches was clearly in league with, possibly even married to, the person responsible for scheduling school holidays.

So, across late July and August, I again caught every minute of a summer holiday Test series, this time a three-match encounter against New Zealand. I made it my task not to miss a single ball. A change of bowling from the Nursery End, and the rearrangement of fielding placings that this would require, offered the perfect opportunity to have a wee and refill my glass of orange squash. And, when the players themselves took a drinks break, the pause in play was exactly the amount of time it took to make a cheese toastie in the Breville sandwich toaster. I was back in position without missing a beat.

One thing that was missing, for the first two Tests at least, was the presence of Ian Botham. He was in the authorities' bad books, handed a 65-day ban for admitting in an interview that he'd smoked cannabis. In early August, while the Kiwis were lining themselves up for a win in the second Test at Trent Bridge, he had returned to the crease after this enforced sabbatical. As the Test took a Sunday rest day, elsewhere in the East Midlands Botham was setting fielders aflutter by dispatching the ball to every corner of the Wellingborough School ground at a John Player League match. Wearing the creams of Somerset after the selectors had elected to install Derek Pringle into the all-rounder berth in the Test side, Botham fired an unbeaten 175 off just 122 balls, a two-fingered – or even, because he could be quite a rude boy, a single-digit – salute to the Test selectors who felt his recreational misdemeanours still precluded him from being rushed back into the England side. That afternoon, he hit 12 fours and an astonishing 13 sixes.

I never saw this masterclass of what the Monday morning's papers referred to as controlled fury. It may well have been televised; indeed, the combination of a returning Botham and the comparative proximity of Wellingborough to Nottingham, where the elephant-grey trucks of the BBC's Outside Broadcast unit were already close to hand, suggests there's a fair chance it actually was.

I wouldn't have known whether this extraordinary display hit the small screen, though. On that particular afternoon, I was otherwise engaged. *Sunday Grandstand* had slipped, just a notch, down the pecking order. Not that – *of course* – it was replaced by anything other than sport. But I was making the shift from permanent spectator to sometime player, by now turning out for a Sunday league cricket XI.

I was the lad who put the XI into their name. The last place on the team sheet was mine, all mine. I knew my place. If ever numbers needed making up, our home phone would burst into life at about 11am on a Sunday. Quite often, they'd dangle a fiver before me if I also acted as scorer for our innings. I knew how to spin it, though. Taking a fee meant I could legitimately claim to have joined the ranks of the professional cricketer.

Professional until I stepped out onto the pitch, that is. There were no tilts at personal glory. I was last into bat. I fielded out of harm's way at fine leg. And I never had so much as a sniff of bowling even a single over all summer. Indeed, the entire bowling attack would have to have left the field with mild dysentery for the captain to chuck the ball in my direction and invite me to properly join the fray.

This was a shame. At Friday night nets, I had been very much modelling my technique, if not the hair on my top lip, on the most graceful but deadly bowler I'd ever clapped eyes on. I rolled my sleeves up the way he did and I fixed my glare on the stumps the way he did. Growing a similar 'tache was possibly a step too far, though, even if nature had been willing.

Richard Hadlee looked like he belonged to the Victorian or Edwardian era. Those rolled-up sleeves set down his manifesto: honest and hard-working, reliable and no-nonsense. Maybe it was the fact that, as he plied his trade during long English summers, Nottinghamshire was his adopted county, which led me to see him as the hero/anti-hero in a D.H. Lawrence novel. Perhaps he was the woodsman who, having toiled throughout the working week, let off steam one afternoon every weekend, chopping the cut-glass-voiced cricketing opposition down to size instead.

That summer, Hadlee chopped England down to size, particularly during that second Test on his adopted home turf of Trent Bridge, where he took ten wickets for the loss of 140 runs – a fine return for his endeavours. And he had done so at the comparatively creaking milestone of 35.

At that point, he was exactly double my age. I had some serious catching up to do. And I couldn't even get to bowl a single over for a put-together-at-the-last-moment Sunday side. I realised I might just not make the grade.

DR EXCITEMENT

'AND LOOK at that! Out . . . that . . . and colossally. That's Mansell! That is Nigel Mansell!'

Sometimes, commentary doesn't flow exactly right. Sometimes, a sudden, unexpected incident can't be instantly articulated in perfectly formed, grammatically correct sentences.

And so it was with Murray Walker when describing the dramatic puncture which befell Nigel Mansell in the 1986 Australian Grand Prix. No matter. It became one of Walker's most cherished pieces of commentary, one that proved he was no automaton, that he was human, that he was telling it from the heart.

No one could ever doubt that Walker meant everything he said. There was arguably no more passionate, no more excitable sport commentator on British television. This was a man who broke into motorsport commentary as a hobby and who, despite being the established voice of Formula One, continued his day job as an ad agency executive until he was

59. This was no career commentator. This was someone who was following their obsession and who loved every moment of it. If his words were momentarily fragmented and faltering, it was because he was right in the moment, affected by the action just as much as us watching.

And to be fair to Walker, within a matter of seconds he had retrieved the situation in Adelaide. It was the final race of the season, in which Mansell needed to finish third to win the world title. Anything less than that would leave the door open for both Alain Prost and Nelson Piquet. By the time the Williams had, after some heroic wrestling for control by Mansell, dinked into the side wall, Walker's composure had returned and he was already evaluating the incident's significance for the overall race.

'This could change – and *will* change – the World Championship.'

SATURDAY AFTERNOON FEVER

No matter how thrilling an afternoon's action on *Grandstand* may have been – a last-minute try for St Helens, a nine-dart finish for Bobby George – the fulcrum of the whole day was always found in the last half-hour of transmission. *Final Score* was a feeding frenzy of data and numbers that came so thick and so fast that it could be a shock to the system, especially if the afternoon had otherwise been spent in rather sedentary surroundings. Masters snooker, perhaps, or indoor bowls.

The first stage of *Final Score* was the most exciting: the vidiprinter. At this particular point in time, science fiction was very much in vogue with television producers, but much of this fanciful futurology was too impatient with its time frames. We were, after all, apparently only 13 years away from the arrival of *Space: 1999*'s particular vision, that of the Moon being knocked off its orbit thanks to a massive explosion of nuclear waste dumped in the lunar landscape by us earthlings. While the workings of the vidiprinter felt decidedly futuristic in such analogue times, this was science fiction with very much a real-world application. No laser guns, no colonisation of other planets. Just football results gathered and disseminated in the quickest possible fashion.

The flashing cursor retained all the power; even Coleman and Lynam were slaves to it. But while we waited for particular results to come in, there was always the hope that elsewhere a heavy defeat, a right walloping, had been exacted on some poor unfortunate team. We were after a defeat so heavy that, in order to reassure the viewer that a typo hadn't been made on the vidiprinter screen, the number of goals conceded would be spelled out and presented in capital letters within a pair of brackets. It was jackpot time if you spotted one of those.

In his terrific book *Saturday, 3pm*, the author Daniel Gray shows his understanding of the dehumanising effect that those brackets, and their almost exclamatory capital letters, can impose. To him, 'they loudly and slowly enunciate like an impatient middle-aged woman telling her half-deaf father how the microwave works'. As if his or her team getting thrashed wasn't humiliation enough, a supporter would sink even lower if the vidiprinter operator had to switch on caps lock. 'Brackets twist the knife and then unleash a rifle just to make sure,' writes Gray. 'They are particular, too; six goals and they leave the victim be, seven and sword is yanked from scabbard.'

Even if the vidiprinter had told you all the scores you wanted to know, there was still a burning duty to have them formally confirmed by the reading out of the classified results. These were handled by the unflappable Len Martin, a man whose working week revolved around the five minutes it would take him to run through the results of England's top five divisions and Scotland's three.

Martin wasn't just unflappable. He was unfailingly metronomic for the 37 years he was in the job. His cadence was consistent throughout: trailing off if the away team had lost; even-toned if it was a draw; rising if the away team had grabbed a win. It meant that, if for some reason (and it would have to be a very good reason, of course) you'd failed to catch the vidiprinter in full flow and didn't already know the results, you could close your eyes and confidently guess the away team's score.

That Martin didn't permit any hint of emotion to trespass into his delivery was not only a mark of impeccable professionalism, but was also actually down to his ambivalence towards the game. The words he was reading out didn't actually mean much to him. After his death in 1995, one obituary pointed out that 'his enthusiasm for football, the results sequence apart, seldom exceeded an enquiry as to how Watford, the club nearest his home, were doing'.

JOBS FOR THE BOY

WHILE LEN Martin's job appealed both for the crucial function it served the nation and for its far from exhausting hours, I was looking towards a career that did actually call on a little more enthusiasm, that made passion a pre-requisite.

By the closing months of 1986, my top three dream jobs had changed slightly. These were now them:

1. Football commentator.
Still first choice. Still top priority. The poetry of Barry Davies and Bryon Butler had only encouraged me more

that summer. A disclaimer, though: the immense heat of the Azteca Stadium, like that high gantry at Goodison Park, had caused me to draw up a fresh list of football grounds (or even countries) to avoid. My diva-ish demands were increasing.

2. Sports reporter.
In my 18th year, though, I was concerned that my voice hadn't developed enough distinctiveness for a life behind the microphone. It had dropped fine and any squeaky falsetto tendencies had evaporated, but it was far from having the kind of middle-age authority that the best commentators had. Was I aiming for too much, too young? Perhaps print journalism was the way to earn my stripes, to learn the language, to develop a taste for getting in free to sports events all over the map.

3. Record reviewer for the *NME*.
I didn't necessarily understand the album reviews in the *NME*, especially the long, labyrinthine ones whose reference points and allusions went over my head and seemed to exist purely to plump up the word count. What I did understand though was that, if I joined the reviewing brethren, I'd get sent lots of records for free and get to hear them before hardly anyone else did. And that I'd have the power to make or break a band, simply from the words my fingers would choose to type out. For the first time when considering my dream career opportunities, I had slipped a furtive glance elsewhere, away from sport. There was more of this to come.

THE BARE NECESSITIES

DURING THE barren months of winter, with that summer's sun-kissed sporting action a distant dream away, TV sport addicts contented themselves by watching words on a screen. Words that, every so often, when something happened in a faraway sports stadium, might change slightly. There were no pictures, no video clips. Just words. And not that many of them. This was how we kept in touch with the action.

This lifeline had a name. It was called Ceefax.

Ceefax was, for those of too few years to have lived in a largely analogue world, the only way to stay abreast of live sporting action if it wasn't being broadcast on TV or on the radio. It was, as the journalist Barney Ronay has so perfectly framed it, 'the original horse-drawn internet'. It's another age away now, one far removed from today's world where, within a minute of a jaw-dropping goal being scored in Istanbul or Montevideo or Airdrie, someone will have posted a clip of it online for the entire world to see. Ceefax couldn't do that. While it did announce the latest significant development in a match pretty speedily, it came with the sketchiest of details. We had to make do with merely *imagining* what a goal – perhaps represented by the on-screen words 'Waddle, 32' or 'Speedie, 77' – looked like. A mazy dribble and cross-shot? A quickly taken free kick? An impudent lob from 35 yards over the head of an advancing keeper?

In a time where you might otherwise have to wait for the next morning's paper to find out the results, Ceefax was invaluable. It was bare, it was spare, but it served a crucial purpose. In his eulogy for the service after it passed away at the age of 38, Ronay celebrated it being 'courteously and brusquely non-interactive, unscarred by the current urge to embellish all with the legitimising babble of transient public opinion'. No analysis, no conjecture. The facts, the whole facts, and nothing but the facts.

Page 312 was my regular haunt. This was where the football news in brief lived, four or five revolving pages of titbits concerning the careers of people not important enough to have a page all to themselves. If Ceefax was a precursor of the internet, then page 312 was how we learned to love speculation and tittle-tattle, an obsession even stronger in the digital age with our online devotion to fast-spinning rumour mills and scurrilous gossip columns.

Page 312 was my first port of call whenever the TV went on to see if, for example, that much-rated Shrewsbury Town left back had been spirited away from Gay Meadow by a First Division club, or if last night's X-ray on the Leeds winger's leg had confirmed a clean break. I knew I was far from alone. We were a constituency. Every sporting occasion at the time had someone in the front row of the crowd holding up a makeshift cardboard placard with the biblical reference John 3:16 scribbled on it in marker pen. If that were me, my sign would say Ceefax 312. And many true believers catching sight of my placard while sitting at home would smile a smile of recognition and comradeship.

The eye-to-hand coordination of the PlayStation generation has surely advanced human evolution, with the fingers of gamers rarely pressing the wrong button on their handsets. But the seeds of this were clearly sown, and then passed down in the genes, by the children of the '80s, their thumbs unconsciously tapping out, on the TV remote, the number of their favourite Ceefax page.

I've just gone into the front room and picked up the remote, pretending to myself that it's 1987 and I need a quick hit of inconsequential, single-sentence news stories. My thumb finds 312 without engaging my brain. It's a muscle memory. Like riding a bike. Or instinctively re-enacting that Marco Tardelli celebration.

HISTORY REPEATING

I DON'T know why I did it. I hadn't done it before and I didn't do it again. But the experience was, well, absolutely fine.

On Cup Final Day 1987, I opted for the unthinkable. I watched the match on ITV.

Perhaps I felt I owed it to Brian Moore. Ever since John Motson's first Cup Final in 1977, the first one I sat down and watched properly, I'd stuck religiously to him and his microphone. Kept the faith. But after ten years, I fancied hearing an alternative sermon, being part of a different congregation. Or, perhaps I thought, having interpreted Moore's bald head as a sign of his advancing years, he might be retiring soon and I hadn't once heard him conduct the season's final showpiece. (He didn't retire soon. In fact, I've just checked and seen that he was actually only 55 at the '87 final.) Whatever my reasoning for the last-minute switch of channels – indeed, it may just have been an uncharacteristic whim – my experience of Spurs versus Coventry City was in Moore's hands. And he took great care of me.

It certainly helped that it was a fizzer of a game. Had it been a drab, attritional encounter, it might have required Motson and his stats book to liven things up, to drop in a particularly tasty fact for us to chew over for five minutes, our collective attention diverted from the average fare being served up. As it was, we got high action right from the off, with plenty of thrills, spills and goals. And no British commentator did thrills, spills and goals as well as Brian Moore.

He hit maximum volume after just two minutes when the Footballer of the Year nodded Spurs ahead for his 49th goal of the season. 'Clive Allennnnn!' Moore had barely got back to his normal speaking level when Coventry equalised. 'A chance for Bennett! And it's 1-1!'

The fast-flowing game was the equal of Moore's fast-flowing commentary. Both teams put their stall in pacy attack, an approach further enhanced by referee Neil Midgley's insistence on keeping his whistle in his pocket. He kept his cards in there too; not a single yellow was issued. His leniency was misguided at one point, though, when Gary Mabbutt was the victim of a tardy and agricultural challenge from Coventry captain Brian Kilcline. A red could have been justified, but not even a yellow was shown. It was certainly a more brutal foul than that carried out by Kevin Moran a couple of years before that had earned him that sending-off. This point wasn't missed by co-commentator Ron Atkinson, Moran's manager in the '85 final. The Irishman must have been spitting feathers back home in front of the box.

Being mown down by the grizzly bear Kilcline wasn't Mabbutt's only significant contribution. He reprised the Tommy Hutchison role from 1981, scoring for his side before deflecting one into his own net. Just a little bit of history repeating. In Hutchison's case, the repercussions had been limited; his misfortune only led to a replay. Mabbutt's own goal, though, won the Cup for Coventry, the ball slicing off his leg and looping over Ray Clemence's head. His agony wasn't contained to that one day. It lingered. For many years, the fans at Highfield Road were avid readers of the fanzine *Gary Mabbutt's Knee*.

It was a cruel way to decide the fate of the trophy. A far more fitting conclusion would have been for Keith Houchen's magnificent diving header, one that brought Coventry level for the second time, to have been the difference between the two teams. I'd always been a sucker for a diving header. It was an art form lesser seen, but when expertly executed – whether by Roberto Bettega for Italy against England to help deny them qualification for the '78 World Cup, or Frank Lampard Sr's Cup semi-final effort to send West Ham to Wembley in 1980 – it gave great pleasure. Houchen's was the pick of the bunch, though. That night, I caught the *Match of the Day* highlights to hear how Motson had described the goal. He did so in exclamatory, to-the-point fashion. 'Houchen! Brilliant goal!' I'd missed the old boy. His voice *was* the Cup Final.

Poor Brian Moore. He hadn't put a foot wrong all afternoon, not a word out of place, but I was still back in Reverend Motty's congregation the following year, the faithful parishioner returning to his regular front pew seat after the mildest theological wobble.

SOUL BOYS

THERE WAS one particular lyric, from one of 1987's totemic songs – Eric B and Rakim's 'I Know You Got Soul' – that was particularly resonant for me that year. Its simple message was profound for a teenager who was struggling for identity and who would soon be searching for his place in the wider world.

'It ain't where you're from, it's where you're at.'

Originally a line that declared how you weren't defined

by which New York borough you called home but instead by the mindset you'd adopted, it was a motto that could also be applied to anyone not wishing to be defined by growing up in a sleepy, soul-flattening, Tory-voting landscape. I took Rakim's lyric as some kind of single-line manifesto pledge. It was the fuel for my escape, the wind beneath my wings.

It was also how I came to justify my support for the Welsh national rugby team.

At the start of the decade, those odd-numbered years were a drag for the TV sport addict. Yes, there was all the annual action you could rely upon – the Wimbledons, the Cup Finals, the world indoor bowls – but no once-every-four-years tournaments that you could lose yourself in. Life was bereft of those intense, day-after-day-after-day affairs that made even-numbered summers so special.

The IAAF's introduction of the World Athletics Championships in 1983 formed a bridge across this void and, four years later, their counterparts on rugby's upper floors did likewise by bringing another new competition to our screens: the Rugby World Cup. Its first incarnation was to be held in Australia and New Zealand.

I was enjoying rugby a little more by then. It's unsurprising that you enjoy something more when it's not compulsory to participate in it – in this case, not having to become human cannon fodder, suffering punches and elbows and knees at the bottom of a pile of bodies. Broken bones, broken spirits.

The rules of union had sunk a little deeper into me by then, even if I was still perplexed by the odd unexpected blast of the referee's whistle for a misdemeanour I hadn't seen nor understood. One thing I definitely did know was that I found it hard to support the England rugby team. Perhaps it was the comprehensive schoolkid in me, but they didn't seem to be my kind of people. They appeared arrogant and untouchable, too easily reminiscent of the collars-up, sweaters-over-the-shoulders brigade I'd often encounter in local pubs (and later at university); those dullards who found no greater purpose in life than honking their approval whenever one of their number dipped his genitalia into his pint. Perhaps it was an unfair assessment on my part, but I tarnished each England player with the same brush – and did so even more when, the year after that first Rugby World Cup, Will Carling, the most collars-up of them all, emerged on the international scene.

I'd always enjoyed watching the Welsh at the tail end of the 1970s as the sun was setting on their extraordinary golden age – obviously the wily Gareth Edwards and the swashbuckling J.P.R. Williams in particular. And, of course, I couldn't fail to be moved by the way rousing renditions of 'Hen Wlad Fy Nhadau' charged a pre-match Cardiff Arms Park. I was already sympathetic to the cause. There was a unity, a sense of belonging, that seemed absent on the eastern side of Offa's Dyke. This only seemed to grow stronger into the 1980s. While Margaret Thatcher insisted that 'society' was a concept that didn't actually exist, the sense of community across the defiant South Wales heartlands that had come under such merciless attacks from the National Coal Board suggested otherwise. I could see that from a distance. I might not have been from Merthyr or Pontypool or Ammanford, but I grew to feel more affinity with these places than I did with the self-satisfied affluence that dotted large parts of my own patch. Elsewhere was where I was at.

I later married into a family of fiercely partisan Welsh rugby fanatics. Through them, it was apparent how rugby in Wales was the sport of the people; it was the ubiquitous talk of both the street corner and the tap room. It represented a large dollop of social glue and helped unify a population. And, with both my kids being born in Welsh Grand Slam years, the timing of their arrivals surely further cemented their connection with the land of their mother – although we did stop short of calling the first-born Shane.

The '80s equivalents of Gareth Edwards and J.P.R. Williams were an exciting bunch, their most mercurial player being the wonderful Jonathan Davies. This wasn't a man who'd glided through life. He hadn't trotted an easy path from public school to Oxbridge, a journey lubricated by privilege and expectation. He'd left school at 17 to become an apprentice painter and decorator, but rugby was his life, what would utterly define him. And he was the best rugby player I saw play in that entire decade.

Davies was brilliantly creative and devastatingly fast. During that first World Cup, he formed part of a superb backline, with Ieuan Evans and Adrian Hadley on the wings and the unerring place-kicker Paul Thorburn at full back, plus the zip and guile of Robert Jones at scrum half. They attacked at a pace that few defences could keep up with, at angles that others simply couldn't predict.

With my A-level exams just out of the way, I really connected with the tournament once it was in its knockout stages. Not that it required too much commitment. Simply avoid the score during the day and sink into the BBC2 highlights that evening, all described by Bill McLaren and Nigel Starmer-Smith down what still appeared to be a phone line. And it was all the better for sounding like that. (While I was pleased that this global celebration of muscle and force and athleticism wasn't being soundtracked by that quirky old *Rugby Special* theme tune, the music that the BBC had commissioned – nasty, easily dated synths married to some generic Antipodean motifs – left me cold. That would need to get fixed by the time of the next World Cup in 1991.)

Wales's march to glory Down Under felt irresistible, especially when they turned England over in the quarter-finals.

In the semi-final, though, they hit a wall – a wall consisting of 15 black-shirted New Zealanders that they couldn't get over or round or through. Nonetheless, they were taking home bragging rights having been the only home nation to reach the semis, and there was still the pride-saving matter of the third/fourth place play-off against Australia, who'd been beaten in Sydney by Daniel Dubroca's French side.

The encounter with Australia proved to be a terrific rugby match, arguably the most gripping I'd seen – and one given extra spice by the dismissal of Australian flanker David Codey in the very first minute. It was an even, full-bloodied encounter, with Wales pipping it by a single point, thanks to a last-ditch Hadley try in the corner and, naturally, an immaculate Thorburn conversion from the touchline. It wasn't a feat that would be replicated, though. Jonathan Davies switched codes a couple of years later and a new generation – exemplified by Rob Howley and the two Scotts, Gibbs and Quinnell – emerged. Accordingly, 1987 remains Wales's highest-placed finish in a World Cup. Thirty-plus years of hurt.

No matter. I never regretted siding with the Welsh, not even when England lifted the Webb Ellis Cup in 2003.

I knew they had soul.

THE CLIMBER

WATCHING AND appreciating sport is all about living vicariously through the achievements or disappointments of others, putting yourself in their shoes, boots or spikes. What would we have done had we just won that tournament? How would we celebrate? Stay ice-cool and just calmly soak it all in as if it were an everyday occurrence, or lose our heads and go flipping mental?

Football in the twenty-first century has seen the rise of the choreographed, pre-planned celebration, those annoying and embarrassing set-ups that players have spent way too much time preparing, time that fans would prefer their team's strikers to have spent developing a closer working relationship with the latest offside rule. Such celebrations leave me cold, and always have done, stripping away and devaluing any beauty the goal itself might have had. And there are the individual ones too. The heart shapes made with thumbs and forefingers. The rocking baby. The thumb-sucking. The skyward salute to an unspecified deity or presumably deceased loved one. These are celebrations born out of both duty and habit. Calculated, choreographed.

It's the spontaneous celebrations that properly touch the soul, those that find their practitioner lost in the moment, expressing the enormity of what has just happened. Like Charlie George lying flat on his back in the '71 Cup Final after scoring what would be Arsenal's winner. Or Bob Willis at Headingley in '81, wheeling around like a kid pretending to be an aeroplane, having just taken the last Australian wicket. Or Mike Powell's ecstatic sprint down the track after discovering he'd eclipsed Bob Beamon's 22-year-old long jump world record. These are the ones that history remembers.

And history certainly remembers Pat Cash.

The Australian charged through the 1987 Wimbledon men's singles championship like a man possessed. He dropped just one set throughout his passage to the final and, once there, swatted aside the world number one, Ivan Lendl, in straight sets. But the dominant recollection of that final concerns what happened after Cash hit the winning cross-court volley. Not a man renowned for an excess of convention (the earring, the chessboard headband, the spiky, shoulder-length hair), he partly wanted to escape the preparations for the formal presentations that were being carried out on the court, but mainly he wanted to share these moments of exhilaration with those that mattered up in the stands – his father, his coach, his girlfriend and his sister.

To reach them, Cash chose route one. The easiest, if more circuitous, way might have been to duck down into Centre Court's internal corridors and race up its stairways to re-emerge, blinking into the bright sunlight, in the box reserved for the players' families and friends. Instead, he decided on a little climbing expedition, making his way up via the rows of courtside seats. 'Maybe I should have planned it out clearly before I started heading off,' he later admitted. 'But I wasn't thinking too clearly then.'

Had he been forced to make a U-turn and return to the court without reaching his folks, Cash would have been remembered for history's most embarrassing celebration. But, having at one point stood on the shoulders of a priest (or, at least, someone masquerading as a man of the cloth), he scrambled onto the roof of Dan Maskell's commentary box and shifted himself across into the family and friends seating.

I wholeheartedly welcomed the fact that Pat Cash wasn't thinking too clearly that day. Instinct had kicked in and adrenalin was pumping through his veins so fiercely that any fear of failure – whether during the match or during the celebration – had completely dissolved. His wasn't the smoothest, swiftest ascent. It was ragged, but it was right. After all, sport isn't choreographed. It's improvised. And it's those improvised moments that make the biggest impact on memory – on what your brain retains, and why it does.

TWO WHEELS GOOD

IN THE summer of 1987, I waited for my A-level results without any impatience or nervousness whatsoever. I was sure

I had passed them. I'd set my academic sights so low that I only needed two E grades to send me on my way to a higher education college in North Yorkshire. I was calm and relaxed, and thought a summer spent gently tilling the land would be the perfect lyrical preparation for studying the rural landscapes of the works of Laurie Lee or Thomas Hardy.

It turned out that long days picking tomatoes in the stifling, high-summer temperatures of an enormous glasshouse was a circle of hell that Dante had neglected to mention. They were nine dragging weeks of insufferable heat and loose-change wages. A further obstacle was avoiding the snooping attentions of the nursery owner's young son. As the mercury inside the glasshouse hit the 100-degree mark, he was sent up to the top of the patch to report on exactly who was taking an unauthorised two-minute break to take on life-saving fluid or to rinse out their sodden T-shirt.

Techniques had to be drawn up to make all this torture remotely bearable. All manner of distraction was needed. Most of this came via the radio, unfailingly tuned to Radio 1 and turned right up as we worked our way up and down each row of super-sized tomato plants, stooping and sweating and swearing. The Mystery Year on Simon Bates's show played its part, as did Bits and Pieces, the daily music quiz on the Radio 1 Roadshow. Aside from that particular item, the roadshow was another glimpse of hell, not just down to the relentless cheesiness of whichever daytime presenter had been allocated to present it that particular week, but because all you could think about was those lucky dabs gathered on a beach somewhere, having to put up with the inanity of warm-up guy Smiley Miley but doing so while sucking on endless Cornettos and Strawberry Splits. I knew where I'd prefer to be. Give me the sands of Cromer or Skegness over the glasshouses of Sussex any day.

The afternoons brought a little relief if you were fortunate enough to be on packing duties. The work was dull and repetitive, but at least it was inside a brick-built shed, not a glass-panelled hothouse. A little respite in the shade. And each hour that passed was another hour closer to the pot of gold at the end of the rainbow, one that could be found in the same place at the same time every night. Channel 4, 6.30pm. The hour of the day's Tour de France highlights.

On my bike ride home, to help my weary legs to get me quicker into the clutches of commentators Phil Liggett and Paul Sherwen, I'd devised a game that anaesthetised me from the aching five-mile ride. For the next 15 or so minutes, I wasn't on my sit-up-and-beg butcher's bike negotiating the windy country lanes of Sussex. I was on the very latest Bianchi or Peugeot, heading to glory through the Loire or the Dordogne on that day's Tour de France stage. The rules of the game were simple. I started off in an arbitrary fifth place in the peloton. For every car that overtook me, I dropped back a place. For every car that passed me in the opposite direction, I gained a place. And, if I was hurtling along at a speed that meant I could actually overtake a car (usually a learner driver hitting the brakes when they saw me looming up in their rear-view mirror), I'd leap a full two places up the field.

Making it seem even more real, the voice of Liggett was forever in my head, every day urging me towards the first British stage win since Robert Millar three years before. Some days, Phil's imagined voice got impossibly excited as I powered along our street at journey's end to take the stage win. Mostly, though, he grew despondent as a trail of cars, driven by end-of-shift fruit and veg pickers from the surrounding nurseries, sped past me, dragging me back into the anonymity of the peloton and a slow ride home.

Halfway through that summer job, I started wearing contact

lenses. Up until that point, when I was on my bike playing my sad Tour de France game, my specs dictated that I'd have to take the part of Laurent Fignon, or that of the similarly bespectacled Irish *domestique* Martin Earley. By ditching the specs, I felt liberated. I could now be anyone I wanted to be. And that summer I wanted to be Stephen Roche.

Dubliner Roche was having a hell of a year. He'd already won the Giro d'Italia and was in very serious contention of taking the Tour as well (this he indeed did, before also winning the World Championship to complete a Triple Crown last achieved 13 years earlier by the incomparable Eddy Merckx).

Physically, it was a difficult ask to become Stephen Roche. I didn't have his dark curls, nor his doleful eyes. And I certainly didn't have a tenth of his brilliance on two wheels. But I was prepared to give the latter a go. And there was one day in particular from that summer's Tour that I wanted to replicate – to be in his saddle, to be in his cleats.

On Stage 21, Roche stood in second place overall, 35 seconds behind the Spaniard Pedro Delgado. Going into the day's final climb up to the Alpine resort of La Plagne, Delgado had increased his advantage, further marginalising the Irishman's hopes of repeating his Giro success. But, prior to the advent of race radios and without a TV camera on him, Roche gallantly came back at Delgado, appearing to have come out of nowhere. He lost just four seconds that day. Not that he realised when he crossed the line; oxygen had to be administered to him straight away.

Back on the flat, decidedly un-Alpine lanes of Sussex, if I had just one car to catch before I reached my own personal finishing line (the second lamppost on the right along our street), La Plagne was the Tour de France stage I'd re-enact. It was an instant classic, one done thorough justice by Channel 4's commentary that afternoon. Naturally, I recited it word for word as I took the last turn, anxious to minimise the – admittedly meaningless – deficit between me and the car in front.

'Just who is that rider coming up behind? Because that looks like Roche. That looks like Stephen Roche! It's Stephen Roche! He almost caught Pedro Delgado! I don't believe it!'

This was Phil Liggett's Kenneth Wolstenholme moment, the piece of commentary that, when he leaves us for the great bike race in the sky, no obituary will be able to leave out. There are few better examples of a commentator being in the same moment as the viewer, having the identical reaction at exactly the same millisecond. I might never have truly been Stephen Roche, but that afternoon Phil Liggett was definitely one of us.

REHEATED RATIONS

AS WELL as making me resolve to never undertake manual work again – at least not manual work that required slaving away in life-threatening temperatures that surely contravened employment law – that summer job had even more serious repercussions. For the first time that decade, I couldn't spend the summer watching Test matches for 20-odd eight-hour days. I'd have to make do with the evening highlights. Smaller rations. Reheated rations.

As it was, though, that was probably for the best. The Test series between England and Pakistan was flat and depressing from a home supporter's perspective. The first two matches were largely washouts before the tourists comfortably won the third Test by an innings in little more than three days, having twice bowled out England for under 200. Mike Gatting's men had a chance to take the fourth Test but, needing 124 from the final 18 overs, were pegged back by the veteran Imran Khan and the dashing young blade Wasim Akram, and were forced to cling on for the draw. The series victory for Pakistan was complete when they amassed 708 in their first innings of the fifth and final Test. Job very much done.

That wasn't it for international cricket, though. In October and November, India and Pakistan jointly hosted the World Cup, 28 matches that pitched together the eight best teams to fight it out to be proclaimed cricket's one-day kings. Surprisingly, though, neither of the hosts made it to the final. Instead, the old enemies – Allan Border's Australia and Mike Gatting-led England – were to fight it out at Eden Gardens in Kolkata, then Calcutta.

The BBC's live coverage started at 3.25am, with Tony Gubba (who else?) drawing the short straw of getting up at an ungodly hour on a Sunday morning in London to open proceedings before handing over to Tony Lewis, Ray Illingworth and Jack Bannister at the stadium.

I declined Gubba's kindly middle-of-the-night invitation, instead preferring to make it a breakfast meeting. It was a Sunday, after all. The news that greeted me wasn't fantastic. Australia had notched up 253 for five in their 50 overs, leaving England to score at a rate of more than five an over. This situation worsened when opener Tim Robinson went first ball. Progress was steady after that, via the bats of Graham Gooch, Bill Athey, Mike Gatting and Allan Lamb. Until, that is, Gatting greeted the first ball from makeshift bowler Border with a reverse sweep. The ball skied high into the air and landed in the safe haven of the wicketkeeper's gloves.

Installed in Botham's all-rounder role, Phil DeFreitas gave it a serious go, spraying the ball into various points of the gigantic, and packed, stands of Eden Gardens. But he fell with ten balls left, holing out to long off. England had the delicious challenge of scoring 17 off the last over. At least it would have been a delicious challenge had DeFreitas still been out in the middle, or some other recognisable batsman. Instead, it was the fast bowlers Gladstone Small and Neil Foster who were charged with performing this Herculean task. They swung their bats but it wasn't enough. The damage had already been done higher up the order. 'Some of the England batsmen will look at the decisive margin,' sighed Jack Bannister in the commentary box, 'and just wonder how they got out and why they got out and when they got out.'

It was the first of five World Cups to date that Australia have won. The seven-run defeat in '87 remains the closest England have ever come to getting their hands on the trophy. We continue to live in hope . . .

THE MOTHER OF REINVENTION

THAT I watched the Cricket World Cup from home, from my early-morning bedroom on the Ferguson TX, tells a story. I was still in Sussex, not North Yorkshire. The relaxed expectation I carried with me – that those A-level results would undoubtedly be granted – had been misplaced. The two E grades I needed turned into the one E grade I got. The life of the fancy-free undergraduate went on hold, the escape route up the East Coast Main Line blocked. And it had been blocked by no one else than me.

I had jacked in the paper round before taking the tomato-picking job and now, having enrolled at the local tech college to retake my exams (and, illogically, to even undertake two additional, *new* A-levels in just eight months), needed part-time work. A five-evenings-a-week job stacking supermarket shelves after college did the trick. The weekends stayed free. I couldn't give up *Grandstand* just yet, despite how it had led me astray the previous year.

After seven years at an all-boys comp, I was now sitting in classes with girls, girls whose academic work had also underwhelmed the external examiner the previous summer. I didn't necessarily know the reasons why they were also retaking, but it was obviously not because a bondage to TV sport had got in the way. My new classmates definitely weren't the kind of people with whom you could compare your scores on the quick-fire round of the previous evening's episode of *A Question of Sport*. Those with whom I'd previously had such conversations had largely disappeared off to higher education. For me, stuck at home, reinvention was needed to establish a different kind of credibility. The card-carrying TV sport nerd – or, at least, the public recognition that I was a card-carrying TV sport nerd – had to be left at my old school, a mile or so across town from my new seat of learning. This fresh cohort of pals, both male and female, need never know my anorak tendencies. That was now a private matter. A new public me would have to emerge. It was time to let the sunshine in.

The nerdish specs had gone too, of course. The spots were clearing up and, rather unconsciously, I was now sporting a decent quiff. With my growing ability to hold a conversation with the opposite sex without resorting to listing my top ten favourite pieces of sporting commentary, I was in danger of appearing – only *appearing*, grant you – a reasonably rounded individual. And all that despite still secretly spending plenty of waking hours worshipping at the altar of St Desmond of Lynam.

PULL UP TO THE BUNKER

FOR SEVEN years or so, Sunday nights had meant one thing: watching any old crap on the TV to put off doing the homework that was due in the following morning. The quality of both the writing and acting on *Ever Decreasing Circles* meant that the procrastination was perfectly justifiable for that half-hour, but the excuses were wearing thin by the time *Howards' Way* came sailing by. Yet still I favoured this laboured, clunky drama, populated by characters about whom I cared not one jot ('So you're not even going to put up a fight, Tom?' 'How can I when the surveyors have already found me guilty?') over improving my academic standing.

Howards' Way was the jewel in the BBC1 crown on the evening of Sunday 27 September 1987. This was a good reason to be tuned in to BBC2 instead. Another good reason was that Europe's golfers were just about to beat their American counterparts to secure their first-ever Ryder Cup on US soil.

Even better, it was a guilt-free watch. Having only recently started at the local tech college – and still revelling in the near-horizontal demeanour of my lecturers, all of whom insisted we call them by their first names and several of whom could be spotted in the nearest pub at lunchtime – there was no work outstanding that evening. With no essay question that needed answering, and no required reading I'd be quizzed about in class, my conscience wouldn't be poking me in the ribs every five minutes. From around 4.30pm onwards, on a specially extended *Sunday Grandstand*, with Harry Carpenter on presenter duties from the Muirfield Village course in Dublin, Ohio, I stretched out and sank right in.

I wasn't one for American courses; the weather was usually benign and invariable, and the holes were too manicured, too *designed*. Give me a windswept links course on the Lancashire coast any day of the week. But the pay-off of American tournaments was – and, indeed, still is – the time difference. We were watching into the night. It was a bonus, an extra helping of sport beyond what had been on the box that afternoon. And there was no time limit. It was open-ended, like a small hours world snooker final at the Crucible. It would take as long as it would take.

And, thanks to the BBC's priorities at the time, nothing would be allowed to get in its way. All other programmes pulled over to the hard shoulder to give the golf clear passage.

The European team were in a healthy position going into the third and final day, needing only four points from the day's 12 singles matches to retain the cup won two years earlier at The Belfry. If that did happen, it would be the first time the US had lost the Ryder Cup on home soil. Historic stuff.

It wasn't straightforward, though. As the day lengthened, the American team built up a head of steam and narrowed the gap as each pairing moved into the last few holes. Although my inner neutral appreciated a tight finish, my heart wanted Europe to humiliate their hosts. But a humiliation it wasn't going to be. Europe were clinging on as the US closed to within a point.

All that whooping and hollering from the galleries had got right on my wick over the previous days. This was why I wanted them to cop the full force of a European onslaught. More so – and this was a development I'd not taken on board in the past – those celebrations didn't just make their presence felt whenever one of their players hit a good shot. The American spectators whooped and hollered just as loudly whenever a European player landed in a bunker or fluffed a putt. If one of the visitors landed their ball within two feet of the pin, it was met by the weakest smattering of applause.

No class, no decorum.

You didn't get this so much in normal golf events. The patriotism, the 'us versus them' mentality, only seemed to kick in once players were brought together in a team and issued with the same sports-casual uniform. This meant the vast majority of the crowd were unified by a common goal; not watching objectively, nor loyally following the hole-by-hole exploits of one favourite player. There was nothing fundamentally wrong about this. This was a team competition, after all. The biggest team competition in all of golf. It was the lack of respect for their 12 opponents that got my goat.

After both the Zola Budd affair and Mary Peters-gate, those feelings of schadenfreude reappeared, making it difficult to suppress a chuckle when a petulant Ben Crenshaw broke his putter in frustration during his match against Eamonn Darcy. He had to putt with his one-iron for the rest of the round, ultimately losing to the Irishman by a single shot on the 18th. This was a crucial point for the visitors, one that slowed the American charge, and significantly staunched the Europeans' metaphorical blood loss.

Seve Ballesteros was the one to finally edge Europe over the line, his grin as wide as mine. The whooping and hollering was still very much audible. It was just that now it didn't come with an American accent.

IRON MAN

JUST AS some commentators get remembered for one line in particular they once uttered, sportspeople can also find their entire career boiled right down into a few seconds, a single moment, a snapshot. It might be a penalty miss or a sending-off, a title-winning try or a final-second drop goal. Something they'd always be remembered by.

For Sandy Lyle, it was the most glorious seven-iron shot he ever hit.

And it wasn't just the clean way it left the bunker, soared through the Georgia sky and landed beyond the flag, before slowly retracing its path towards the hole. It was all in the timing. It was all about the moment that Lyle had pulled that particular shot out of the bag. The final hole of the US Masters. A par for a play-off. A birdie needed for immortality.

Lyle had been leading the tournament since its second day but, as the shadows lengthened and the sunlight turned to gold on the final day, he was ready to deliver high drama. To be fair, the drama was largely of his own making. With a clear if not formidable lead at the turn, Lyle stuck his ball in the water at the 12th. The double bogey put him on the retreat, soon to be passed by both the muscular Mark Calcavecchia and Craig Stadler, a man who resembled a cross between a walrus and a redneck police chief straight out of Central Casting.

This pair were the crowd's favourites. Men of power, men of force. Men who could do little wrong. If they so much as sneezed, the assembled masses at the Augusta National would probably break out into another fit of unrestrained delirium. Imagine the volume, then, whenever they holed a long putt. The speaker on the Ferguson TX couldn't take it, this roar that would distort with ear-popping regularity whenever the Augusta crowd got excited in those last few holes. They got excited rather often.

But the brilliance of Sandy Lyle, retrieving his equilibrium from somewhere deep down inside after that double bogey, would quieten the galleries. The most elegant player of the three, he birdied the 16th to tie with Calcavecchia, making a play-off the most likely scenario. I would have normally been wholeheartedly in favour of that. At least another hour of nail-nibbling tension. Extra bang for our bucks. But I was also desperate for Lyle not to lose, to not be immortalised as the man who had choked, who had meekly surrendered when the bigger boys came along. His career-defining shot couldn't be the one that put his ball in the water hazard.

Thankfully, it wasn't. The bunker shot on the 18th – the one that set up the title-winning birdie, the one that effectively anointed him as Britain's first Masters champion – would become his everlasting calling card, the most famous stroke he'd ever play, the one everyone still wants to talk about.

RED SEVEN

THERE ARE several totemic symbols connected with Liverpool Football Club. The small but legendary boot room on which the dynasty is founded. The passive-aggressive 'Welcome to Anfield' sign in the players' tunnel. And then there's the number seven shirt, the fabled jersey worn by gods.

Liverpool's shirt numbering wasn't a slave to convention. Ray Kennedy wore number five but didn't play a single match at centre half. Steve Heighway almost always had number nine on his back, despite operating as a 'get to the byline' winger rather than a goal-poaching centre forward. And the number seven shirt wasn't reserved for the right-winger, as it would be at most other First Division clubs. Instead, it seemed to be reserved for whoever was their current best player.

Over the course of six seasons on Merseyside, Kevin Keegan made it his own, transforming himself from Fourth Division hopeful to European Cup winner. If it was a tough shirt to fill when he joined in 1977, Kenny Dalglish didn't feel the pressure. As Keegan's replacement, he in fact forged a legend even deeper and more profound.

By 1988, with Dalglish's playing career fading away while he increasingly filled his time with management duties, the number seven was handed to its next guardian. That that player was the just-signed Peter Beardsley – to my mind, the best English footballer of the 1980s – did the tradition justice. He was worthy of the accolade. The master had named his heir and the circle went unbroken.

Beardsley's finest 90 minutes in a Liverpool shirt, in *that* Liverpool shirt, were surely during the league game against Nottingham Forest at Anfield on 13 April 1988. It was quite possibly Liverpool's finest ever 90 minutes too.

I was just back home from my shelf-stacking evening job when *Sportsnight's* opening titles cranked into action. In his introduction, Steve Rider teed the match up as something very special. That was an invitation you couldn't ignore. I quickly fixed myself a bowl of cornflakes and perched on the edge of the sofa. For the next 30 or so minutes, my dad and I were just purring.

I was only five at the time of the 1974 World Cup, so I never got to see the Dutch team's masterclasses in 'Total Football'. By the '78 tournament, and without Johan Cruyff (who, 30 years later, revealed his absence was due to his family receiving kidnapping threats), the Dutch, to my young eyes at least, placed less emphasis on fluid interplay and were more reliant on Arie Haan scoring outrageous goals from ridiculous distances.

You can't have gradations of absoluteness, but on that particular Wednesday night at Anfield, Liverpool played football perhaps even more totally than the Dutch had in their mid-70s prime. Their players interlocked and interchanged in a way I'd never seen before. Everyone seemed to be everywhere. And everyone seemed to know where everyone else was.

While it was a performance to which every player contributed energy and pace and precision, it was the twinkle-toed pixie Beardsley who was at the heart of all that happened, more than ably assisted by his lieutenants John Barnes and Ray Houghton. Beardsley forced great saves from Steve Sutton, he hit the bar, and he scored Liverpool's sumptuous fourth. But his most dazzling moment was the most delicious, eye-of-the-needle 50-yard through ball to release John Aldridge for the first of his two goals. I'm happy to declare it to be one of the passes of the century – and this is coming from a Hoddle acolyte. Eleven days earlier, at the corresponding fixture at the City Ground, Beardsley hadn't even made the starting line-up.

'The Liverpool anthem booms out again,' noted John Motson in the dying minutes as the Kop choir broke into a lusty recital of 'You'll Never Walk Alone'. The 5-0 victory had put them within a point of the title. 'It surely hasn't saluted a more complete side than this.' I had studied several different Liverpool teams and had to agree with him. This was no 'caught up in the moment' judgement. You just instantly knew how very, very special this display had been. And it wasn't just 19-year-old lads like me saying so. After the game, the BBC interviewed Tom Finney. He wasn't green behind the gills, but his conclusion unequivocally chimed with mine nonetheless: 'The spectators here saw an exhibition tonight that'll never be bettered.'

The verdict was unanimous; the non-Liverpool quarters were especially effusive. 'No one could have competed against them,' conceded Forest chairman Maurice Roworth whose own side, finishing third in the league, were no slouches. 'They are the best team in Europe, which is why they are not in Europe. They are too good.'

That, of course, wasn't why they weren't in Europe. But it is a sad irony that the heights this particular team was hitting coincided with arguably the most tortured period in the club's history, three years on from Heysel and one year before Hillsborough. They never had the opportunity to test themselves against the cream of the continent, never had the chance to match the achievements of the side half a generation older than them.

There was one test for them still to come. A month and a day later, Liverpool faced the ankle-biting mongrels from Wimbledon in the FA Cup Final. The footballing philosophies couldn't have been more contradictory. Such was the flow and brilliance of Dalglish's team that I dispensed with my usual neutral's support for the underdog and chose instead to roar Liverpool on towards their second Double in three seasons. I was to be out of luck, with Lawrie Sanchez's goal and Dave Beasant's penalty save denying this super-slick Liverpool side their deserved prize for a season of domination and delight. Motson's final-whistle line lives long: 'The Crazy Gang have beaten the Culture Club.'

DURKHEIM AND THE DOUBLE BAGEL

STEFFI GRAF really, really wanted me to pass that sociology A-level.

It was Saturday afternoon, the eve of the eve of my next exam. I'd been really diligent. Unusually so. My head had been lost in a pile of revision notes and textbooks since 9am. No distractions, no diversions. I'd even ignored the previews to the upcoming European Championship that both Bob Wilson and *Saint & Greavsie* had served up at lunchtime. Missing those would have been heresy just 12 months back.

But I was on my last life. I was using my 'Get out of Jail Free' card, the passport to not be anchored to the same home town for ever. After the famous A-level debacle of 1987, this was it. I had to pass. And I had to pass with some decent grades. This time, I needed more than two E's. Way, way more. A month of head-down, eyes-out revision with all – well, almost all – TV sport removed from my schedule. Cold turkey.

I could have ignored the women's singles final of the French Open. I could have pressed on and on with reading and re-reading and re-rereading until my eyes went square, at which point the words in the Michael Haralambos classic *Sociology Themes and Perspectives* would have morphed into indecipherable hieroglyphics that lost all meaning and significance. I needed a break, I told myself. Yes, I needed a break. A screen break. A break from the books by staring at the screen.

Also, the nerdy sports historian inside of me knew the significance of the next hour or two and insisted I watch it to witness history unfurling. That day's match was to be the first women's Grand Slam final since 1981 at which neither Martina Navratilova nor Chris Evert would be striding out onto court, such was their domination of women's tennis for two-fifths of my life. This was a potentially epoch-ending moment, the baton leaving their hands and being lunged for by the new generation, represented that afternoon by Germany's Steffi Graf and the Belarussian Natasha Zvereva, at the time playing under the Soviet flag. As it turned out, only one of them made a grab for glory that afternoon.

As the pair warmed up on the rust-coloured clay of the Stade Roland-Garros, with its seating stretching up impossibly high into the heavens, I cast aside the collected wisdom of Emile Durkheim and stretched out on the bed in front of the faithful Ferguson TX portable, still offering great service five years into its overworked life. A little guilt did linger at the edges, but Durkheim, Weber and the others would understand. I'd be back in their company soon enough.

As it was, it didn't take long for any remaining guilt to dissolve into the warm June air. Steffi Graf was making her claim for the throne and was in no mood to hang around. Zvereva was being blasted away. A slow, unwinding, extended final, such as those trademarked by Borg and McEnroe at the start of the decade, this wasn't. The first set flashed by in the blink of an eye. The second set zipped past just as quickly. Graf hadn't shown the common decency of letting her opponent win a single game. She only allowed her 17 points in the entire match. Thirty-two minutes was all it took. I was vindicated. History had indeed struck that afternoon. 6-0, 6-0. The first double bagel in a Grand Slam final during the Open era.

In casting aside Zvereva, Steffi Graf had reserved all her decency for me. She had made her grab for the crown in the quickest, most ruthless way possible. In doing so – deliberately, I always felt – she'd ensured that there had been minimal disruption to my revision regime. Little more than half an hour after that screen break started, I was back at the desk, nose-deep in the textbook, trying to tell my *gemeinschaft* from my *gesellschaft*.

Two months later, notification of the required B grade came through the letterbox. University now beckoned, an escape route without which I wouldn't have met my future wife, without whom my future kids would never have existed.

She helped make my life, Steffi Graf. Wherever she is, I'm sure she knows.

MR TANGERINE MAN

THE REWARD for the most intensive academic year of my life would take a full 16 days to completely unwrap.

Aside from a keenly observed lunchtime ritual that involved a pint of Courage and a game of bar billiards in the old men's pub near college, all weekday daylight hours had, for the last eight months, been committed to reversing my academic woes. This unstinting regime deserved a good pay-off. And it got it. As soon as those words rang out in my final exam – 'Please put down your pens' – and before a summer job tied to a supermarket checkout kicked in, there was the not insignificant matter of football's European Championship. This was my reward. I had no agenda other than watching each and every match. Tough life.

The best matches involved the best team: the Netherlands. The '88 incarnation played rather as I imagined the class of '74 had. Fluid and flowing. In Ruud Gullit, they had their Cruyff, the player around whom the rest of the team would pivot. And in Marco van Basten, they possessed a striker in the form of his life. Like a pear, he ripened at exactly the right moment.

Van Basten hadn't started the first match, a disappointing single-goal defeat to the Soviet Union, but he played almost a full 90 minutes in their second game – a 3-1 victory over England. He scored all three. Merciless, clinical. That performance, from both team and man, buried an England side that had already suffered its first defeat to the Republic of Ireland in 40 years, thanks to that collector's item – a header from the less-than-towering Ray Houghton. England, give or take a couple of changes in the centre of defence, were largely the same team that had given us plenty of joy in Mexico two years earlier, but their customary slow start to a tournament had ensured they'd dug their own grave. A third defeat, to the Soviets, meant a giant points tally of exactly zero.

The Netherlands, however, were far from pushing up the daisies. A second victory, this time in an all-to-play-for, winner -makes-the-semi-finals encounter against the Republic, took them to a monumental tie in Hamburg, one loaded with historical significance and poignancy. Their opponents? West Germany.

It wasn't the first time in recent years that two countries, their relationship pockmarked by military conflict, had met at the knockout stage of a major football competition. In Mexico, of course, England had met Argentina, just four years after the Falklands War. Afterwards, Maradona admitted that revenge had been very much at the forefront of the collective mind of his team. 'Although we had said before the game that football had nothing to do with the Malvinas War, we knew they had killed a lot of Argentine boys there, killed them like little birds.' Casualties were felt close to home. José Ardiles, the air force pilot cousin of Maradona's former international teammate Ossie, had lost his life when his plane had been shot down.

The Netherlands taking on West Germany was a fixture as scarred by history as sport got this side of the Middle East. This was no mere cross-town rivalry, such as you'd find in domestic football; this wasn't just catcalling across city neighbourhoods. The 1940 Battle of the Netherlands, and the subsequent Dutch surrender, brought about five years of German occupation, during which more than 200,000 civilians, many of them Jewish, were killed. In peacetime, the scars had faded a little. But they were still there, still visible.

The two sides had played each other in the postwar period, of course. And they had played each other on German soil in a tournament since, too: the 1974 World Cup Final. But perhaps it was the confluence of military history, of that mid-70s defeat in Munich, and the manner in which Germany took the lead in Hamburg that evening in 1988 that made this encounter particularly spiky. Under very little pressure from Frank Rijkaard, Jürgen Klinsmann went flying, twisting wildly in mid-air like a determined salmon heading upstream. Like a determined salmon hit by sniper fire, in fact. Actually, like a determined salmon hit by sniper fire but which had also been electrocuted for good measure.

Lothar Matthäus fired home the penalty. After the events at the Azteca Stadium two summers earlier, my sense of justice felt as if it were about to be betrayed again. But then the Netherlands were awarded an equally soft penalty. Two injustices appeared to make a right. Ronald Koeman. 1-1.

It was then up to van Basten – the tangerine man shortly to be awarded the Golden Boot – to score the winner, offering both euphoria to the Dutch and a recalibration of my moral compass. It was clear what the victory meant to the Netherlands, even if it wasn't overtly expressed by too many in their party. Rinus Michels was largely the only one who was happy to hint at the significance of the win in non-footballing terms. The team manager – and the architect of the concept of Total Football – had a similar world view as Maradona over the separation of sport from wider society. Or, rather, how they weren't, and how they couldn't be, split into two stand-alone entities. It was exactly the point I had tried to make with that Zola Budd essay. After the game, Michels admitted that he was experiencing 'an extra feeling of satisfaction for reasons I don't want to sum up now'. His words were cloaked in very little ambiguity. Nothing was lost in translation.

It was a seismic victory – and not just because it put the Dutch in another major championship final. 'Back in Holland,' the author Simon Kuper wrote, 'the staid nation surprised itself: nine million Dutchmen, over 60% of the population, came out onto the streets to celebrate. Though a Tuesday night, it was the largest public gathering since the Liberation.'

Their true 'Victory in Europe' celebrations kicked in a few days later in the final. It was their second match in the competition against the Soviets, who had sent Italy packing in the other semi-final. Gullit, imperious throughout the tournament, emphatically headed them in front, before the second half witnessed the most sublime goal of the entire decade – after Maradona's in Mexico City, at least. It was that man van Basten again, connecting with Arnold Mühren's deep, hanging cross with a sumptuous volley from an impossibly tight angle. John Motson was incredulous. We all were. How on earth had he hit the ball with such pace and precision from that position?

Perhaps we needed to persuade Ebenezer Skeet out of retirement to explain the geometrical reasoning underpinning the goal. No matter how many times we watched the replay, no one could understand just how van Basten had made the impossible possible.

OPEN SEASON

WATCHING THE 1988 Open at Royal Lytham & St Annes was, for me, a perfect storm: an irresistible final-round charge to glory from Seve Ballesteros, and the BBC's chief commentator

Peter Alliss on effortlessly sublime form. The fact that a day had been lost to the weather, precipitating the first-ever Monday finish in the competition's history, was not a problem for me. I was, once again, currently occupying the doldrums between exams and summer job. Yeah, I could do Monday, no problem.

From the sound of it, Alliss didn't mind the extra day either. He was his usual laid-back, informal self, albeit an informality that still had professionalism and discipline as its backbone. Occasionally, though, he could slip into cliché. 'The paella's on me!' he said, seemingly without a tinge of embarrassment, after Ballesteros birdied the eighth. I suppose you could forgive Alliss. After all, Ballesteros's phenomenal final round was using up the superlatives; he hit five birdies and an eagle in eight mid-round holes.

Alliss redeemed himself later when Ballesteros's approach shot at the 16th landed just a couple of inches from the cup. 'Oh, look at that. This hole is certainly the one that Seve will remember all his life.' The hole had also been a defining one when he won there in 1979.

The surge of spectators down the final fairway of an Open Championship is one of the great sights of British sport, a tide of people eating up the ground like a relentless springtime tidal bore. Despite the thinner Monday crowds, the cheers, whistles and applause were among the strongest heard at the Open, saluting the ever-popular, soon-to-be-three-time champion. The commentators put down their mics, soaking in Ballesteros's welcome. When he almost chipped in from the edge of the green, it got even louder. The realisation, the grin, the win.

Alliss opted for brevity and function, largely letting the moment speak for itself. He knew there was no need to overpower the moment of victory.

'In she goes. Sixty-five strokes. Seve is once more the champion.'

THE OTHER ELTON

IN 1988, the *Match of the Day* theme tune fell silent – for league games at least. Until then, the BBC and ITV had shared rights for First Division matches but, with Rupert Murdoch expressing a preference for taking live league matches off terrestrial screens, ITV had to act. Their successful bid of £44 million over four years was the deal that began the television revolution in English football; the previous deal was a two-year arrangement costing just £6.2 million, a cost shared between ITV and the BBC.

With the deal came some slight rebranding. *The Big Match* became *The Match*. It no longer needed to qualify its size against the output of others. It was now the only show in town.

With live matches now a fixture of Sunday afternoons, Elton Welsby was thrust forward as the face, the main man, of ITV football. He wasn't flash but he was decidedly polished – suited, booted and rarely without a light tan. He was definitely 'ITV'. You couldn't see him as a potential future defector to the BBC, following the route Steve Rider had taken in 1985. He didn't quite have the gravitas for the corporation. And he was cutting a more deliberate career plan: early in his career, he'd ditched his birth name of Roger in favour of the marginally more rock n roll Elton, and later he'd find himself doubling up as the presenter of the gameshow *Busman's Holiday*.

For the four years of the ITV contract, Welsby was in command of his own destiny. To many, he epitomises televised football of that particular time. Once Sky and the Premier League revolutionised the way the game was presented, and the BBC took the terrestrial rights, Welsby retreated back to regional sports programmes and the after-dinner speaking circuit. His career traced a slightly Partridgean parabola.

Indeed, one of the fictional guests on the radio incarnation of *Knowing Me Knowing You* had once described the host as 'the non-thinking man's Elton Welsby'.

THE BREAKFAST CLUB

TO SET the alarm or to set the video?

As South Koreans headed to lunch on Saturday 24 September, Californians were sitting down for their Friday night dinner. In the UK, we were between those meals, between those two time zones. It was the hour officially known as 'the middle of the bloody night'. So, as the eight sprinters contesting the men's Olympic 100m final filed out into the middle-of-the-day heat of Seoul, North American TV viewers had it comparatively easy. Kick back with a post-work beer and take in the spectacle of track and field's heavyweight clash: Ben Johnson taking on the defending champion Carl Lewis.

In comparison, European viewers had to put the effort in – and had to make do with pre-dawn coffee. The Olympic organisers' scheduling clearly evaluated, probably correctly, the North American prime-time audience to be the more valuable. This placed British sport fans in a quandary. You could either put your trust in the video machine doing exactly what you had programmed it to do (this was never, ever a given), or set the alarm for somewhere before 4am to watch the event live. There was only one correct answer, of course. You had to witness history at the moment it was made.

Everything pointed in the direction of big history, that this might be one of the most significant races in nearly a century of the Olympics in their modern form. The contest was universally viewed as a two-horse affair between the muscular, barrel-chested powerhouse Johnson and the defending champion

Lewis, a leaner man who, when in full flow, appeared to float above the track. Both looked in peak condition: Lewis had twice gone below the ten-second mark in reaching the final, while Johnson had survived being flagged for a hairline false start in his semi to effortlessly power his way into the final eight.

As the author Richard Moore would later write, the other six sprinters were 'extras, with walk-on, non-speaking parts'. Back in the UK, the bleary-eyed who were gathering before their TV sets, that strong coffee in their hands, hoped that Linford Christie might put in a performance that was slightly above that of an extra, that he might take the bronze.

When the starter's gun cracked, Johnson and Lewis were out of their blocks together. After 50 metres, though, it seemed as though there was a problem with the feed from Seoul, as if the pictures bouncing off satellites weren't behaving themselves. The race looked speeded up. Or, rather, Johnson alone looked speeded up. The rest were at 'normal' speed, the speed of mere mortals, trailing in his wake, eating his cinders. There was silent shock when the Canadian broke the tape. 9.79 seconds. A new world record. A beyond-human world record. And, as we observed and Johnson later confirmed, he could have gone quicker. In the last few strides, he began to decelerate, raising his right arm in salute and looking across towards Lewis's lane. Big history, indeed.

The time seemed hyper-real and, strong coffee or not, took a while to sink in. Our last Sunday cricket match of the season had been brought forward 24 hours and, as we gathered at the ground that lunchtime, the whole team still seemed somewhat stunned by what had happened at dawn. There was only one topic of conversation among the bags-under-the-eyes players. And even then the conversation wasn't exactly the most erudite or illuminating.

'So, 9.79.'

'Yeah, 9.79.'

An expulsion of air to indicate incredulity.

'Nine. Seven. Nine.'

Three days later, Des Lynam broke the news. 'I've just been handed a piece of paper here which, if it's right, it'll be the most dramatic story out of these Olympics or perhaps any others. It says: "Ben Johnson of Canada has been caught taking drugs and is expected to be stripped of his 100m gold medal, according to International Olympic Committee sources."'

I was crushed. It didn't matter that Linford Christie's bronze-winning performance would now be upgraded to silver. It mattered that the purity of the Olympic ideal – or, at least, my perception of its purity – was tarnished, sullied, spoiled. I was five days away from leaving home for university, five days left as an inbetweener. I had wanted to shut the dirty adult world out until the last possible moment, but it had made its presence felt a little earlier than announced.

The fraud of the rings.

GOING WITH THE FLO

BEN JOHNSON took most of the headlines during those Olympics, first dominating the back pages for the sensational time he clocked before shifting onto the front pages as newspaper editors amplified the scorn and shame of the failed drugs test. After the announcement, his story overshadowed, and partly obscured, that of another sprinter, one whose astonishing performances in Seoul would have been the take-home tale of another Games. That she never got the wholehearted acclaim that she deserved was just one of the tragedies of Florence Griffith Joyner, the woman known the world over as Flo Jo.

In 1988, she was as dominant, and her breakthrough as swift, as Usain Bolt would be 20 years later. Flo Jo was supreme from the moment she first set foot on the Seoul track, breaking the Olympic 100m record in her opening heat. She then broke it twice more on her way to taking gold the day after the men's race. It was a weekend that belonged to two athletes so far ahead of their respective packs, the fastest man and the fastest woman to have ever lived.

The aftershocks of the Johnson affair were still rocking the foundations of the Olympic movement when Flo Jo's assault on the 200m title started a few days later. This was the crown she really craved – and she wanted it in style, by taking both gold and the world record, at that point shared by the East German pair Marita Koch and Heike Drechsler. One of these she achieved in the semi-final, benefiting from a 1.7m/s tailwind to register what David Coleman memorably described as 'a world record without any effort at all'. She then reduced it by a further two-tenths of a second in the final. But she wasn't done yet. Another gold in the 4x100m relay, plus a silver in the 4x400m, made her the first female track athlete to take home four medals from a single Games.

Fuelled in part by the events on the men's side, the rumour mill cranked into action. If a male sprinter could only dominate his cohort through use of pharmaceuticals, the logic went, then how could his female equivalent, whose margin of superiority was even more pronounced, achieve what she had without recourse to chemical assistance? Lending weight to the whispering campaign was the fact that Flo Jo hadn't shown anything like this kind of speed throughout a career that had at one point been set aside in favour of a job as a bank teller with a sideline in doing people's hair and make-up during the evenings. Her form had only arrived during that 1988 season. Earlier in the year, she took nearly half a second off her personal best for the 100m at the US Olympic Trials. 'She really is a transformed athlete,' said Coleman after that world record in the 200m semi in Seoul.

This transformation had come through a change in emphasis in her training. Under the advice of her new coach – her husband Al Joyner – Flo Jo elected to place more focus on muscle development. By the time she arrived in Seoul, she was quite a physical specimen, her long legs pumping like well-oiled pistons, while those extended fingernails, each decorated with its own design, gave her genuine star quality.

But the fact that she abruptly retired from the track the following February, along with the announcement of her premature death in 1998 at the age of just 38, kept the doubters doubting. I had absolute sympathy for her, though. Maybe, after Johnson, I *had* to believe. But it wasn't just my faith in her that should have silenced the critics. She never once failed a drugs test – and she was extensively tested in Seoul by Olympic officials desperate not to have a duplicate drugs case on their hands.

Flo Jo was simply a one-off. The fastest woman in history. Her records still stand today.

THE GOLDEN HOUR

I ALSO had a lot of sympathy for Peter Elliott during the Seoul Olympics. I had a lot of sympathy for Peter Elliott throughout his entire career, actually. He was my favourite of all that decade's highly decorated British middle-distance runners. While, like Flo Jo, he had a distinctive, individual look (luminous yellow spikes and spiky copper-coloured hair), he was the polar opposite of the Californian when it came to his character traits. He was discreet, self-effacing, shy almost.

Even his running style, with his arms down by his sides rather than pumping furiously at chest height, seemed timid and unsure.

In Seoul, Elliott finally got what he deserved: an Olympic medal. In 1984, he had controversially failed to be selected to represent Britain in the 1500m in Los Angeles, despite beating Coe at the AAAs Championships in the unofficial 'run-off' for the vacant final berth. Coe's seniority – and the fact that he was the reigning Olympic champion, to be fair – had got him the nod and that had narked me. Elliott had proved his worth back then but couldn't force the door open. He seemed to be forever the fourth man of Britain's middle-distance gang, a man invariably, and perhaps disparagingly, referred to by broadcasters in the context of his home town and his trade. Too many commentaries contained the phrase 'the Rotherham joiner', rather than referencing his many achievements on the track.

Four years later in Seoul, with Coe and Ovett beyond their prime and unable to convince the selectors to be included (even Coe's luck had run out by then), this was Elliott's chance. And he took it, putting in a brave, kerb-hugging performance to secure silver in the 1500m behind Kenya's Peter Rono. I was absolutely delighted, but my cheers failed to drown out David Coleman's post-race analysis. Not only had he concentrated a great deal on Steve Cram throughout his race commentary – what he was going to do and when he was going to do it – but he also busied himself with discussion of Cram's fourth place before celebrating Elliott's silver. 'Cram walks away without a medal.' Yes, David. And Elliott walks away *with* one.

Silver was as good as it got for Britain's athletes in Seoul. After the three golds in Los Angeles, there were none this time around. Plenty of bridesmaids, though; Colin Jackson, Liz McColgan, Fatima Whitbread, Linford Christie (after a fashion) and the men's 4x100m squad all contented themselves with their respective second places. In fact, the BBC producers had little reason to reprise the back catalogue of Spandau Ballet that year. There were just five British gold medals across all 21 sports. Shooting, sailing and rowing took one each, as did swimming, when Adrian Moorhouse became the third British man in four Olympics to take breaststroke gold.

There was one other British success in Seoul. And it was one that unfolded over a two-week period, giving the nation a full fortnight to fall in love with the medal winners and their sport.

The Great Britain men's hockey team had made itself known to the nation four years earlier in Los Angeles, where they had gallantly taken bronze. It was in south-east Asia, though, where they would make their own indelible contribution to Olympic history. Their passage to the final stages of the competition was relatively smooth, with only a couple of stumbles before a magnificent do-or-die 3-0 victory over the much-fancied India in the last round-robin match.

Once the competition reached the knockout phase, the nation began to become gripped. After the England football team's abysmal showing at the European Championship, we needed it. Obviously I'd been gripped from the start, but not everyone was occupying that glorious dead zone between receiving decent A-level results and packing their bags for university. The summer shifts in the supermarket had dried up so, other than time spent buying a couple of cook-for-one recipe books and trying to pin down exactly which 50 albums I'd take away with me in order to educate my new flatmates, it was wall-to-wall Olympics for me.

Over that fortnight, we as a nation became increasingly familiar with these new heroes. Even now, I can still remember which clubs they played for back home and what their occupations were. The goal machine Sean Kerly, the team's own Gary Lineker, played for Southgate, as did their creative force Stephen Batchelor, while goalkeeper Ian Taylor was an East Grinstead man and flying winger Imran Sherwani played for Stourport. Sherwani, I can confidently tell you, was a policeman at the time, Taylor a teacher and captain Richard Dodds a qualified doctor. That they had regular jobs offered a shortcut to getting us on board, to securing our support for a sport most knew little about. They were regular Joes and we were witnessing the high-water mark of their sporting careers – this second life away from their usual day-to-day, whether that be apprehending criminals, handing out lunchtime detentions or scrubbing up for the next medical procedure.

Two men guided us through the competition, their incisive, insightful commentaries a winning blend of knowledge and openness. Nigel Starmer-Smith was our man for the semi-final against Australia, formidable opponents who'd already given the usually strong Pakistan a 4-0 walloping. The semi was a terrific match, probably the best the GB team had played in the entire tournament, with Sean Kerly's hat-trick ensuring a 3-2 win. Starmer-Smith's words told it like it was to the breakfast-time audience back home. He was caught in the moment too: 'That reverse-stick flick-back I'll never forget,' he cooed.

His colleague out in Seoul was Barry Davies. In the ongoing Motson or Davies quandary, he had an advantage that swung people in his favour. Motson was a one-sport pony, a man who worked the August-May shift, as well as tournament summers, but always in the service of football. Davies was a round-the-clock, round-the-calendar presence. Like Starmer-Smith, he was versatile and could shape-shift. As the nation's football pitches fell fallow in the close season, he headed for SW19 and an annual two-week booking marshalling the mic on Wimbledon's outer courts. He also called the shots for the BBC's coverage of badminton and gymnastics.

Davies had been given the mic for the hockey final – against another bitter sporting enemy, West Germany – and it was then that he made his most notable contribution to non-football sport commentary. It was a rare, but delightful, show of bias on his part, expressing a sentiment we were all feeling when the third GB goal went in. He knew his audience. 'Where were the Germans? And, frankly, who cares?'

After the titanic battle against Australia, that 3-1 win in the final – featuring two goals from Sherwani – curiously felt like it was always going to happen. The result seemed a foregone conclusion, possibly because it had the weight of a nation willing it to. Not that this ever happened in international football tournaments, though. Never before – at least not outside of a one-sided Liverpool title campaign – had I sensed a sporting outcome to be so inevitable. Perhaps it was the red shirts that recalled a certain afternoon in 1966, but doubt had no place in our hearts that particular Saturday. The golden hour.

The hockey boys had won gold on the first day of October, the day before I was due to depart for a new life in higher education, the day before I was leaving home. Imran, Sean and the rest had given me one final Boy's Own story with which to sign off childhood.

A LITTLE MORE CONVERSATION

WHILE THOSE recipe books and those 50 records successfully made it into the boot of my parents' car that October Sunday for the drive across the country, my cherished Ferguson TX – that loyal companion through thousands of hours of sporting agony and ecstasy – kept its position at home.

It wasn't a matter of space. I could have happily spent the

three-hour journey with it perched on my lap if I'd had to. It was that I had deliberately left it behind.

I'd left it behind for a reason. Even I knew that burying myself away in my student room, chained to a 14-inch box to get my around-the-clock hit of televised sport, wasn't a healthy regimen for someone now purporting to be an adult. Nor was it what I was coming to university for. I envisaged a new life where conversation was king; where, by candlelight, young undergraduates talked through the night about Cartesian dualism or the future of the novel. This might have been happening in the quads and cloisters of Cambridge's colleges but, 50 miles to the south-east, in the tower blocks of Essex University's concrete jungle, it most certainly wasn't.

But I did find a social outlet; one that required me to interact with other human beings, to leave the security blanket of solitary confinement. For the next two years' worth of Saturdays (during term-time, at least), I did something that the 11-year-old me, the 14-year-old me and even the 17-year-old me would have viewed as heresy. I largely left *Grandstand* well alone.

The reason? I'd handed Saturdays over to rock 'n' roll, signing up as a member of the university ents crew.

I stayed off the telly for nearly a month. It was easy. I didn't have one in my room. Then, on the last Sunday of October, a drizzly day where, from our 12th-floor flat in a campus tower block, you could barely see through the mist to the ground floor, I caved in. Still bleary-eyed from working into the small hours at the gig the night before (either Steel Pulse or The Men They Couldn't Hang), and showing extreme reluctance to pay the campus launderette my second visit of term, I knocked on the door of my flatmate Simon.

Simon was a third-year who had brought his telly from home; he clearly knew all about the paucity of meaningful debates on Cartesian dualism around the campus. His was a curious TV set, a small black-and-white screen set in a cube that also housed a radio, a cassette player and a digital alarm clock. For the next half hour, as he set about smoking for England, we watched the highlights of the Japanese Grand Prix, where Ayrton Senna secured his first World Drivers' Championship. It felt good to hear the voices of Murray Walker and James Hunt again, but the size of the screen meant it was far from the greatest audiovisual experience.

As Senna got busy with the champagne, I made my excuses and gave the launderette another try. It would have been just too sad to stay on in Simon's room to watch the live indoor bowls from Preston.

THE UPSETTERS

THROUGHOUT THAT first year as an undergraduate, I was disconcerted about how relaxed higher education was proving itself to be. I was able to spend plenty of hours every week in the service of the ents crew, as term-time was far from packed to the rafters with lectures. And those holidays were long. After Christmas, I didn't need to be back on campus before mid-January and so, having been reunited with my beloved Ferguson TX, I had nothing better to do than lose myself in two staples of the first fortnight of a new sporting calendar: the world darts and the FA Cup third round.

Having all the time in the world was handy, as the final of the darts was an out-and-out ten-set classic. In the red corner, stepping out to a chorus of boos and jeers, was five-time champion Eric Bristow who was the 4/9 favourite. In the blue corner was Jocky Wilson, the squat Scot and former champion who always punched above his height; he was four inches shorter than the bullseye on a regulation dartboard. Lakeside Country Club, in stockbroker belt Surrey, was filled with 1,300 refreshed and noisy darts fans, although 60 miles away and without a drink to hand, I felt right at home. It looked just like the students' union bar on a typical Saturday night – just with fewer indie kids with Smiths T-shirts beneath their cardigans.

And there were the familiar, reassuring tones of Sid Waddell, too. He and his commentating colleague, the Mancunian

Tony Green, were relishing the occasion. Wilson defied the odds by racing into an extraordinary lead, taking the first five sets in the best-of-11 match. Bristow, facing the verbal slings and arrows of the Lakeside crowd, began a comeback. 5-0 became 5-1. 5-1 became 5-2. 5-2 became 5-3. 5-3 became 5-4. It needn't have been so close, though. At 5-3, Wilson had a single dart for a double 18 and the world title. But his sums – normally faultless, like those of his mathematically sharp fellow professionals – were out. He went for double top instead, leaving the door open for Bristow to take the ninth set. 'I think he miscounted,' shrieked Waddell. 'He did! Oh, what drama!'

The lengthening match had disrupted the BBC2 schedules. A documentary on the America's Cup was the victim, its moorings untied and left to drift away. Even the nation's yacht owners couldn't complain at the loss, though. No one could ignore what was happening down in landlocked Surrey.

What ultimately happened, though, is that the match failed to go right down to the wire. We didn't get that deciding set. As brilliantly as Bristow was throwing, Wilson managed to ride out the storm and turn the tide, landing a final double ten and his second world title. Both players appreciated the slugfest that the match had developed into. Wilson sank to his knees before Bristow and kissed his hand. As viewers, we didn't get a gummy kiss from Wilson, but we did get peak Waddell. 'Unbelievable! What! A! Match!'

There had been another upset in Surrey seven days earlier, another occasion where the exclamation marks were working overtime. Until then, Hereford's slaying of Newcastle in 1972 was the quintessential FA Cup giant-killing, the one all others were judged against. That Saturday afternoon, at the non-league ground known as Gander Green Lane, the upsetters were out in force again.

Coventry City had won the Cup little more than 18 months previously and had plenty of household names in their side. Sutton United were in the midst of an unremarkable season in the GM Vauxhall Conference. No one knew who any of them were.

By five o'clock, we knew at least two of them: Matthew Hanlan, the floppy-fringed winger who'd scored that afternoon's winner in a famous 2-1 victory, and Barrie Williams, Sutton's wistful, hopelessly romantic manager. Everybody wanted a piece of them and I gobbled up the breathless interviews on *Final Score* and then the *ITV News*, the camera lens steaming up in the dressing room as the team tried to throw Williams into the shower. We were sharing an intimate moment with them, the highest altitude that all their careers would ever rise to. But it didn't feel intrusive. It was celebrative. Our presence was gratitude for them providing us with an indelible, everlasting memory. And besides, Hanlan and Williams had a good few more opportunities in the days that followed to soak up the limelight, however fleeting it would prove.

Half of the experience of being a fan of sport concerns itself with recollection and recall, with gazing into the rear-view mirror. We don't just live in the moment, or look to the future. We need past events in order to gauge the significance of current ones. They are our yardstick, our measure. And that afternoon in Surrey, on a status-levelling pitch of mud and sand, Sutton United gave us a yardstick against which all future giant-killings would be graded. They were the new David.

A SHEEP IN AN ABATTOIR

ANOTHER SUNDAY on a ghostly quiet university campus. Another Sunday spent putting off the drudgery of the launderette until the dirty washing started to make its own way there.

En route, a black bin bag of laundry over my shoulder, I was issued with a potentially distracting invite: the opportunity to watch the Mike Tyson vs Frank Bruno world title fight. There was a problem, though. While the BBC was showing it 'as live' in the middle of the afternoon, the fight had been done and dusted hours and hours ago. I knew that Bruno was stopped in the fifth round. There was no grand upset to be seduced by.

Knowing the result needn't have been an obstacle to still enjoying the fight, of course. After all, I'd spent the previous ten years or so watching *Match of the Day* having already learned twice over, via the vidiprinter and the classified results, all of that day's scores in the First Division. It rarely impaired my enjoyment. Had Tyson/Bruno been a humdinger of a fight, a tight, well-matched bout between two equally powerful adversaries, there might have been purpose in watching the entire fight a fair time after it finished. But that morning's radio reports had made clear the gulf in class. Indeed, the great sportswriter Hugh McIlvanney later described Bruno's travails against Tyson as being 'no more competitive than a sheep in an abattoir'.

I declined the offer and carried on my way. I might have missed Bruno's defeat, but at least my clothes smelled summer-meadow-fresh in Monday's lectures.

That the BBC hadn't shown the fight live in the wee small hours, nor first thing in the morning, was significant. Rupert Murdoch's new company Sky had started broadcasting earlier that month and had secured the rights to show it live – albeit only after an intense legal battle with ITV. In a mirroring of their later relationship around Premier League highlights, the BBC had entered into a deal with Sky to show the fight at a decent distance afterwards. As the changing broadcast landscape took its first faltering steps, the BBC astutely worked out which side to fall: be the terrestrial partner of this major new satellite player with seemingly bottomless pockets or duke it out with the other main terrestrial channel and potentially end up with nothing.

New realities were acknowledged and bets were hedged. But as long as Sky stuck with boxing, a low priority sport for me, I felt it could do what it liked. Just leave football well alone. I'm sure it would . . .

HILLSBOROUGH

IT WAS a walk I'd done plenty of times over the previous couple of years. The few hundred yards between Victoria coach station and Victoria train station, the middle part of a familiar journey from the farthest reaches of Essex to the farthest reaches of Sussex.

That day, my housemate Darren was with me, heading south to revisit old friends we shared, him having left for university a year before me. As we trundled through the upper floor of shops above the train station, Darren – a Forest fan – wanted to check on the early stages of the FA Cup semi-final, in which his boys were taking on Kenny Dalglish's all-conquering Liverpool. We made a beeline for the window display of Dixons to see if there'd been any score yet. It wasn't on live, but there was the outside chance of seeing a score flash up during the coverage of the first day of the world snooker from the Crucible, just three miles across Sheffield from where the match was being played. Gazing through the glass at a silent screen, it was a surprise to see live pictures from Hillsborough being broadcast. And what we could see was essentially the pitch with several hundred fans on it. The events might have become clearer had we been able to carry on watching, but the arm of a Dixons salesman, in a cheap, flecked suit, lunged into view and his hand reached for the off switch.

What we'd seen reminded me of the scenes at Heysel four years previously. The train journey south was largely spent in quiet contemplation, but quite what we were contemplating remained unclear. We wouldn't know for sure for at least a couple more hours. These were the days of no internet, no mobile phones. And we didn't have a transistor radio either; nor, it appeared, did anyone else on the train. But we knew something was wrong, possibly very wrong. We rattled our way through the Surrey commuter belt and, as a first-year student of American literature, I couldn't help but think of one particular Mark Twain quote. 'History doesn't repeat itself. But sometimes it rhymes.' I hoped to God that this was no echo of Heysel.

Of course, it was much worse.

GOD IS FROM LEEDS

WHEN IT came to rugby league, I only had eyes for one man. Balance, poise, intelligence, aggression and pace, all wrapped up in one. He seemed to operate on a higher plane to everyone else. A man apart. The fact that he had a name more suited to a nineteenth-century northern industrialist, perhaps a mill owner or an eminent engineer, made him even more other-worldly. He was Ellery Hanley.

I hadn't intended to watch the match. It was a Saturday afternoon, after all, the time of the week when the rest of the ents crew and I should be opening the rear doors of the venue and guiding a reversing Luton van, crammed with amps and instruments, into position. But there was no sign of that night's band yet. I was kicking my heels. The whole crew was.

I hadn't even realised it was Challenge Cup Final afternoon. It was only when I heard the cheers coming from one of the students' union meeting rooms upstairs that I twigged. Some of Essex University's northern contingent had taken residence in the Oliver Tambo Room and managed to coax its ageing TV into life. I'd never seen it work before.

The cheers were from the Wigan-supporting side of the room. Only two minutes had gone, but they were already ahead against their bitter rivals St Helens, a try created by a fabulous run from Hanley. I stood in the doorway and caught the reverse-angle action replay, watching him brilliantly stretch the opposing defence before offloading. He was well worth watching. I decided to hang around.

Better was to come. About 20 minutes later, Hanley singlehandedly took on St Helens and scored an astonishing individual try. There's that famous picture of Diego Maradona at the '86 World Cup where he appears to be taking on half a dozen Belgian players at the same time, an image that supposedly encapsulated his supremacy at that moment in his career, the notion being that it would take more than half a team to stop him. (The context of the picture was later explained, though: the Belgian players were clustered together simply because they were just breaking out from a defensive wall following an Argentinian free kick.)

Hanley didn't need a judiciously cropped photograph to show his superiority. Collecting the ball just inside the St Helens half, he set off on a mazy run that bamboozled and beguiled. He was soon surrounded by a diamond of opposition players, a quartet that seemingly had him boxed in. But no. A shuffle right, then left, then right again and the diamond was smashed, leaving St Helens' players tackling each other as he charged for the line.

It didn't get better than that. I left the room right then, allowing the perfection and the poetry of the moment to stand intact, faultless – the memory of it unsullied. Plus, I'd just heard the horn of a late-arriving Luton van downstairs.

Once the bulk of the gear had been unloaded and piled high on the stage for someone more qualified to position it and plug it all in, I popped back up to see what the final score was. Hanley was on screen, offering his thoughts on Wigan's 27-0 whitewash of their near-neighbours.

It turned out that God spoke with a Leeds accent.

HALF PAST THE 11TH HOUR

IN EARLY May, I took my affiliation with the students' union ents crew a little further. I made it official, getting myself elected as ents officer. It was an unpaid job undertaken at the same time as studying. After TV sport had disrupted my academic progress at school, I seemed intent on letting live music do the same at university.

One morning, with my academic duties done for the day after a single one-hour lecture on Roosevelt's New Deal legislation, newly elected me headed up to the ents office. Among the messages was an offer to put on the Death Valley Boys, the slimmed-down alter ego of the Colorblind James Experience. I liked the Colorblind James Experience a great deal, a sprawling collective from Rochester, New York whose song 'Considering A Move To Memphis', a near-seven-minute slab of lounge jazz and beat poetry, had been a cult hit on night-time Radio 1 the previous year. It would have been a nice little gig to do, a final let-your-hair-down shindig in the main union bar before the exam period made its evil presence felt.

This time, though, sport defeated music. It was the victor in an imaginary game of rock/paper/scissors between the two monoliths in my life. I was being unusually sharp here. We were being offered the band a fortnight before the show, but I knew there was something about that date: 26 May. There was definitely something about it.

The date is scored forever on the hearts of Arsenal supporters. Liverpool fans choose to ignore it. It was the night that the First Division title was won at half past the 11th hour.

Perhaps my main motivation was selfishness, but I turned down the Death Valley Boys. Now without a band's backstage demands to fulfil, I gave myself the night off and knocked on flatmate Simon's door. I had to watch the match, just in case a little bit of history was to be made. I held my breath through the mushroom cloud of Benson & Hedges smoke and found a spot where I could just about see over someone's shoulder. Five of us were crowding round the tiny screen.

There were a couple of Arsenal acolytes among us, but I was secretly holding a candle for Liverpool that night, the chance to secure the domestic Double, the chance to properly salute the fallen of Hillsborough. Arsenal weren't as sentimental as me. You couldn't blame them. In their nostrils was the scent of their first league title in 18 years. But needing to win at Anfield by two clear goals, against the near-impregnable home side, was a fanciful notion.

After the events of Hillsborough had understandably created a fixture backlog, this rescheduled match was the last league game of the season. No other teams were in the mix, making it a scenario not tricky to decipher. Or, as Brian Moore had it, 'a night of chilling simplicity about it'.

Even when Alan Smith glanced Arsenal ahead in the second half, the dreamers knew the dream was still but a dream. One goal, yes. But two? Liverpool would never permit that.

And yet it came to pass.

As much as the drama was about Smith's through ball, about Michael Thomas's poke past Bruce Grobbelaar and about his forward roll celebration, it was also about Moore's commentary doing justice to the drama. It was the whole package. Those seven words remain the most quoted line of a man who commentated on thousands of matches for ITV. 'Thomas . . . It's up for grabs now! Thomas!' The improbable, the impossible, had happened.

We all breathlessly headed down to the union bar. It was a good job that I had turned down the offer of the Death Valley Boys. No one would have heard a single note, let alone picked up on any subtlety or nuance in their art. Instead, our American friends would have been drowned out by the hearty choruses of Arsenal fans who had previously not gone public with their affiliation. Out of the closet, this was their moment.

THE UNLIKELY LAD

FOR OTHER, more exciting 20-year-olds, the summer of 1989 was a season of illicit raves, of acid house, of horns-locking confrontation between their right to party and the authorities' determination to say no. It wasn't the way I spent the Second Summer of Love. Yes, the records of The Stone Roses were never far from my turntable, but the disused warehouses of the Home Counties never felt my patronage. I was otherwise focused on a brilliantly exciting Tour de France, one with more twists and turns than a hairpin-heavy Alpine summit.

The final stage of the Tour dispensed with tradition in 1989. The usual benign procession into Paris, and the ubiquitous bunch sprint, wasn't happening. Instead, a short individual time trial was being held, riders heading off in turn from the Palace of Versailles to do battle against the clock.

The race leader Laurent Fignon, seeking the immortality that comes with notching up a third Tour victory, had a healthy 50-second lead over the American Greg LeMond. While the

Parisian had never beaten LeMond in a time trial, 50 seconds was surely an unassailable lead over just 15 miles. No one could pull that back, could they?

It was an intriguing scenario, but surely an impossible one too.

While this was going on in Paris – and only being shown on Channel 4 later in highlights form – I had to go to ground and avoid the result. The final round of the Open golf was happening at the same time, but I didn't dare watch it for fear of the Tour result being flashed up on the screen. In the event, I missed Greg Norman's course-record 64 in the final round but, from the cheers downstairs, I could sense he'd put himself in contention.

But I kept my distance. This was my *Likely Lads* moment. I knew the 'No Hiding Place' episode of the sitcom inside out, where Terry and Bob try to avoid the score of an England away match in Bulgaria for the best part of ten hours, from the lunchtime kick-off until the TV highlights that evening. All the while, they had to contend with the near-constant attentions of Brian Glover's mischievous Flint ('You'll never last out until tonight. Let me put you out of your misery'). I didn't have anyone trying to undermine my viewing pleasure. I just needed to stay in my room.

For the sake of all the time and effort and emotion I'd invested over the previous three weeks of an extraordinarily topsy-turvy race, I put in place a plan to ensure the successful evasion of learning what had been occurring in Paris that afternoon. Going against type, *Sunday Grandstand* stayed off. I put on a record instead. In fact, I put on several albums – I was still obsessed with The House Of Love's debut from the previous year, so there were a couple of spins of that, plus the 67 minutes of De La Soul's *Three Feet High And Rising*, which healthily advanced the time towards the golden hour at which Channel 4's extended highlights package would be broadcast.

I was shaking as I switched the set on. Tense and nervous. And these were emotions that were only amplified as I watched first LeMond and then Fignon leave the start house at Versailles. When the first split times came through, it confirmed what the naked eye could see: that LeMond was taking time out of his great rival. By the second split, LeMond had narrowed the deficit some more. My toes tightened. It was on. It was very much on.

Then the bedroom door opened. It was my dad. But I wasn't in the mood to chat. I didn't look round. My gaze was fixed on the mesmerising patterns being produced by Fignon's red, white and blue disc wheels.

'The golf's tight.'

'Oh yeah?'

'Going to a three-way play-off. Norman, Grady and Calcavecchia. It's anyone's title. Just about to start if you're interested.'

'Right.'

Fignon was turning off the embankment of the Seine now, heading for the Place de la Concorde. Ahead of him, LeMond – charging up the Champs-Élysées like a man possessed by some extraordinary inner demon – was pulling back time with every pedal stroke. This was going to the wire.

'This one's close too,' I said.

What happened next wasn't deliberate or malicious or bloody-minded. Just six words were uttered, but they were six words that nonetheless ruined arguably the greatest-ever climax in sporting history.

'Oh yes, the American wins it.'

And so that's how I learned that Greg LeMond had performed a sporting miracle, overturning that 50-second deficit and putting him in credit to the tune of a full eight seconds. The narrowest Tour de France victory ever, and all achieved with LeMond's body still carrying 30-odd buckshot pellets after a near-death hunting accident a couple of years before.

The Open was going out live, so I couldn't get a chance to exact cheap revenge by stomping downstairs to loudly reveal the name of the winner. And such was my combined and confused state of both annoyance and exultation that I couldn't bear to watch the climax of the golf. It might have been an extraordinary end to the tournament, but it simply couldn't compare with events in Paris, even if I didn't find out the result in the proper way: by watching it.

FRIENDS REUNITED

IN MY second year at university, I left my TV at home again. This wasn't because I wanted to try once more to find those corners of the campus where engaged, intelligent debate was flourishing into the small hours. No, I left it at home because the shared house I moved into already had a massive old goggle-box that dominated the living room.

I soon settled into a Saturday routine that satisfied both my worlds, my twin needs. First off, I'd get two or three hours of TV sport under my belt. With little protest from the other members of the house, I'd segue from *Football Focus* and *Saint & Greavsie* to whatever sport was scheduled for the first couple of hours of *Grandstand*. Perhaps it was a few holes from the Suntory World Matchplay from Wentworth or touring car action from Silverstone.

And then, around 3pm, I'd make the half-hour walk to campus, where the ents crew and I would do our Saturday routine, our weekly dance to get that night's gig on.

Nothing got in the way during those busy hours. Indeed, so immersed was I in the process that not even the slightest thought was put the way of the afternoon's football. Imagine that even 18 months before . . .

PROPHET WARNING

SID WADDELL wouldn't have realised just how much foresight was contained in his words. 'We have a new era in the sport of darts!' To most within earshot of the BBC's coverage of the world darts final of 1990, Waddell might have sounded rather premature in declaring a changing of the guard, but history has proved the prophecy correct.

The master had been undone by the protégé. Unfancied Phil Taylor had beaten Eric Bristow. He'd walloped him, in fact. 6-1. Bristow never won another world title. For Taylor, it was the first of 16.

In his adopted town of Stoke, Bristow had taken local boy Taylor under his wing, shown him patronage, shown him tough love. In the process, he'd created a world champion. Not just that. He'd created the greatest player in the history of the sport. It seemed apt, if not a little embarrassing, that it was Bristow himself who handed the baton on directly, up on the stage at Lakeside. It was as if he'd named his successor.

New decades need their own heroes. Different chapters close and open, and blank pages need writing. It's just that the tenses change: future into present, present into past.

WHERE'S THE BEEF?

BY THE opening months of the 1990s, I was not the boy I used to be. I was out in the world, in the sunlight, out of my bubble. But there was one night in this new life that the young boy would have loved, an event we promoted that brought together my past and my present. It was an event that didn't need towering PA stacks or smoke machines or hordes of brick-shithouse bouncers. It was a more genteel affair that required little preparation on our part. It was, to give it its proper billing, 'An Evening with Ian Botham'.

This was a chance for old Beefy to indulge himself for an hour or two: reheating old war stories, offering up pen portraits of various former teammates and opponents, and taking questions from the floor.

It had seemed like a good idea at the time. Botham was undeniably the most famous person we'd ever booked. He was certainly more famous than Pop Will Eat Itself or the Wee Papa Girl Rappers. But he was also the person to pull in the least number of punters of any of our events that year. The evening's questions, answers and anecdotes echoed around the vast lecture theatre we'd hired on campus for the night. Just 26 people came.

Those that were there seemed to enjoy the evening and Botham did what was expected of him, fulfilling the terms of the contract. We did too. I remember there was one particular obligation we had to uphold: no one was allowed to leave the auditorium straight after the show. The exit doors had to stay shut for a couple of minutes. Botham appeared to be keen on getting a quick getaway, preferring not to get trampled in a furious stampede of autograph hunters and well-wishers that would delay his long journey home to Lincolnshire. I'm not sure that 26 people dotted around the hall – most of whom were men of a certain age, meek types whose questions invariably began with 'Mr Botham, I've been an admirer of yours for many years . . .' – could have caused a stampede.

And, come on. Just how little time would signing 26 autographs really have taken?

OH! CALCUTTA CUP!

I VISIT Edinburgh a couple of times a year for work, flying up from the south-west of England rather than taking the train, transferring any pangs of guilt I might feel about taking to the skies onto the shoulders of the rail companies and their eye-watering pricing strategies. Unfortunately, it's a no-brainer, both financially and logistically.

There is one clear highlight of the tram journey from the airport up to Princes Street, the point at which it skirts the site of one of the notable battlefields in Scottish history. Not Bannockburn 1314 or Culloden 1746, obviously. It's more significant than that.

Murrayfield 1990.

That March day, the script was word-perfect. Scotland and England had won three Five Nations matches apiece; the Calcutta Cup, here in the Scottish capital, offered the winner-takes-all prize of the Grand Slam. England hadn't won the championship in ten long years. The last time they had, the title had been secured by a comfortable win right here at Murrayfield. The sulphurous smell of revenge hung in the Edinburgh air a decade on. But this wasn't simply some idle sport on a rugby field. There was something more to it than that.

In early 1990, being part of our students' union executive committee, I'd been involved in organising, and mobilising people for, local Poll Tax demonstrations. As this was far from a student-specific issue, we had plenty of support within the town. That was an otherwise rare commodity. But the winds were blowing; frustration and anger was growing against Margaret Thatcher's keynote policy of the day, even in the Home Counties.

It was nothing compared to the anger and frustration in Scotland where she had introduced the tax the year before.

Unsurprisingly, the Scots – who had returned just ten Tory MPs at the general election three years previously – weren't exactly over-impressed with being treated as guinea pigs, that their communities were being used as a dry run before the policy was rolled out across the rest of the United Kingdom. My sympathies naturally sided with the men in deep navy blue.

The fact that the back pages were full of English trash-talk made it even harder to remotely find favour with Will Carling's men; one newspaper likened their trip to Murrayfield to an SAS mission. To Scottish eyes, at least, they were seen as Thatcher's representatives, sent north to put the natives back in their box, back in their place.

Before the game, 'Flower of Scotland' was played and sung for the first time in a Calcutta Cup match. 'God Save the Queen' was left for England's exclusive use. It was a masterstroke, a rallying call, a battle cry. The camera panned across the Scotland team as they heartily sang out, their faces hewn from granite. Man mountains. Finlay Calder and John Jeffrey and Gavin Hastings and the rest. These weren't men who would wilt, who would lie down and die, no matter the levels of the visitors' cocksure confidence.

Two early Scottish penalties stirred England into action, with Carling and Jeremy Guscott cutting open the home defence with guile and speed to chalk up the game's first try. Perhaps, after all, England were the much superior side, able to turn on the style at will. Perhaps the devil really did have the best tunes.

But England got very little else that day. Three pivotal moments turned the tide and had me cheering alone on the sofa in Colchester: Tony Stanger chasing a tricky kick to go over; a try-saving tackle by Scott Hastings on the electric-paced Rory Underwood; and, earlier in the match, a misguided, possibly arrogant decision by England to take a scrum rather than slot three easy points over. This public display of that arrogance simply girded Scottish loins and they sent England back up the pitch.

On the final whistle, that man of Hawick, Bill McLaren, was notably calm and reflective in the commentary box about his countrymen's 13-7 victory. 'Scotland have won a famous victory,' he declared without exclamation. He kept a lid on it. His heart was surely pounding like a marching drum, though.

On that mid-March day, the verses of 'Flower of Scotland' rang out across the battlefield, words that couldn't have defined the encounter any more precisely. Carling, Guscott and the rest had been sent 'homeward tae think again'.

THE DOOR FRAME OF DESTINY

BACK IN 1985, when Boris Becker had upset Wimbledon's natural order, I'd made peace with his supremacy at such a tender age (he was just 13 months older than me, don't forget – he still is, in fact). He was simply a freak of nature, an anomaly, a one-off. Accordingly, I needn't have felt insecure or insignificant about his achievements. He was a man-child prodigy. One in a million. One in 50 million, perhaps.

Besides, anyone older was simply *older*, no matter how narrow the margin between them and me. I'd always be the younger one, the one who didn't need to lead the way, who could always play catch-up. Until, that is, the day that Stephen Hendry became world snooker champion for the first time. There was a problem. He was 28 days younger than me.

I'd started the 1980s as a myopic sub-teen who only had eyes for untouchable sporting deities. By the start of the following decade, Hendry's victory at the Crucible had served notice that sports stars were increasingly my contemporaries. These were people who'd sat the same O-level exams on the same day as me; kids who – in their corner of the country and me in mine – answered the same essay questions about *Hamlet* or the Treaty of Versailles or the ideal location for a market-gardening business. Now they were on their way towards the gods. I was left on earth with a very moderate opinion of my worth and a bondage to cheese-flavoured baked snacks.

While something of a Becker-like prodigy at the snooker table (he still holds the record for being the youngest world champ), Hendry was far from being a one-off in terms of his age in the wider world of sport. Confirmation of this had come three months earlier at the City Ground in Nottingham. The visitors for an FA Cup third round tie were Manchester United whose boss – a pre-sainthood Alex Ferguson – was reportedly just about to receive his P45 in the post. A date with Brian Clough's Forest was the last roll of the dice.

Ferguson's saviour that day was a young player who'd ended his teenage years just a fortnight before, making him more than a year younger than me. That Mark Robins was my junior to this degree didn't sit well with me. This was a young lad whose headed goal that afternoon – scored while holding off the attentions of that most carnivorous of full backs, Stuart Pearce – subsequently went down in history as the one which gave Ferguson an 11th-hour reprieve. Without that stay of execution, the next 20 years of English football would have looked much, much different.

It's human nature to measure yourself against your contemporaries. In adult life, this is often quantified in material terms: the size of a house, the flashiness of a car, the destination of an annual holiday. It's like marking your height on a door frame as a kid, seeing how you stand up to older siblings; an exercise in comparative development that reveals, or confirms, your place in the wider scheme of things.

In the first few months of a bright, shiny new decade, Mark Robins and Stephen Hendry confirmed my place in the wider scheme of things. I still largely felt like a kid operating in a minuscule world and here they were making enormous contributions to the sporting landscape of the nation. One of them was already a world champion, for Christ's sake. Together they showed my earliest adult years were following the pattern of my teenage ones: that I was locked in an eternal game of catch-up, lagging further behind as others disappeared over the distant horizon.

'AND IT'S GONE IN . . . PARDEW!'

ON FA Cup semi-final day in 1990 (both matches were still played on the same day back then, before the era of Wembley semis), I was making the same journey that I had the 12 months previously – the coach/train shuttle between university and home, between Essex and Sussex. I was retracing my steps and, inevitably, retracing my thoughts about Hillsborough.

Liverpool were in the semis again, a year on from their very darkest day. It was their fifth appearance at this stage of the competition in six seasons, and they were red-hot favourites to reach Wembley. Crystal Palace were their opponents at Villa Park, a team Liverpool had decimated earlier in the season, dishing out mortifying embarrassment in the form of a 9-0 walloping.

So inevitable was the outcome that I almost considered not catching the game live on TV. It was a 12 o'clock kick-off, meaning that I'd need to leave Colchester at the kind of ungodly hour only ever encountered by students on their way back from some all-night hootenanny. But that nagging inkling that an historic upset might, *might* just happen ate away at me like it always had. You had to watch *just in case*.

So I put in the hard miles. The tricky part – the getting up and the getting to the bus station – had been successfully negotiated. By the time I reached London, I was still on schedule. But now, half a mile out of Clapham Junction, this stationary train was scuppering my plans. We sat there for ages, for no apparent reason and with no apologetic explanation. And when we did finally start moving again, the driver – clearly not a football fan – saw no reason to try to make up time. Instead, we pootled and trundled when we should have sped and galloped.

The result was that I missed the kick-off and, as with that England/France game at the 1982 World Cup, a goal had already been scored by the time I slipped my key in the door. Inevitably, Liverpool had scored it. Equally inevitably, it came from the boot of Ian Rush. My shoulders slumped. All this effort for the one-sided bore-fest everyone had expected. Why on earth had I listened to the whispers of that nagging inkling?

Right from the start of the second half, Crystal Palace – through the left foot of Mark Bright – showed me why I'd listened. 1-1. From there, and eventually into extra time, the score pinballed back and forth in mesmerising fashion. 2-1 to Palace. 2-2. 3-2 to Liverpool. 3-3. And then, in the second period of extra time, ex-glazier Alan Pardew – then bottle-blond rather than trophy-silver – headed home the seventh goal of the afternoon to put Palace into their first-ever Cup Final. Liverpool's dream of a Double, denied by Wimbledon in '88 and Arsenal in '89, lay shattered in pieces for the third successive year. Plus, the prolonged pain felt by Palace after that 9-0 defeat had been anaesthetised. It had been 120 breathless, pulsating minutes, rightfully described by John Motson as 'one of the most amazing matches surely in the recent history of the FA Cup'.

The other semi-final came along just an hour later – Manchester United versus Second Division Oldham Athletic. Lightning struck twice. This too was one of the most amazing matches in the recent history of the FA Cup, another twist-and-turn affair that ended three-all after extra time. Barry Davies was on duty at Maine Road. 'What an unbelievable day this is,' he announced with unrestrained delight. 'This is the stuff of schoolboy comics!'

When the final came around a month later (United having nudged Oldham aside in the replay, thanks again to that young sprite Mark Robins), Wembley bore the burn marks of a third lightning strike. It was another six-goal thriller, with the honours again shared. The big story was that of young Ian Wright – Motson anointed him as 'the whiz-kid from Woolwich' as he came on as a second-half sub – who, after having missed the previous ten matches with a fractured shin bone, scored twice.

It was the first Cup Final I'd watched en masse. It was usually a solo pursuit observed in reverential silence. In 1990, though, Darren and I hosted a few pals, serving our visitors with cheap, room-temperature lager and an industrial quantity of sandwiches. Going by the example of both semi-finals, extra time was a distinct possibility and we had to ensure there was adequate sustenance. There had been a definite spring in my step that afternoon. I'd missed the Cup Final the previous May, otherwise engaged in fulfilling the refreshment demands of some middling, never-going-to-really-make-it indie band. Whoever they were (and the annals of rock history seem rather light on the details of that particular show), they were surely not an outfit worthy of me missing my first Cup Final in more than two decades.

But now, with my year-long tenure as ents officer having expired, I was back to being a normal student again. And this

– beer and sandwiches and a full front room – was how normal students watched the Cup Final. Me and Darren and Al and Phil and Josh. It was how it should be.

Afterwards, like a bunch of sugared-up ten-year-olds, we went and had a kickabout, suitably inspired by Palace's super-sub. The days of playing 'Allan Wells' along my old street, or 'Ian Botham' in Alex Cooper's back garden, were being revisited. We took a ball out to the sloping, grassy area beyond our row of houses, ignoring the 'No ball games' sign with carefree abandon. We invented a new game that evening. It was called 'Ian Wright'.

OF MICS AND MEN

THIS HAS been a boy's story largely populated by men. This is not deliberate. It is a reflection. That was the sporting landscape back then.

Coverage of women's sport was far from as widespread as it is today. And female commentators, pundits and presenters were then rare pennies indeed. You would certainly never hear female voices at a male sporting event. Female pundits would be used solely for women's events and even then sparingly. The BBC's Wimbledon coverage would call upon the observations and analysis of former players like Virginia Wade and Ann Jones, but the men still dominated. And the anchors were exclusively male.

(This was also true when it came to non-white male representation. The only time you would hear the voice of a black football pundit other than Garth Crooks would be if a former or current player was drafted in during the World Cup to offer his thoughts on a match involving an African side. It was as crude as that.)

Today we have the likes of Gabby Logan, Clare Balding, Sue Barker, Hazel Irvine, Elly Oldroyd, Caroline Barker, Kelly Cates and many others rectifying the gender balance, presenters who bring the utmost skill and expertise across a range of sports. Each one of them surely has to thank one true trailblazer for chopping through the undergrowth for them: Helen Rollason.

On 19 May 1990, 32 years after its birth, Rollason became the first female presenter of *Grandstand*. After long-term presenters like Dimmock, Coleman, Bough, Lynam and Rider – and ad hoc anchormen like Carpenter, Icke, Vine, Gubba and many others – it had finally been deemed appropriate for a woman to take charge of the flagship programme. Any scepticism that met the appointment (and there was some) was soon extinguished by the calm authority that Rollason brought to the role.

It was a tragedy that hers was not a longer career in sports broadcasting. She succumbed to cancer in 1999 at the horrifyingly young age of 43.

GROUP THERAPY

OVER THE previous decade, the vast majority of the thousands and thousands of hours of TV sport I'd watched had been on my own, in solitary confinement, in my own self-determined republic. But the experience of watching the Cup Final with others, with beer and banter enhancing the proceedings, had shown me that the alternatives weren't unattractive. And so it was, on 16 June 1990, the last Saturday of the academic year, that I found myself in the company of a couple of hundred others in front of England's World Cup group match with the Netherlands. We were in the Dancehall, that main venue that I'd given so much service to over the previous two years, where a giant screen had been procured and set up on the stage. The picture wasn't great, but the atmosphere was sharp and salty. After a disappointing draw with the Irish, England needed to assert themselves to ensure safe passage to the knockout stages of Italia '90. After the ease with which the Dutch had brushed aside England in the European Championship two years earlier, this was no given.

Thanks to a little insider information, I had the best seat in the house. Using my ents knowledge, I knew there was a near-invisible ladder set into the wall at the back of the hall, which led to a hidey-hole about ten feet up. When the masses rose to their feet every time Paul Gascoigne was given the ball, it didn't affect my view at all. And it actually meant that I was, I have to admit, still kind of watching alone. It was just that I couldn't hear the Motson/Brooking commentary over the general hubbub. But the others in the room were adding atmosphere and colour for me. I remember – with half the room seemingly puffing away, their smoke drifting towards me in my lofty perch – there being audible admiration for the Dutch coach who'd also lit up a ciggie in the dugout. Admiration turned to apoplexy when a Gary Lineker goal sent chairs and beer flying, only to be ruled out for handball.

And then, with the match sliding into its dying seconds, Stuart Pearce fired a long, low free kick into the bottom corner. The place exploded. I leapt down from my eyrie to join in the communal throng, all hugs and euphoria. The screen disappeared behind a mass of pogoing England supporters. Qualification from the group stage was guaranteed with a match still to go. Our world was in motion. When the room settled down and everyone retook their seats, the game had restarted but the final whistle was soon to come.

A delighted procession made its way up four flights of stairs to the main bar. It was quiet in there, but not for long as pints were enthusiastically ordered and songs were sung. It was a full ten minutes later, when those who'd been watching the game up in their tower block flats arrived in the bar, that we realised something was up. These new arrivals had been bemused by the carnival atmosphere that greeted them and swiftly put us right. Pearce's goal had actually been disallowed. It was awarded as an indirect free kick, but he had smacked it home without a touch from another player, either a teammate or an opponent. In the hullabaloo that had ensued down in the dance hall, no one had spotted that the game hadn't restarted with a Dutch kick-off.

The beer quickly turned flat. England had simply recorded another mildly unsatisfactory draw, albeit in a game they had dominated and should have won. So much for watching in the company of others.

BEATING THE SHITE OUT OF O'LEARY

THERE'S A split-second moment when, while watching sport, a significant incident occurs and your brain tries to compute the situation and its consequences. It might be Phil Taylor slotting home that final double ten to send Eric Bristow on the career downslope. It might be Zola Budd's legs tangling with those of Mary Decker, sending her sprawling and out of the Olympics. Or it might be David O'Leary scoring the decisive spot kick in a penalty shoot-out against Romania to send Ireland into the last eight of the World Cup. 'Did x really just happen? And does that mean y is now on the cards?'

In *The Van*, the final instalment of his *Barrytown Trilogy* based around the fictional Rabbitte family from Dublin's South Side, Roddy Doyle beautifully expressed that momentary confusion after the successful conversion of arguably the most important penalty in the history of Irish football:

> Jimmy Sr looked carefully to make sure he'd seen it right. The net was shaking, and O'Leary was covered in Irishmen. He wanted to see it again though. Maybe they were all beating the shite out of O'Leary for missing. No, though; he'd scored. Ireland were through to the quarter-finals.

You didn't have to have Irish blood to appreciate the cool way that O'Leary, a centre half by trade, of course, dispatched that penalty in the manner of a dead-ball expert number ten. The way he stroked the ball home was nothing short of Platini-esque.

I was back home for the summer holidays by now and had elected to hold off taking a summer job until we were the other side of the final, keeping the days and nights free for every remaining minute of the tournament. Being home meant watching without the attendant hubbub of a mass screening, and thus being able to hear every word of the commentary away from the din of the beered-up masses. 'It defies belief,' announced ITV's Alan Parry as he tried to get his head around the ongoing Irish success. 'It really defies belief.'

Ireland, in their first-ever World Cup, were hard not to take to your heart and no one begrudged them this irresistible run. They had universal appeal – a raggle-taggle bunch of Scousers and Londoners and Glaswegians and Italians, all moulded into shape by a Geordie. Look hard enough and you could even find a couple of Dubliners in there too. The united colours of Ireland.

THE LAST TEMPTATION OF CHRIS

'GOOD EVENING. This is, of course, the most momentous day for English football since 30 July 1966. It's estimated that more than half of the entire population of the country will be watching tonight's semi-final against West Germany. What the other half are doing we'll leave up to them . . .'

If anything, the 'back of a fag packet' calculations Des Lynam was alluding to seemed a tad conservative. For starters, I didn't know a single person who wasn't watching it (and, let's be frank, I wouldn't have *wanted* to know anyone who wasn't). Those staying away couldn't all be at work at that time in the evening, driving Underground trains or working hospital shifts or stacking supermarket shelves. If you could watch, why on earth wouldn't you?

England's passage to the semi-finals hadn't exactly been assured and dominant. David Platt's brilliant volley against Belgium in the last 16 had only come with a single minute of extra time remaining while, against Cameroon in the quarter-final, only a pair of soft penalties had seen England narrowly squeeze past Roger Milla and his countrymen. Bobby Robson's boys had got out of jail twice. This good fortune couldn't last.

To avoid a repeat of the Netherlands game – where watching en masse had removed the subtleties and nuances (not least knowing what the final score was) – I elected to watch in comparative solitude. I did, though, assume my old place at the far end of the sofa. The match was too important, potentially historic, not to share it with my parents.

That summer, I worked two jobs: supermarket checkout boy by day, theatre usher by night. But as dedicated as I was to checking ticket stubs and selling ice creams in the interval, there was no way I was working that particular Wednesday night. I, like many others, phoned in sick that day, but I made sure I called up early, the first to sag off. And, anyway, were they truly expecting the audience to turn up too, on such a significant evening? Or, maybe that's where the other half of the population was, sitting in darkened theatres in front of mediocre plays where the action wouldn't be one tenth as gripping as what was about to unfold in Turin.

Whatever the actual proportion of the population was that watched the match, most of these surely tuned into the BBC. It was a no-brainer. No adverts, better pundits, and no Jimmy Greaves wearing a succession of bespoke T-shirts with universally unfunny slogans on them.

The BBC coverage was a class act, exemplified by the choice of its accompanying music. If ITV had comfortably won the battle of the World Cup theme tunes four years previously, the BBC took its revenge in 1990. That year, ITV commissioned Rod Argent from The Zombies to write theirs. It seemed like a prudent choice; it had been Argent who'd written and recorded 'Aztec Gold' in 1986 under the pseudonym Silsoe, and who presumably lived handsomely on its royalties in the years since through its use on both *The Big Match* and *Saint & Greavsie*.

Argent's 1990 effort – 'Tutti Al Mondo' – was rather Italia-light, a drifting ambient piece with a slight operatic theme. And it was up against the hard stuff. The BBC went with full-strength, high-proof opera in the form of Luciano Pavarotti's soaring tenor and the emotion and drama of 'Nessun Dorma'. It was a masterstroke, a prime cut of Puccini to soundtrack the month-long tournament when none, indeed, would sleep. It felt as if that piece of music's primary reason for existence was to accompany this titanic semi-final, those 120 minutes (plus penalties) that put us through the wringer several times over.

(The FA also got it spot-on music-wise in 1990. This time, the England squad wasn't required to struggle its way through a massed-voice, flat-voice dirge for their official song. Instead, New Order had been commissioned to come up with a tune infinitely more contemporary. And 'World in Motion', complete with John Barnes's still-cherished rap, remains the best-loved football song ever. It was partly so successful because it played down the Italian motifs. These were largely limited to the liberal use of the word 'arrivederci'.)

Almost 30 years later, the key points of the match remain burned into the nation's consciousness. The German goal, freakishly deflected by Paul Parker over Peter Shilton's head. David Platt's header that fell on the wrong side of a borderline offside decision. Gary Lineker's balance and instinct in fashioning an equaliser despite the attentions of three German defenders. Gazza's impulsive, overstretching tackle that precipitated a yellow card, a suspension and many tears. Lineker's message to the bench to keep an eye on the youngster. And the penalty shoot-out. We'll always have the penalty shoot-out.

There was no David O'Leary moment for an English player. No moment of realisation that their successful kick had put their side into the next round; no being buried under an avalanche of ecstatic teammates and coaching staff. Instead it was anguish and solitude for penalty-takers four and five. Stuart Pearce's spot kick hit the German keeper's legs, while Chris Waddle's clean strike went high, wide and unhandsome into the dark Turin night.

'Would you want to be Chris Waddle now?' John Motson had asked as the ball was placed on the spot for the final time. No one would have, of course. Gazza, too emotionally distraught, wasn't in a fit state to take one and neither was anyone at home. And even if we were, how would we have taken ours? Try to place it and hope the keeper hadn't read our intentions, or, like Waddle, succumb to the temptation of blasting it into the top corner?

Waddle's miss is the contribution of his to Italia '90 that's always remembered and recalled. This is grossly unfair. The semi-final was undeniably his best performance of the entire tournament. Having shorn off English football's most famous mullet before the game, the loss of his locks hadn't, unlike Samson, removed his power and potency. While the collective memory has Paul Gascoigne as the pivot and lynchpin, it was the newly aerodynamic Waddle who posed the biggest threat to Beckenbauer's Germans. Not only should one of his mazy runs have ended with the awarding of a penalty, but twice he hit the German woodwork. The first, an audacious 45-yard thumper that shook the crossbar, was called back for an earlier foul, but the second, a cross-shot halfway through extra time that hit the inside of the post and stayed out, could have endowed this England squad with immortality.

England's world was no longer in motion. They were out. Fine margins had decided the day: an inch or two to the left and that cross-shot would have gone in off the post, and Waddle would have been the hero of the hour, of the day, of the summer. It was the proximity to the World Cup Final that made the hurt sting more sharply. The players were inconsolable. Forlorn on the fourth of July.

We'd been here before. Not spiritually, of course; this was England's first semi-final since 1966. Nor in a penalty shoot-out either; this was their first of many. We'd been here geographically. Turin was where we started out ten years previously where, in the summer of 1980, Ray Wilkins had scored the goal that had started the process, encouraging an 11-year-old lad to lose himself to a decade of TV viewing and hopeless dreaming.

That lad – The Sundance Kid – was now nearly twice as old. As an adult, he was out in the world, no longer cocooning himself away, no longer living life on the interior. But that obsession, that hopeless devotion to TV sport, hadn't been a dead end, nor time poorly invested. He never became that football commentator, but lessons had nonetheless been learnt about life and justice, and his moral compass had been accordingly reset. Everything he had watched and absorbed over the past decade – every triumph, every disaster – had informed his world view and had shaped whom he became. If his passage into adulthood was guided by voices, they were the voices of Coleman, Motson, Davies, McLaren and Lynam, the philosophers of his age. And, in his mind's eye, he had the pictures that went with them.

He wouldn't have missed it for the world.

THIS IS all ancient history. The landscape is unrecognisable now.

It's nearly 30 years since the 1980s ended. Back then, the notion of paying to watch TV sport, in this country at least, was in its embryonic stage. Sky was a young, snotty-nosed kid on the block. Almost everything you wanted was already there on the terrestrial channels. For the time being, at least.

I'm far from the first person to make the connection between the strength of sports coverage on terrestrial television and the number of kids taking to the nation's pitches and tracks to emulate the heroes they'd just seen on the small screen. Tens of millions have observed that correlation. It's a blatant link to make, and impossible to argue against. The less access that kids have to free-to-air coverage of Test matches or tennis or football or athletics, the more distanced they are from those sports.

Even when terrestrial television comes up trumps these days, the young folk's attention is often beckoned elsewhere. We had very few alternative temptations; the 21st-century teens and pre-teens are lured in multiple directions. Today is the tenth day of the Easter school holidays, a day that my 12-year-old son is largely spending on the sofa in the front room. Yesterday, he finished watching all 105 episodes to date of the sitcom *Brooklyn Nine-Nine*. Today, he's started watching them all over again.

The Commonwealth Games, from Australia's Gold Coast, are happening right now. This would have been manna from heaven to the 12-year-old me – the confluence of a near-fortnight of sporting action and being home all day with few duties or tasks to fulfil. It would have been even sweeter-tasting manna if, like him, I lived my youth in the age of the BBC Red Button, when I would have had the superpower of watching whatever event – table tennis or triathlon or powerlifting – whenever I liked, all at the touch of a button.

But he doesn't know the Commonwealth Games are on. He might not even know what they are. He's his own person with his own interests and his own agenda. I leave him be.

It's a sunny day outside, but he's drawn the front-room curtains, burying down into his bunker to feed his obsession. At least that's one thing I've passed on. He is The Sundance Kid's kid.

ACKNOWLEDGEMENTS

I came up with the title of this book four or five years ago and, in a very unhappy coincidence, the day after I finished writing it, Ray Wilkins left us, having suffered a huge heart attack a week previously. As you will have just read, it's not a book about Ray, although he does make an appearance in a couple of places. We've kept the title as a salute to him, as someone who loomed large throughout the decade in question and whose spirit pervades the pages. He remains a hero to a generation, representing a time when life was simpler – and so was sport.

Hearty thanks go to:

– my editor Pete Burns for being a pleasure to work with, and to everyone else at Arena Sport who made sterling contributions, including Ian Greensill, Kristian Kerr, Vikki Reilly and Jamie Harris.

– Nathan Burton, for his knockout cover design.

– my agent Kevin Pocklington at The North, for his diligence, wisdom and laughs.

– several old school pals for whom much of this story will be familiar: Jon and Johnny and Ab and Jez and Gange and, of course, Stephens the Bookie, for whom the mere mention of Mary Peters continues to bring about a cold sweat.

– for general encouragement, as well as demanding regular progress reports: Witts, Griff, Rob W, McG, Jimmy C and the two Keiths.

– for favours either specific or general, or for just good tidings: Ned Boulting, Matt Williams, Jim White, Andrew Collins, Andy Dawson, Nigel Blackwell, Jude Rogers, Anna Pointer, Matt Gardiner, Daniel Gray, Andy Murray, Alex Narey and the ever-generous Danny Baker.

– most importantly, though, to Jane, Finn and Ned for their patience and unswerving love. This book is about the past. You are my present and my future.